UNDERSTANDING LANGUAGE

3
T/o

UNDERSTANDING LANGUAGE

*Towards a Post-Chomskyan
Linguistics*

Terence Moore
and
Christine Carling

**MACMILLAN
PRESS**

First edition 1982
Reprinted 1983, 1985, 1987

Published by
THE MACMILLAN PRESS LTD
Houndmills, Basingstoke, Hampshire RG21 2XS
and London
Companies and representatives
throughout the world

Printed in Hong Kong

ISBN 0-333-27188-2 (hardcover)
ISBN 0-333-33108-7 (paperback)

The essence of language is human activity – activity on the part of one individual to make himself understood by another, and activity on the part of that other to understand what was in the mind of the first. These two individuals . . . and their relations to one another, should never be lost sight of if we want to understand the nature of language and of that part of language which is dealt with in grammar. But in former times this was often overlooked, and words and forms were often treated as if they were things or natural objects with an existence of their own – a conception which may have been to a great extent fostered through a too exclusive preoccupation with written or printed words, but which is fundamentally false, as will easily be seen with a little reflexion.

> Otto Jespersen, the opening sentences of
> *The Philosophy of Grammar* (1924)

It is not sufficiently considered that men more frequently require to be reminded than informed.

> Samuel Johnson

Il faut beaucoup de philosophie pour savoir observer une fois ce qu'on voit tous les jours.

> Jean Jacques Rousseau

Contents

Acknowledgements

Anyone who has become disillusioned with the dominant framework of enquiry in his field will be familiar with the problems and pains that accompany the slow withdrawal. There is a keen sense of loss of familiar methods of investigation and modes of argument, and an acute awareness that able and talented people are still continuing to work within the old framework, apparently undisturbed by what has come to seem its unacceptable degree of irrelevance.

At such time a group that offers constructive and sympathetic discussion of fledgling ideas and encourages the questioning deep-rooted theoretical assumptions has a value beyond measure. One such group in Cambridge was the Tuesday group who, starting in the Michaelmas term 1978, met regularly over a sandwich and coffee lunch to thrash out general problems in understanding natural language and to examine their treatment in particular versions of transformational generative theory. Many of the ideas and some of the early versions of chapters of the book had their first public airing in this company. We owe a debt to all the participants but we can single out here only the hard core members of that group: Anthony Appiah, Iain Boal, Gemma Geoghegan-Dubois, Rob van Oirsouw, Martin Spaul and Phil Turetsky.

Many other people in Cambridge have directly or indirectly contributed to the making of this book. For constructive and destructive criticism on particular sections we want to thank especially Sylvia Adamson, Stephen Levinson, Francis Nolan, Nigel Vincent and Jim Woodhouse.

There are in addition mentors whose influence has been subtle and pervasive but whom it has not been easy to acknowledge through the usual paraphernalia of scholarship. We have in mind particularly R. G. Collingwood, M. Polanyi and Angus Sinclair.

The figure however that casts the longest shadow is Noam Chomsky. We disagree with him. But we disagree, not with his aim of explaining the cognitive basis for the acquisition and workings of language, but with his methods and model of explanation. We are conscious that we have come to formulate our own

x   Acknowledgements

views on language more clearly by trying to understand the nature
of his. Chomsky is a great stimulant and great stimulants are
sufficiently rare to be worthy of a measure of homage. As we
ourselves are only too aware, and as Chomsky himself once remarked: 'There is of course nothing wrong with being wrong.'

There is finally one individual to whom we owe a special debt – a
debt that cannot be repaid. Ritva-Liisa Cleary has, with patience,
calmness and gentle efficiency, transformed an often wild manu-
script, full of arcane signs to backtrack, skip and sidetrack, into a
clean, orderly and elegant Diablo printout. But for Liisa this book
would have been even longer in the making.

This book is the work of two authors. We do not know how
other co-authors have managed but find it hard to believe that any
other joint work could surpass the degree of united effort that has
gone into each chapter, each section, each sentence and, in the
end, where it counts, given its theme, each word of this book. The
deepest and final acknowledgement each of us find we can make is
to the other.

T. M.
C. C.

Prologue

The starting point of this book was a growing sense of disquiet with a great deal of the work being done in current theoretical linguistics. Generally our feeling was that such work was throwing very little light on the object of enquiry: language. It was clear that many of those who had turned to theoretical linguistics on the quite reasonable assumption that it would help them to understand the nature of language had been dissapointed. We were aware that psychologists, teachers, sociologists, computer scientists and philosophers interested in language had come largely to disregard the theoretical work that was being done in linguistics.

Our sense of disquiet appeared to have its roots in a growing divergence between theoretical concerns on the one hand and the unsolved mysteries of the workings of language understanding and language production on the other. Considerable talent and energy was being devoted to the elaboration of theoretical models relevant to highly restricted domains. At the same time, a multitude of problems in language production and language understanding were being left almost totally uninvestigated. This divergence might not be grave were it the case that an account of fundamental principles of language use was, however slowly, beginning to emerge from the theoretical work. For a number of reasons, optimism on this score is becoming less and less justifiable. In Part I of the book we want to pinpoint the chief causes of the divergence of the science of linguistics from its subject matter, language.

We begin our evaluation of work in theoretical linguistics by considering some of its more fundamental assumptions. Foremost among these is the assumption that linguistics should aim not simply to describe but to explain aspects of language. For us this is not an issue. We too assume that the pursuit of linguistics has as its goal the formulation of clear and satisfying explanations of language behaviour. The problem lies in establishing what counts as an adequate explanation. In linguistics, largely under the influence of one man, a particularly strong position was taken on the form of an adequate explanation. We shall call into question the appropriateness for linguistics of that form of explanation. Our thesis is that the divergence of linguistics from its subject matter

1

has been exacerbated by the adoption of an inappropriate form of explanation.

In general terms the form of explanation adopted into linguistics is known as deductively formulated theory or, informally, as the received view. It is a type of explanation that has been successful in some, but by no means all, of the physical sciences. A signal advantage of such theories is that they make it possible to see that apparently disparate phenomena may be explained in terms of common underlying principles. In order for such theories to be appropriate however a number of conditions must be satisfied. Two are of particular importance. First, the phenomenon to be explained must be well-defined, and second, it must be of a type that lends itself reasonably easily to expression in terms of a formal notation. We shall be arguing that the conditions that make deductively formulated theory appropriate as a model of explanation are not approached in linguistics. In pursuing this argument we find ourselves raising an issue that is a particular case of a much more general problem, namely, what is an appropriate model of explanation in the human sciences?

The originator and continued advocate of the view that deductively formulated theory can and should be transferred from some of the best developed of the physical sciences to the much more recent human sciences of linguistics is Noam Chomsky. For more than two decades. Chomsky's transformational generative theory of language has dominated the field of theoretical linguistics. A great deal of work has been carried out either as a response to or as a reaction against the successive versions of his theory. Much of his work, however, has been more impressive for its rhetoric of claim and counter claim than for the light it has thrown on language. Yet these battles, savage and bitter as internecine battles often are, seem to us to be of relatively little significance. Much more important is that the form of explanation supporting Chomsky's work has actually stood in the way of productive research.

The reasons for this are twofold: excessive concern with the form theories should take coupled with insufficient concern for empirical confirmation. The view of explanation which Chomsky took over from certain of the physical sciences – a view incidentally which is the subject of controversy among philosophers of science as to its general explanatory power – has profoundly influenced the kinds of problems linguists have considered worth investigating. On examination many of these problems prove to be generated, not by the unsolved mysteries of the subject matter, but by the theoretical framework imposed on linguistics by the assumption that an explanatory linguistic theory should be deductively formulated. There has been in linguistics a shift from interest in the nature of language to interest in the form of a linguistic theory. This shift of interest to the form theories should take could have been justified if reasonable procedures for testing had been devised. What is striking about theoretical linguistics, and in the context of public support, sobering, is that there has been little emphasis on reasonable standards of empirical confirmation. This is all the more important since, as we shall show, the deductively formulated theory Chomsky developed was never clearly related to uncontroversial data. We argue that from the outset his theoretical approach was never securely grounded.

What is particularly interesting from the standpoint of the history of ideas is that a theory that was insecurely grounded should nevertheless have been so influential. Part I offers an explanation of how it was that such an insecurely based theory should nevertheless dominate the field of theoretical linguistics.

As a general framework for our analysis of transformational generative grammar as an explanatory linguistic theory, we have found useful F. S. C. Northrop's account of scientific method. Northrop begins by discarding the 'hasty and erroneous conclusion' that there is a single correct approach to scientific investigation. He insists on two points. Firstly that enquiry begins with a problem and that it is the nature of the specific problem that determines the method of enquiry that is appropriate. Secondly, that enquiry proceeds in stages and that there are appropriate and inappropriate methods for each stage of enquiry.

Northrop distinguishes three basic stages of enquiry and thus three basic methods of enquiry. The first stage he calls the analysis of the problem. This is the most crucial stage of any enquiry. It involves tracing the problem back to its roots and extricating it from the traditional assumptions which generated it. At this stage, the scientist is likely to call upon his extra-theoretic knowledge of the phenomenon under investigation as well as his familiarity with related areas and existing theory.

The second stage Northrop calls the natural history stage. This involves essentially collecting data made relevant by the analysis of the problem and devising appropriate theoretical concepts in terms of which the data may be ordered.

The third stage is called the stage of deductively formulated theory. This stage involves the search for abstract principles which might be said to explain aspects of the phenomenon under investigation.

It is interesting from the point of view of the approach being developed in this book that the third stage is not seen by Northrop as necessarily appropriate to all types of enquiry. Whether it is or not depends very much on the nature of the problem under analysis and the kind of explanation which the subject matter allows. Indeed Northrop writes of the dangers of moving to the third method of enquiry prematurely. It results he says in 'immature, half-baked, dogmatic and for the most part worthless theory' (Northrop, 1959:37).

With Northrop's distinctions in mind we begin by placing Chomsky's work within a historical context. This context is provided by a number of linguists – Harris, Joos, Hockett, Bloch, Trager, Smith – who worked on the detailed description of the phonology and morphology of a number of languages, often those of the North American Indians. These linguists we group under the label: North American descriptivists.

In Northrop's terms, the North American descriptivists may be said to have adopted a 'natural history' approach to the investigation and analysis of language. Chomsky's concern with the construction of a formal linguistic theory certainly appeared to make his approach very different. This apparent difference gave rise to a claim which remained a commonplace of linguistic textbooks at least as late as 1979, the claim that *Syntactic Structures*, Chomsky's first major publication heralded a revolution in linguistic thinking. We want to challenge this claim. We believe that Chomsky's work was strongly influenced by a number of assumptions which he took over from the North American descriptivists. We press the view that while Chomsky's work was in some ways innovative and evolutionary, it was, as far as the study of language generally is concerned, not revolutionary.

Because of the importance Chomsky attached to the characterisation of an explanatory theory, we devote a good deal of space to discussing the kind of formal model he devised and the aspects of linguistic behaviour it purported to explain. This leads us to pay particular attention to the specific idealisations he was obliged to make in order to be able to present aspects of language in formal notation. The fact that Chomsky made idealisations is not in itself of course open to criticism. It is a commonplace of scientific enquiry that the systematic investigation of any phenomenon requires it to be idealised to some degree. It is unlikely that any scientific work could proceed without such a step.

Idealising is not however without its pitfalls. Foremost among these is the danger that a theorist may sooner or later fail to notice the gap between his idealised object of enquiry and the object unidealised. A central problem in any act of idealising is that of establishing and maintaining a clear relation between a phenomenon idealised for the purposes of analysis and that same phenomenon unidealised. We call this the problem of congruence.

Neither the importance nor the difficulty of arriving at a productive congruence can be exaggerated. Failure to do so is like setting out on a trek on a bearing that is apparently only slightly inaccurate. The further one proceeds, the wider grows the divergence from the true path. In considering Chomsky's theory of language, we shall be giving a good deal of attention to the problem of congruence. The reason for this is that Chomsky at the outset made a number of ill-justified idealisations. Perhaps the most important of these was his decision to view native users of languages as having a highly specific ability: that of being able to distinguish the grammatical from the non-grammatical sentences of their language without reference to meaning. He did not do this because it had been established in any pre-theoretic way that such an ability existed, or that this ability was a source of mystery or had given rise to any problems or questions or indeed that anyone was interested in it at all. He did it in fact for rather a curious reason. He assumed that native speakers could distinguish between grammatical and non-grammatical sentences independently of meaning because the formalised theory which he was devising required this ability to exist in order to be testable. The idealisation which he imposed upon native speakers thus arose out of the requirements of the particular type of theory he was attempting to construct. This arose in its turn from the assumption that a particular view of explanation, borrowed from the physical sciences, was appropriate for linguistics. Chomsky went one stage further however: he claimed that the theoretical model also explained the ability which in order to be valid it required.

The direction in which explanation flows – from the requirements of a particular type of theory to an ability to be explained –

is sufficiently striking to warrant examination. We shall look carefully at whether the idealised native speaker ability which Chomsky's theoretical model required is congruent with the actual abilities which speakers of a language have. If it is not, then his theory can be shown to have been ill-grounded and incongruent from the outset.

Related to the general question of congruence is a further problem which may be specific to theoretical linguistics but is, we suspect, rife in the social sciences more generally. We call it the problem of relevance of description. Irrelevance can arise when a theorist devises a model which is congruent with only peripheral aspects of his subject matter. This is quite common in the social sciences where theorists have often been obliged, in order to produce a formal theory at all, to give unjustified prominence to those aspects of their subject matter which have the apparent virtue of lending themselves to formalisation. In linguistic theory we shall show that Chomsky's account of creativity illustrates this problem. More broadly we believe that the reason the results of research in theoretical linguistics have had so little to offer those in other fields seeking to understand language can be traced to the problem of relevance.

We give considerable attention to the problems involved in idealising as it will be a recurrent theme of the first part of this book that time and again the idealisations made by theoretical linguists have not emerged from an analysis of problems but have been imposed by the kind of explanatory model that was adopted. Unfortunately this kind of idealising has not led to a productive simplification enabling linguistic abilities to be investigated more easily. Indeed the reverse has happened. Under Chomsky's idealisations, the subject matter of enquiry became distorted. The roots of the divergence of linguistics from language lie partly here.

The treatment of meaning in Chomsky's theory provides a complex illustration of this problem. Initially and explicitly *Syntactic Structures* set out to give an account of aspects of linguistic knowledge in terms of purely syntactic categories and syntactic operations. Earlier Chomsky had written:

> Meaning is a notoriously difficult notion to pin down. If it can be shown that meaning and related notions do play a central role in linguistic analysis, then its results and conclusions become subject

to all of the doubts and obscurities that plague the study of meaning, and a serious blow is struck at the foundations of linguistic theory. (Chomsky, 1955:141)

There was thus, we shall argue, from the outset in generative theory, a problem of congruence. The idealised object of enquiry was lacking an interdependence between structure and meaning that we shall show is integral to the unidealised object. We shall argue furthermore that the related problem of relevance, which is such a serious one in theoretical linguistics, can be traced to this original assumption, required by the theory, that form be readily separable from meaning.

In spite of Chomsky's strongly expressed misgivings on the possibility of introducing meaning into linguistic analysis, later versions of transformational generative theory included attempts to broaden its domain to embrace a tentative account of aspects of meaning. In the mid-sixties, a semantic component was added to the syntactically-based formal model. This might be seen as an attempt to overcome the problem of congruence, resulting from the original idealisation which entirely excluded meaning. We argue, however, that the congruence problem remained in spite of the addition of a semantic component. There are two main reasons for this. The first lies in the failure of generative linguists to recognise the significance of introducing into a formal model a component relating to something as ill-defined and elusive as meaning. Chomsky had originally excluded appeals to meaning from linguistic analysis on the grounds that meaning was vague and obscure. For similar reasons, the North American descriptivists had sought to diminish as far as possible any reference to meaning. Furthermore, among philosophers interested in meaning, Tarski, in an influential paper, had concluded that a formal semantics of a natural language looked impossible. Yet when meaning was introduced into linguistic theories, very little detailed consideration was given to how its vagueness and obscurity were to be eliminated such that it could be integrated into a formal model. The second and related reason is that generative linguists interested in semantics were unduly influenced by the formal techniques already developed to account for syntactic structures. Discussions of the relations of syntax and semantics in the transformational generative literature of the sixties and seventies were almost invariably discussions of the adequacy of this or that piece of syntactic apparatus to describe an aspect of meaning. The addition of a semantic component was in effect an attempt to graft an account of meaning on to an apparatus of description specifically set up to account for syntactic characteristics of language without reference to meaning. This attempt led eventually to a fragmentation of the field. Out of it have emerged interpretative semantics, case grammars, generative semantics, trace theory, as well as a host of short-lived 'new theories' or 'new grammars'. We shall argue that an important cause of the present dissarray in theoretical linguistics has been failure of generative linguists to recognise the difficulties inherent in devising a deductively formulated theory once something as indeterminate as meaning was no longer excluded from the domain of enquiry.

Chomsky made other idealisations which further contributed to the divergence of language from its subject matter. He was obliged to disregard language variety and language change. He had to assume, counterfactually, that speech communities were homogeneous in order to satisfy the conditions his explanatory model required. Furthermore, he assumed that speakers of a language have knowledge which is 'purely linguistic' and that such knowledge was readily separable from other types of knowledge, separable from the beliefs, attitudes, experience and expectations of language users.

This idealisation is best seen as an extension of his original assumption that native speakers of a language are able to distinguish grammatical from non-grammatical sentences without reference to meaning. As Chomsky's model developed to include semantic and phonological elements and a lexicon, so the domain of his theory shifted from the explanation of the concept 'grammatical in language' to the explication of the much more general 'purely linguistic knowledge'. Indeed, from this point of view, his earlier insistence on the independence of syntax from semantics can be seen as a special case of his more general view of the independence of purely linguistic knowledge from other types of knowledge that bear on language use.

As with his interest in grammaticality, Chomsky's concern with purely linguistic knowledge did not arise from having established pre-theoretically that such knowledge exists independently of other knowledge. It stemmed instead from his commitment to a particular type of explanatory theory which led him to develop a formal model in the form of a set of rule systems. Just as this originally purely syntactic model to be testable required native speakers to have the ability to distinguish grammatical from non-grammatical sentences, so his extended model required them to have knowledge which is purely linguistic and which they may apply independently of other knowledge. The extended model is then said to explain native speaker ability to apply purely linguistic knowledge to judge the phonological, syntactic and semantic well-formedness of sentences.

Once again, explanation flows from the requirements of the theoretical model to the assumed existence of a set of linguistic abilities and not vice versa. There are however even more problems with the extended domain than with the original restricted one. It is, for example, extremely difficult to make a clear distinction between linguistic and non-linguistic knowledge. In his more recent work in particular Chomsky has recognised that such factors as common sense understanding and systems of belief play a part in language use. He even admits that: 'It may well be impossible to distinguish sharply between linguistic and non-linguistic components of knowledge and belief' (Chomsky, 1975:43). Yet his continued commitment to the devising of a deductively formulated theory has meant that in actual practice he has had to assume that such a distinction can be made or at least that the implications of such a distinction are worth pursuing. We shall be arguing that the attempts to broaden the domain of enquiry to which deductively formulated theory was applied have done no more than lead generative linguistics further up a blind alley.

Exposing the limitations imposed on Chomsky's work by the idealisations he was obliged to make in order to construct a deductively formulated theory is a necessary but preliminary task for us. It is preliminary because our conviction that many linguists have been working within an inappropriate overall theoretical framework does not lead us to the conclusion that work in theoretical linguistics should be abandoned. On the contrary, we believe there is a great deal to be gained from knowing more about the character and functioning of language. Such knowledge could have important social consequences. If, for example, we understood how it is that speakers of a language understand one another, then we might better understand how they misunderstand one another or how they use a common language but fail to communicate. If we understood more about how language works

we might be in a better position to distinguish the processing of
linguistic input that goes on in ordinary conversation from the
kind of processing that has to go on when learning is taking place.
This should have important consequences for education. Too
many courses in too many subject areas seem to be conducted on
the assumption that a student who hears, necessarily understands
and simultaneously learns. Yet most of us have learnt precious
little from our exposure to many, many hours of language in
classrooms and lecture halls. We therefore approached our own
analysis of the problem stage with questions such as these in mind.
It seemed clear that in order to throw light upon these problems,
more had to be known about the processing involved in language
use. The phenomenon whereby language users make sounds and
others associate meanings with these sounds is still largely a
mystery. If we were to throw any light at all on this mystery, we
needed to distance ourselves very firmly from the idealisation of
language which in one form or another had prevailed for so long in
linguistics, the idealisation that allowed language to be characterised apart from its individual users and which futhermore
appeared to place linguistics within the realms of the physical
sciences. From that idealisation, which we argue is a distorting
one, we moved to viewing language in use in terms of the processes
likely to be taking place within language users in the course of
language production and understanding.

Thus in the first stage of our enquiry – the analysis of the
problem stage – we rejected the view that language was best
studied as an independent system or network of relations of
different sorts in favour of a view of linguistic behaviour as a
self-organising complex of interactive processes. In attempting to
give some substance to this view we have concentrated our attention on understanding. We approached the problem from two
directions. We considered first some of the general characteristics
of language which emerge more clearly once it is no longer seen as
separable from the attitudes, beliefs, expectations and overall
experience of language users. Two immediately stand out. First,
language is an epiphenomenon. In Chapter 4 we consider what it
is epiphenomenal on. We assume that the processing involved in
language use takes place within a complex framework of the
knowledge, experience, expectations, attitudes and beliefs that
language users have and, to a limited extent, share. This
framework we term *support* and argue that without its supportive

framework, language would not be a viable system of communication or expression. The view that language without support would be empty is very much in keeping with a general thesis of Part I of the book. There we show why attempts to study linguistic form in isolation have been necessarily sterile.

The second important characteristic of language in use is that meaning is not an inherent but an emergent property of words and sentences. We approach our investigation of this characteristic of language by setting it against what we call a 'container' or 'conveyor' view of meaning. In various forms the container view is widespread both among ordinary language users and among linguists and philosophers interested in language. This is the view that words, in some ill-defined way, contain meaning within themselves; a meaning which, in the course of language use, is conveyed or transmitted to another individual. In contesting this view, we shift the emphasis from language to language users. We view language users as individuals trapped within the confines of their own experience and limited in their knowledge of the world to their own perception of it. We assume that each individual has what we might crudely refer to as a 'knowledge base', representing his accumulated and categorised experience of his environment. If he is to understand language, then the string of sounds or written characters must enable him to gain access to appropriate areas of his 'knowledge base'. The 'knowledge base' of any individual is however not a static 'store of information'. It is rather a self-organising and self-regulating system, constantly shifting and modifying as a result of fresh input. Thus, understanding a fragment of language requires an individual to access an information base which is continually adjusting. Each understanding of an utterance in turn has the effect of causing further reordering of the 'knowledge base'. Much of the time the modifications caused by any act of understanding may be slight. In some sets of circumstances, for example, in the course of effective learning, the reorganisation of the 'knowledge base' may be more substantial.

Keeping these general characteristics of language in mind, we turn to more detailed aspects of the understanding process. The other prong of our attack on the analysis of the problem is to concentrate our attention on what we call 'linguistic units'. These are the units that an understander – an individual hearing and processing language – will process in the course of understanding. Without knowing more about understanding, we cannot define

such units with any precision. At the same time, we could not
proceed far in the investigation of language understanding without at least a working hypothesis as to their nature. In an effort to
surmount these problems, we devise a number of tentative theoretical concepts. We make a basic assumption in relation to what,
for the sake of exposition, we call the 'understander'. We assume
that the understander's task involves at least using the utterance
to locate in his own information base an area of knowledge or
belief that corresponds to some extent with what he hears. In other
words, an understander does not receive information from an
utterance, but rather uses the utterance to gain access to information which in some form and to some degree he already possesses.
From this perspective, language serves to draw out meaning from
the understander. Meaning is thus not, as the container view
would have us believe, in language, but rather language serves to
tap the existing knowledge and experience of language users in
such a way that understanding – to some degree – is possible. This
cannot be anything but a crude expression of a very complex
process. One of the particularly complicating factors is the lack of
any straightforward correspondence between language and the
world as it is likely to be perceived by language users. Consider a
simple example. Suppose someone were to announce: 'I'm going
into town', at least part of an understander's task would be to
locate, in his information base, the particular type of activity
evoked by the combination of units I – go into – town. If, on
another occasion, the passenger in a car were to say: 'Be careful,
the car's going into the wall' then part of the driver-
understander's task would be to locate in his store of accumulated
experience, the particular type of activity evoked by the combination of units – car – go into – wall. Note that 'go into' occurs in
both the above examples. In the first, in combination with 'I' and
'town' it forms part of a unit evoking a complex activity: an
individual journeying to, stopping and doing something in town.
In the second example, in combination with 'car' and 'wall' it
forms part of a unit evoking a simple activity collision: or impact.
'Go into' could of course occur in many other types of unit: 'I'm
going into nursing' would cause a different kind of activity to be
evoked in the understander, while 'I'm going into the possibility
very carefully' would be likely to be construed differently again.

The observation that the same unit, in this case 'go into', occurs
in different combinations each of which would cause an under-

stander to gain access to a different area of experience, is of
considerable significance. If units made essentially the same contribution to all the many combinations in which they occurred,
then the problem would be simple as nothing for example that in:
'He picked the fruit' 'pick' is effectively the same as in: 'He picked
the flower.' The problem however is clearly not that simple. 'Go
into' in 'I'm going into town' is not effectively the same as 'go into'
in 'the car is going into the wall'. Not only would an understander
access different areas of his information base in each case, but also,
the first combination would evoke a complex of actions making up
an open-ended activity: journey plus arrival plus activity or series
of activities in town, while the second would evoke a simpler, more
clearly defined and circumscribed activity. Thus we have the
following state of affairs: language users employ what appear to be
the same linguistic units in diverse combinations to mean different
things. As a consequence, understanders cannot proceed in a
linear fashion by 'looking up' in a sort of 'mental lexicon' the
meanings of the words making up an utterance being processed,
since the meaning of any part of the utterance may depend on the
meaning of the whole. In the example, 'Be careful, the car is going
into the wall', an understander needs to recognise that the utterance establishes a relation between 'car' and 'wall' which is one of
impact, but this interpretation emerges from the whole utterance
and not from knowing the meaning of 'go into'.

In Chapters 4 and 5, we explore the concept of 'emergent
meaning', contrasting it with the much more widespread 'container view' of meaning. The advantage of the emergent view is
that, unlike the container view, it does not require the idealisation
that words have a number of distinct senses which could be
isolated and listed. In Chapter 5 we demonstrate some of the
weaknesses of this idealisation and suggest ways in which the
emergent view could be further explored.

Linguists would recognise what we have been discussing as
related to the fact that linguistic units may be what they would call
polysemous or have multiple meanings. Yet surprisingly little
serious attention has been given to what we see as a rather striking
characteristic of language: that the contribution of words to the
utterances in which they occur is not constant, that words
apparently mean different things on different occasions. Linguists
have tended to adopt what might be called a dictionary approach
to the question: acknowledging that words may have a number of

senses and assuming that the separate senses can be isolated and specified. If language is approached and analysed as a set of processes or operations however then this characteristic must be seen as bearing on the organisation of the data stores accessed by understanders, and on the kinds of accessing strategies that would be required to locate the area of accumulated and categorised experience appropriate to the utterance being processed. If it were the case that linguistic units were monosemous, then we might hypothesise that words act as addresses – to use computing terminology – to appropriate stored meaning representations, developed as a result of experience and that these stored representations could be combined to provide the understander with the meaning of an utterance. The fact, however, that linguistic units are variable means that this simple hypothesis cannot be supported, and that we must envisage accessing and locating strategies of much greater complexity. Some of the factors which these strategies must be able to take into account are discussed in Chapter 5.

The emphasis which we have placed, in the course of our investigations, on the epiphenomenal nature of language, as well as the variability of linguistic units, has led us to view language as a very rough and ready instrument whereby individuals, trapped within the confines of their own experience, are able, within limits, to communicate with others. Language, as we understand it, is a necessarily imperfect instrument. Language users – much more than linguists – are eminently conscious of the limitations of language: expressions such as 'Do you know what I mean?' or 'Do you see?' are frequent, and are likely to occur when there is uncertainty as to whether sufficient support in terms of shared beliefs or experience is present to enable a speaker's language to function successfully. Language users are likely to become aware of the shortcomings and inadequacies of language as soon as they move out of the domain of the commonplace and the familiar. Linguists have not, in general, given serious attention to these limitations. Yet in seeking to understand how language works, its limitations can provide clear pointers to some of its basic properties.

In idealising away from these limitations, linguistics have assumed language to be a rigorous and well-ordered system. While there is no denying the attraction, from one view of science, of looking at language in this way, it is a theme of this book that this view is in the end counter-productive. It conceals the open-

ended and self-organising nature of the processes involved in
language understanding and production. We argue that failure to
recognise these properties had led to the growing divergence
between the science of linguistics and its subject matter: language.

In recent years some theoretical linguists have begun to pay
more attention to the importance in the interpretation of language
of what they refer to as 'the world'. This is reflected in the
flourishing of a domain which has become known as pragmatics.
Very broadly, pragmatics is concerned with the characterisation
of language in use. There are certainly aspects of this work with
which we are sympathetic. However, workers in this field have
generally assumed that the results of their work could be integrated in some way into existing formal models. They have seen
their work as supplementing, not replacing the accounts of aspects
of language provided by the deductively formulated theoretical
models which Chomsky originally inspired. One consequence of
this is that a recurrent issue in the theoretical linguistics of the
mid-seventies has centred on the question of where the borderline
between semantics and pragmatics should be drawn. This is to
some extent parallel to the discussion in the mid-sixties on the
interrelations between syntax and semantics. However, since no
reasonably well-defined formal semantic component for a natural
language has been developed, the question of the relations of
semantics and pragmatics – the relations between knowledge of
the meaning of words and sentences and knowledge of 'the world'
– has of necessity remained elusive. From the point of view of the
theme being developed in this book, workers in pragmatics have
not traced their problem back to its roots. Pragmatics, in other
words, has not been radical enough.

In tracing back to its roots the question of the relation of
language not to the world but to the language user's view of the
world, we foresee for linguistics a prolonged natural history stage.
It has been said that physics took the whole of the Greek period
and the entire Middle Ages to develop its natural history stage and
passed to its deductive stage through the particularly brilliant
minds of Galileo and Newton.

For linguistics – a human science – to move forward, the
question to be asked at this early stage in its development is not:
how can language be idealised so as to link it to deductively
formulated theory?, but: how can linguistics open up productive
lines of research into workings of language?

As long as a reductive style of deductively formulated theory is accepted as the one true model of explanation in linguistics, a negative role for theoretical linguists is at least clear: they should firmly resist the lure of that model. To move in a more positive direction linguists will need to develop a mode of explanation more appropriate to the human sciences, one able to integrate, rather than idealise away from, the purposes, beliefs and expectations of language users.

Notes

1. In viewing language terms of interactive processes we may seem to share the standpoint of workers in artificial intelligence who attempt to program computers to carry out tasks which would require intelligence if performed by humans. One such task is the use of language. Computer systems have been developed whereby it is possible for a human interlocutor to converse in natural language, to a limited extent, with a machine. Such systems constitute simulations of language use, and one of the justifications of such work is the light it could throw on the actual processes involved in human language production and understanding. It is, however, outside the scope of this book to assess the likelihood of work in artificial intelligence throwing any light on the problems of natural language productions and understanding.

Part I

Chomsky's Theory of Grammar: the Divergence of Linguistics from Language

1 Chomsky's Theory of Grammar: the Historical Connection

Grammar is best formulated as a self-contained study independent of semantics.

Noam Chomsky

From the outset Chomsky's work aroused feelings of shock, excitement, turmoil, and in some quarters, dismay, hostility and misunderstanding. To his contemporaries he appeared to be directly challenging assumptions and working practices which were fundamental to North American linguistics of that time. It soon became commonplace to observe that Chomsky had revolutionised linguistics in North America. Nor was this a short-lived view. As late as 1979 an introductory textbook was published with the sub-title: *The results of Chomsky's revolution.*

The basis of the difference between Chomsky and his early contemporaries lay in their different view of what constituted 'doing science'. Central to the concerns of the North American linguists of the forties and fifties had been a determination to practise linguistics in such a way as to establish for the subject the status of a science akin to the physical sciences. Chomsky never questioned the assumption that linguistics could and should be practised as a science. He did however turn away from the inductive, positivist view of science which had prevailed in linguistics to adopt a more sophisticated hypothetico-deductive approach.

In this chapter we shall be discussing the way in which the inductively-based view of science of Chomsky's contemporaries and immediate predecessors had imposed upon them a particularly narrow view of their subject matter, language. It had, for example, required them to exclude considerations of meaning and concentrate instead on linguistic form. Furthermore, it forced them to disregard the language user and, in particular, any insight he might have into the workings of his language. It was a view of science that sought to make language a context-independent and user-independent object of enquiry.

19

We shall be arguing that although Chomsky introduced into linguistics a different view of science he equally had his subject matter imposed upon him. Furthermore, although Chomsky's domain of enquiry differs in important respects from that of his contemporaries, there were nevertheless a number of their assumptions he did not question and which have continued to have a profound effect on the direction of his work. Most significant among these was first the assumption that meaning can be clearly separated from form and second that language users and their knowledge, beliefs, values and expectations have to be excluded from the domain of enquiry if linguistics is to be a rigorous science.

Our general thesis is that in sharing with his contemporaries the view that linguistics should be an exact and rigorous science Chomsky continued a tradition which has proved largely barren of insights into the workings of language. In assuming that the physical sciences provide an appropriate model for a human science such as linguistics, North American linguists have been forced to exclude aspects of language which we shall show in subsequent chapters turn out to be fundamental. In modelling themselves so closely on the physical sciences, North American linguists of the forties and fifties began a process which Chomsky continued – a process whereby the new science of linguistics diverged in important respects from its subject matter. In developing their approach Chomsky may be said to have brought into linguistics new insights about science, not new insights about language.

The North American descriptivists

Among Chomsky's contemporaries there was a group whose views had become particularly influential in setting the tone of theoretical and descriptive linguistics in North America. We shall refer to this group as the North American descriptivists, a name they frequently used of themselves in preference to the more general label of structuralists. The linguists in this group included amongst others Zellig Harris, Charles Hockett, Martin Joos, Bernard Bloch, George Trager, Harold Smith and Freeman Twaddell. Of these, two stand out when it comes to understanding Chomsky's relations with other North American linguists. One is Zellig Harris, Chomsky's teacher at Pennsylvania, from whom he absorbed many of his methodological concerns. The other – perhaps surprisingly – is Charles Hockett, in whose writing can be found some of the concern which Chomsky himself came to show with the psychological relevance of linguistics models.

In discussing the views of science of the descriptivists we shall not be presenting a rounded picture of the views of any single one of them. Instead we shall seek a selection and grouping of a number of attitudes and assumptions which are representative of their general view. Among our sources for the views of the descriptivists we have found two works particularly useful. One of these is *Structural Linguistics* by Zellig Harris. The other is a collection of papers, edited by Martin Joos, entitled *Readings in Linguistics*.

It is clear from the introduction to the *Readings in Linguistics* that the editor confidently felt that, in drawing together a number of papers representing the current state of descriptive linguistics in North America, he had caught 'the American style in linguistic thought' (Joos, RIL, 1957:V). It is however one of those curious, ironic, but not unfamiliar accidents of history that the year of publication of *Readings in Linguistics* was the same year as Chomsky published the first version of his theory of language. The year was 1957 and Chomsky's book was *Syntactic Structures*.

The North American descriptivists' view of science

The view of science which prevailed in linguistics well into the fifties owed much to the influence of Leonard Bloomfield. The North American descriptivists fully recognised their debt to Bloomfield. Joos, for example, once described as 'the Newton of Linguistics' and one of his papers as 'the Charter of contemporary descriptive linguistics'. Bloch, for many years editor of the most prestigious journal in the field, *Language,* affirmed that Bloomfield's major contribution has been to make linguistics a science:

> There can be no doubt that Bloomfield's greatest contribution to the study of language was to make a science of it. Others before him had worked scientifically in linguistics; but no one had so uncompromisingly rejected all pre-scientific methods, or had been so consistently careful, in writing about language, to use terms that would imply no tacit reliance on factors beyond the range of observation. (Bloch, 1949:92)

In attempting to outline the general character of Bloomfield's views, a major difficulty arises from the fact that these underwent a number of changes, particularly on the relation of the study of language to the study of mind, and on the role of meaning in linguistic analysis. All we have space to do here is to pick out those aspects of Bloomfield's views that influenced the North American descriptivists.[1] Foremost among these is his view of what counts as a valid scientific description of some object or event. Bloomfield wrote.

> It is the belief of the present writer that the scientific description of the universe, whatever this description may be worth, requires none of the mentalistic terms linguists use to explain the operation of language . . . we can distinguish science from other phases of human activity by agreeing that science shall deal only with events that are accessible in their time and place to any and all observers (strict behaviorism) or only with events that are placed in co-ordinates of time and space (mechanism), or that science shall employ only such initial statements and predictions as lead to definite handling operations (operationalism), or only terms such as are derivable by rigid definition from a set of everyday terms concerning physical happenings (physicalism). These several formulations, independently reached by different scientists, all lead to the same delimitation, and this delimitation does not restrict the subject matter of science but rather characterizes its method. (Bloomfield, 1939:13)

In this characteristic passage Bloomfield is insisting that an appropriate scientific description is one that makes use of abstract terms only if in each and every case they 'are derivable by rigid definition from a set of everyday terms concerning physical happenings'. This approach enabled him to replace the subjectivity that in his view tainted European linguistics by a greater degree of objectivity of description: the keynote of the American style of linguistic thought. As he saw it, objective description was not compatible with the use of 'mentalistic' terms, terms introduced into a description without being directly derivable from the linguistic data.

Looking at Bloomfield's views in a wider context, it is clear that his position is closely related to that of the nineteenth and early twentieth century positivists. Simplifying considerably, we may say that for such positivists what was unacceptable as science was the untestable. Their emphasis therefore fell upon methods of verification. It was a principle of the logical positivists for example that the meaning of a statement lay in the method of its verification. In Bloomfield's case we may construe this as the belief that the value of a linguistic statement lay in the soundness of the methods that had determined it. Bloomfield's emphasis on methods of description was to make linguistics a science that sought objectivity by striving to derive its generalisations by rigorous procedures directly from observable data.

Bloomfield's rejection of the use of mentalistic terms was at base a rejection of what he saw as overly simplistic attempts to explain the use of language. The linguists, generally European, he characterised as mentalistic looked for explanation for language use in terms that appealed to the purposes, beliefs and expectations of language users. In place of this mentalistic, and in his view, unscientific approach to explanation, Bloomfield proposed what he called the mechanist view:

> For the mentalist, language is the expression of ideas, feelings, or volitions. The mechanist does not accept this solution, he believes that mental images, feelings, and the like are merely popular terms for various bodily movements, . . .[2] (Bloomfield, 1935:142)

This had not always been Bloomfield's view of the relation of language and mind. Earlier he had written:

> . . . perhaps the student of mental science could and ideally should refrain from any running psychologic interpretation; but in practice, however, such interpretation is unavoidable . . . , linguistics is of all the mental sciences most in need of guidance at every step by the best psychologic insight available. (Bloomfield, 1914:322–3)

However the Bloomfield that influenced the descriptivists had abandoned this view. As early as 1924, he was moving to viewing linguistics as an autonomous science:

> . . . psychology and phonetics do not matter at all and are, in principle, irrelevant to the study of language. (Bloomfield, 1924:318)

In the paper that Joos had called 'the charter for contemporary linguistics', Bloomfield wrote:

> . . . the postulational method saves discussion, because it limits our statements to a defined terminology; in particular, it cuts us off from psychological dispute. (Bloomfield, 1926:153)

As well as a general concern for objectivity, the descriptivists thus absorbed from Bloomfield a view of linguistics as an independent science separate from psychology, a science with its own methods and subject matter.

This essentially Bloomfieldian view of science is reflected both explicitly and implicitly in the descriptivists' work. Bloch and Trager for example in their *Outline of Linguistic Analysis* describe a linguist in the following revealing terms:

> He is a scientist whose subject matter is language, and his task is to analyse and classify the facts of speech, as he hears them uttered by native speakers or as he finds them recorded in writing. (Bloch and Trager, 1942:8)

A linguist, in other words, deals only with events – the facts of speech – 'accessible in their time and any place to any and all observers'. There is considerable evidence in the writings of the period that the North American descriptivists believed that the scientific method consisted in observing, collecting data and describing accurately, making use of only such terms 'as are derived by rigid definition from a set of everyday terms concerning physical happenings'. Joos wrote:

> . . . we try to describe precisely; we do not try to explain. Anything in our description that sounds like explanation is simply loose talk . . . and is not to be considered part of current linguistic theory.[3] (Joos, 1957a:349)

Joos' almost contemptuous dismissal of explanation – 'simply loose talk' – in favour of accurate description appears to be a somewhat simplistic comment on a highly complex problem: the interaction between description and explanation in science. Chomsky's insistence that linguistics should be an explanatory science seemed to constitute a complete break with the descriptivists' position. However, it is important to note that the kind of explanation that Joos was rejecting was not the reductive hypothetic-deductive mode that Chomsky introduced but the much more discursive, speculative and largely untestable accounts of language offered by earlier European linguists.

In general, the North American descriptivists shared Joos' conviction that linguistic work was, in essence, classificatory. The opening sentence of a characteristic paper of Hockett's begins:

Linguistics is a classificatory science. (Hockett, 1957a:97)

The interest in the ideas that were coming out of Europe, particularly those from the Prague Linguistic Circle, was tempered by the same descriptivists caution. Joos clearly felt that such ideas offered:

... too much of phonological *explanation* where a sober *taxonomy* would serve as well. (Joos, 1957b:96)

A recurrent theme in their writings reflecting their self-conscious concern with the status of linguistics as a science is the obligation 'to speak precisely about language or not at all'. In order to describe precisely they sought to make 'our linguistics a kind of mathematics'. While recognising this as a desirable goal, they were aware that it was not an easy one to achieve. To the question of whether the descriptivists had succeeded in setting up an adequate mathematical style for describing language structure, Joos replied:

Well, not quite; but our science is still young. In its mathematical phase it is just a quarter of a century old, for we date it from Bloomfield's 'A set of postulates for the science of language' (in the journal *Language*, 1926). (Joos, 1957a:350)

Nevertheless the descriptivists undoubtedly felt that among the human sciences descriptive linguistics had a clear lead:

But of all the sciences and near-sciences which deal with human behavior, linguistics is the only one which is in a fair way to becoming completely mathematical, and the other social scientists are already beginning to imitate the strict methods of the linguists. (Joos, 1957a:350)

Not all North American linguists entirely approved of this move to mathematise linguistic description. Haugen writes:

> Present-day descriptions bristle like a page of symbolic logic and lack entirely the leisurely, even charming quality of the traditional grammars. I would not go back to those grammars, but only suggest that economy may not always be a virtue; in some cases it results from poverty, and in any case it must be replaced by an expansion into real sounds and real meanings . . .[4] (Haugen, 1957:363)

Harris was among those linguists most committed to the mathematising of linguistic description. At one stage he summed up the descriptivists' task as follows:

> It is . . . convenient to consider the elements as purely logical symbols, upon which various operations of mathematical logic can be performed. At the start of our work we translate the flow of speech into a combination of these elements, and at the end we translate the combinations of our final and fundamental elements back into the flow of speech. All that is required to enable us to do this is that at the beginning there should be one-one correspondence between portions of speech and our initial elements, and that no operations performed upon the elements should destroy this one-one association, . . . (Harris, 1951:18)

Hockett too, in a mathematical interlude inserted in one paper, pointed out the parallels between mathematical systems and linguistic descriptions:

> Mathematics is a good place to turn for analogs of structures . . . A good many *mathematical systems* are characterisable wholly or primarily as consisting of a set of *elements* for which certain *relations* are defined . . . Another great class of mathematical systems are characterisable as consisting of a set of elements for which certain *operations* are defined. (Hockett, 1957c:394–5)

We emphasise the mathematical aspects of work in North American descriptive linguistics partly to draw attention to a feature of their practice that has often been overlooked by those who focus on the revolutionary aspects of Chomsky's linguistics.

In seeking to bring the exactness of mathematics into theoretical linguistics Chomsky was continuing, not revolting against, a practice of the theoretically-minded North American descriptivists. While he undoubtedly developed the kind of mathematical logics applied to linguistics, he was in so doing extending the descriptivists' commitment to linguistics as an exact and rigorous science rather than introducing any new and radical approach.

The working practices of the descriptivists

The North American descriptivist view of science as non-speculative, exact, objective and rigorous naturally had a profound effect on their aims. These were neatly summed up by Harris:

> The overall purpose of work in descriptive linguistics is to obtain a compact one-one representation of the stock of utterances in the corpus. (Harris, 1951:366)

Making adequate description the overall purpose of work in linguistics was a goal that Chomsky was to reject, but not before he had absorbed enough of the descriptivist approach for it to influence, in important respects, the direction of his work. We call attention to these origins since they help to explain why Chomsky has adopted some of his characteristic positions – and why, under his aegis, linguistics has diverged further from its subject matter, language.

What then did Harris mean when he said that the purpose of the descriptivists' work was to give a compact one-one representation of the stock of utterances in a corpus?

(i) The corpus

Generally speaking a 'corpus' was likely to be a body of utterances of an unknown or unfamiliar language that had been recorded and initially transcribed, often on field trips. A good deal of the descriptivists' interest was centred on the indigenous language of their own continent. Thus much of their work consisted of analysing and characterising languages of the North American Indians.

This did not mean however that a corpus was just any random sample of extracts from a language. In principle at least a corpus

was not an adequate corpus until it could be shown to be representative. Harris wrote:

> To persons interested in linguistic results, the analysis of a
> particular corpus becomes of interest only if it is virtually identical
> with the analysis which would be obtained in like manner from any
> other sufficiently large corpus of material taken in the same dialect
> ... When this is the case, the analysed corpus can be regarded as a
> descriptive sample of the language ... When the linguist finds that
> all additional material yields nothing not contained in his analysis
> he may consider his corpus adequate. (Harris, 1951:13)

The descriptivists insisted, on a theoretical level at least, that
the corpus be representative since only on that basis could one
'predict the relations among elements in any other corpus of the
language on the basis of the relations found in our analysed
corpus' (Harris, 1951:13).

In practice, however, the descritivists were not able to ensure
that the corpus they had collected was an adequate descriptive
sample. Given the extreme difficulties they were often working
under, those who went out into the field had little option but to
collect what corpus they could from their informants, or sometimes only a single informant. In the light of the problems and
hardships of fieldwork, it simply was not practical to pursue an
analysis until it had been established that the corpus was a
representative sample. The descriptivists became, almost inevitably, more interested in methods of analysing the corpus actually
collected than in its status as an adequate sample. In spite of his
misgivings as a theorist, Harris is summing up the actual practice
of the descriptivists when he writes:

> The procedures discussed below are applied to a corpus of
> material without regard to the adequacy of the corpus as a sample
> of the language. (Harris, 1951:13)

For linguists whose concern was to be exact, rigorous and
objective the immediate attraction of grounding descriptive work
in a specific corpus of utterances was that it required them to keep
very close to the directly observable: an actual transcribed text.
And yet trying to ground an analysis firmly in the directly observable did in fact give rise to various types of problems. One such
problem, particularly for theoretically-minded descriptivists, was

how far to idealise the corpus. Any actual corpus of recorded material inevitably contains hesitations, coughs, grunts and other apparently irrelevant non-linguistic noises. The good practical sense of the working field linguist would lead him to eliminate these 'interruptions' from his transcript. To that extent the field linguist idealises his corpus. The theorist on the other hand will have to ask himself on what grounds these phenomena are removed since the claim of the descriptivists is that recorded material is being analysed in precisely the form in which it is found.

There are, in the writing of the two major theorists of this period, Harris and Hockett, discussions of methodological problems of just this sort.

Harris asks:

> But what of a cough, or of the utterance Hmm!, or of gestures whether accompanying speech or not? (Harris, 1951:18)

Harris decides that where there is no regular distribution of a sound, we may exclude that sound as non-linguistic, Hockett, on the other hand, distinguishes marking sneezes in a corpus from coughs and belches on the grounds that the latter are bisocial and therefore an act of speech. The passage is worth quoting in full as an illustration of what the North American theoretical linguist saw as a problem in idealising his corpus:

> Utterances are bisocial. A sneeze occurs in the same area; . . . but the source of the sneeze is purely physiological. Therefore a sneeze is not bisocial, and is not a speech act. On the other hand, a cough in our society, where it may be an indication of polite embarrassment, or a belch in some parts of Africa, where it shows appreciation to one's host, fulfills all the requirements of bisocial behavior, . . . and must therefore be considered an act of speech. (Hockett, 1957a:97)

Hockett concludes however that the cough and belches along with the English interjection *pst* may nevertheless be excluded from an analysis on the grounds of their marginal status.

(ii) Analysing the corpus

One assumption which was fundamental to the descriptivists' approach to analysis was that the text – their corpus – could for the purposes of analysis be taken in isolation from those who had uttered it. In other words the text was to be treated as a self-contained entity. This most basic assumption was forced on them by their view that as scientists they should aim to be objective – impossible if the beliefs, expectations and idiosyncrasies of language users had to be taken into account.

They made in addition a second important assumption which was that the form of the text – the arrangement of its elements – could be characterised with no reference to the meaning of the text. The exclusion of meaning was justified by a methodological principle known as the separation of levels. This assumed that the phonological, morphological, syntactic and semantic characteristics of language could be entirely separated from one another and that for a given language a linguist could analyse for example the arrangements of sounds – the phonological system – without taking any account of its other characteristics. This they coupled with a second methodological principle which assumed that analysis should proceed from the analysis of sounds step-by-step to syntactic structure and that this order should never be reversed since it was only in this way that the links with observable reality in the form of sounds could be maintained.[5] Both these methodological principles stemmed from the descriptivists' view of science. This required them to remain anchored firmly in the directly observable – which for them were the strings of sounds which lay behind the transcribed text.

The assumption that form could be characterised independently of meaning meant in practice that the descriptivists excluded meaning from the domain of their enquiry. There were a number of reasons for this, one of them being that their efforts to 'make our linguistics a kind of mathematics' meant that they had to exclude anything which could not be reduced to a reasonably strict notation. Meaning was much more difficult to categorise than form, much more open to idiosyncratic interpretation and was clearly not directly observable nor very clearly related to anything that was.

There was, however, an additional reason which may have bolstered the descriptivists' exclusion of meaning. Working as they most generally were with unfamiliar languages and 'exotic' cultures the exclusion of meaning allowed them apparently to escape the limitations of their knowledge of the beliefs and ways of life of the peoples whose languages they were describing. This is reflected in their attitudes to their informants whose own insights they disregarded.[6] There are unsavoury aspects of this attitude to members of a community – often a North American Indian community – whose language is studied as if it were 'pure form', as if it bore no relation to their values and way of life. At the scientific level it appears to have arisen from the belief that by proceeding in this way the descriptivist would somehow get at the 'pure facts' of the language under analysis, untainted by anything that might be called 'mentalistic'. This enabled them to see their ignorance, which should have been a crippling limitation, as a virtue that guaranteed their scientific approach.

On the basis of methodological and theoretical assumptions of this kind, which show up in a diluted form in Chomsky's own work, the descriptivists worked on the characterisation of the regularities of form which they observed in their corpus. Harris wrote:

> Descriptive linguistics . . . is a particular field of inquiry which deals . . . with the regularities in certain features of speech. These regularities are in the distributional relations among the features of speech in question, . . . The main research of descriptive linguistics, and the only relation which will be accepted as relevant in the present survey, is the distribution or arrangement within the flow of speech of some parts or features relatively to others. (Harris, 1951:5)

The concentration on form and formal arrangements at the expense of meaning is the keynote of the descriptivists. They might well be known, as a mnemonic for their methods, as distributionalists. A label such as distributional descriptivists would then sum up both their methods and their aims.

By the distribution of an element was meant:

> . . . the total of all environments in which it occurs, i.e. the sum of all the (different) positions (or occurrences) of an element relative to the occurrence of other elements. (Harris, 1951:15–16)

Very generally, the descriptivists seem to have believed that if they observed and represented in a suitable notation the arrangements of elements in a corpus then they were remaining entirely objective. Harris commented that their analytical procedures were in effect 'merely ways of arranging the original data' adding that:

> ... since they go only by formal distinctions (that is make use of statements of distribution) there is no opportunity for uncontrolled interpreting of the data or for forcing of the meaning. (Harris, 1951:3)

One of their major tasks on the phonological level was to establish for an unfamiliar language which sounds were distinct and which were simply variants of one another. Harris explains their procedure:

> We take an utterance whose segments are recorded as DEF. We now construct an utterance composed of the segments of DA'F, where A' is a repetition of a segment A in an utterance which we had represented as ABC. If our informant accepts DA'F as a repetition of DEF, ... and if we are similarly able to obtain E'BC (E' being a repetition of E) as equivalent to ABC, then we say that A and E (and A' and E') are mutually substitutable (or equivalent), as free variants of each other, and write A = E. If we fail in these tests, we say that A is different from E and not substitutable for it. The test of segment substitutability is the action of the native speaker: his use of it, or his acceptance of our use of it. (Harris, 1951:31)

In a typical case Harris cites, the analyst would observe – if the language under analysis were English and he were unfamiliar with English – that there are variations, sometimes only slight, in the pronunciation of the first sound segment of a word such as *can't*. We may represent two different degrees of aspiration in the initial sound *k* as [k] and [kh]. The analyst then compares these variants with the initial segment of a similar utterance with apparently similar variants, say *cameras*, by substituting the [k] or the [kh] segment of the first utterance for the initial segment of the second. If a native speaker of English acting as informant now accepts the new utterance as a repetition of *cameras* then the analyst will conclude that the two segments are freely substitutable and thus descriptively equivalent.

Substitution or replacement of one element by another was the chief methodological tool of the descriptivists and was seen as giving them a distinct advantage over other social sciences in that it enabled data to be duplicated. It was seen by some as a linguistic analogue to controlled experiments in the physical sciences. Haugen wrote:

The method which the metalinguists recognise as fundamental in their analysis, namely replacement, is primarily directed at the discovery of distribution. In some ways this technique is analogous to the natural scientist's controlled experiment. Just as the latter varies a single factor while keeping the rest constant, so the linguist studies the possibilities of variation in utterances. Whenever he can, he finds utterances differing by only a single factor; if he has a native speaker available, he manufactures such utterances by asking for repetition of the same utterance with replacement of a single factor. The fact that such repetition is possible gives the linguist a great advantage over other social scientists, whose situations can rarely be duplicated at will. (Haugen, 1957:360)

What the descriptivists appear not to have noticed however was that the segment substitutability test required personal judgement of a highly subjective kind. It either required the informant, often a North American Indian, to make subtle judgements about what was to count as 'same' or 'different', or it required the linguist to judge that his best imitation of the sound under analysis had been adequate when his informant for a myriad of linguistically irrelevant but sociologically extremely significant reasons might be agreeing or disagreeing with his rendition. In either direction segment substitutability testing was fraught with rampant subjectivity.

The descriptivists generally glossed over the informant's problem of what counts as a repetition. In practice however for the analysis of sound segments to proceed in an illuminating way, the linguist needs constantly to draw on the personal knowledge of the informant in subtle and intricate ways. Although the descriptivists may have believed that they were eliminating meaning they were in the actual process of analysis implicitly drawing on it. As Haugen once remarked:

The minimising of meaning as a factor in linguistic description was at first a healthy reaction against the misuse of meaning in establishing linguistic categories, but has now become almost a fetish with some linguists. It is curious to see how those who eliminate meaning have brought it back under the covert guise of distribution . . . But it is important to note that only a native can make such replacements; and by definition a native knows the meanings of the forms he uses. (Haugen, 1957:362)

At the syntactic level, the descriptivists sought to use the results of the analysis of words at the 'lower' phonological and morphological levels to provide a compact description of the sentence forms in the language. A sentence form was arrived at by assigning each word in the corpus to a grammatical category. Let us suppose for the sake of illustration that we have a restricted corpus of three English sentences with word divisions conveniently marked:

Max – left
Alice – cried
Alice – detested – Max

We can then assign each of the words to categories. If we call these categories syntactic categories, we are then performing a syntactic analysis of a very simple sort of the words in the language. Assuming that we assign 'Max', 'Alice' to the category noun (N), and 'left', 'cried' and 'detested' to the category verb (V), we have three sequences of categories, N + V; N + V; N + V + N corresponding to the three sentences in the corpus. If we call each sequence of categories a sentence form, we can then say that our corpus of three English sentences contains two sentence forms, N + V, N + V + N. Furthermore we may observe in our corpus, or elicit from our informant, that *Max* and *Alice* have a freedom occurrence or distribution in each others' positions. Thus *Alice left*, *Max cried* and *Max detested Alice* are all sentences of the language. While the number of sentences has doubled, the number of sentence forms has remained the same. In general, there will be many fewer sentence forms, sequences of syntactic categories, than sentences, sequences of words, in the corpus. In this sense, the descriptivist is giving a compact one-one representation of the stock of utterances in the corpus.

Syntactic analysis of this sort can be done at different levels of generality. We have taken broad categories such as nouns and verbs. Each of those categories could be broken down into subcategories, then sub-subcategories, and so on. Each sequence of subcategories constitutes another sentence form. As the analysis of syntactic categories becomes more detailed, so the sentence forms become more numerous.

This kind of syntactic description was known as constituent

analysis. Constituent analysis is a form of parsing that breaks down a sentence into its syntactic word classes, its syntactic constituents. The grammars that resulted from constituent analysis of this sort had as their aim to give an account of the distribution of categories and subcategories relative to other categories and subcategories. The problems that confronted descriptivists devising constituent structure grammars were typically problems about how, on distributional not semantic grounds, to assign the syntactic categories to the words in the corpus. In the examples just cited, how do we know that *Max* is a noun and *left* a verb? Clearly, the descriptivists could not use the traditional definitions such as a noun being the name of a person, place or thing.

They sought to resolve this problem in a way that corresponded to their procedures for identifying equivalent and non-equivalent sound segments. That is they used the technique of substitution but this time in syntactic frames to determine whether elements belonged to the same category. The test in this case was the informant's readiness to accept as grammatical the frame that resulted from each substitution. Thus Fries, in *The Structure of English*, attempted to set up the syntactic categories, or parts of speech, without using the traditional names, noun, verbs, adjective etc. Instead he set up a frame and labelled the words that could appear in the frame as, for example, Class 1 words. Thus in the frame.

The — was good.

the class of words that could be acceptably inserted in the blank would be, not nouns, but Class 1 words, and so on for other frames and other classes. More generally, as at the phonological level, mutual substitutability with the preservation of grammaticality according to the native speaker was usually taken to be the basic criterion of grammatical analysis. In practice no descriptivist syntactation seriously examined all possible frames to discover syntactic equivalences and non-equivalences. In effect what he did was to use a few frames that lent support to the category he intuitively knew to be appropriate. Once again as happened with the segment substitutability test at the phonological level, intuitions turn out to play a much greater role than was acknowledged in the assignment of syntactic categories.

A firmer theoretical basis for the descriptivists' work

It has now largely been forgotten that Chomsky's initial contribution to linguistics arose out of his attempts to provide a firmer and more rigorous theoretical basis for the kind of grammars the descriptivists were attempting to construct. We must emphasise, however, that in setting about this task, he was not turning his back on the work of his contemporaries. On the contrary, as he himself once expressed it, he was seeking a more rigorous and explicit formulation of the assumptions underlying their work:

> In *The Logical Structure of Linguistic Theory*, the theory of phrase structure is developed in an effort to capture essential ideas of traditional and structuralist theories of categories and constituents, within the new framework of generative grammar. (Chomsky, 1975:8)

Chomsky's attempt to find a firmer theoretical basis for the work of his contemporaries emerged out of his efforts to write grammars in the mode of the descriptivists. Some of his own earliest linguistic work was on the production of a descriptivist grammar of Hebrew. Chomsky set about this task in the orthodox way using an informant and applying analytical procedures of the type discussed earlier. The results of these attempts were, in Chomsky's own words, 'rather dull and unsatisfying' (Chomsky, 1975:25). As he saw it, merely arranging or re-stating the data in more compact terms had no explanatory force. The question that Joos had ruled out:

> . . . we do not answer 'why' questions about the design of a language. (Joos, 1957a:349)

became the very question Chomsky sought to explore.

He found – to his initial disquiet – that in order to find a way of explaining the distribution of Hebrew forms he needed to postulate abstract theoretical constructs that could be related only indirectly to the observable data. His disquiet arose from his conviction at that time that in moving away from the directly observable he was at the same time moving away from what he called 'real scientific linguistics'. He was well aware that the positivist emphasis of descriptivist linguistics on maintaining clear links with the directly observable ruled out the postulation of abstract elements of the type he was beginning to see as necessary. In the Introduction to *The Logical Structure of Linguistic Theory* he comments that he first thought of his own work as 'more or less of a private hobby, having no relationship to "real linguistics" '. (Chomsky, 1975:29)

In seeking to explain the distribution of forms rather than simply describing them there is some evidence that Chomsky was influenced by his father's work in historical syntax. In historical linguistics there was never any question but that the goal is to find explanations for the different forms in related languages. It was standard procedure among historical linguists to postulate abstract proto-forms in order to explain the similarities, equivalences and anomalies of later forms of related languages. Attested language forms were compared and assumed to have a common origin. This could lead by way of inferences about possible processes of change to the postulation of an original 'first' language. It was then this reconstructed language that purported to explain the similarities, equivalences and anomalies of the later attested forms. By reconstructing forward from his abstract postulated form the historical syntactician can test the adequacy of his hypothesised construct. The kind of explanation Chomsky *père* sought in historical syntax, Chomsky *fils* came to seek in synchronic syntax. At one point in *The Logical Structure of Linguistic Theory*, Chomsky himself draws the connection. He writes:

> A historical analogy may clarify the point in question. Our general conception of grammar is formally somewhat analogous to a description of historical change . . . In its full generality, our notion of grammar has the full power of a descriptive statement of historical change. (Chomsky, 1975:203–4)

The direction that Chomsky's search for explanations of the distribution of linguistic forms was to take is strikingly clear from the title of his major work, *The Logical Structure of Linguistic Theory*. There Chomsky lays out the underlying formal properties of the models of syntactic description used by the descriptivists. Indeed, his first and original contribution to linguistic theory was to show how by using the apparatus of formal language theory as a model the constituent analysis grammars of the North American descriptivists could be recast as deductively formulated rule systems. His own work then came to centre on the elaboration and refinement of such systems as explanatory models. We shall discuss the character and operation of such systems in the next chapter.

There can be no doubt that Chomsky's interest in the development of deductively formulated systems within linguistics represented a decisive break with the practices of the descriptivists. Their work was analytic and firmly linked to data in the form of transcribed texts. Chomsky's grammars would in contrast be best described as synthetic. He was concerned with delimiting the general properties that any constituent grammar would possess. Thus his work was at a higher level of abstraction than that of his contempories. His aim was to provide grammars for their grammars, or meta-grammars.

In attempting to construct a meta-grammar for the local grammars of the descriptivists in the form of a deductive system, Chomsky was however extending not radically altering the theoretical concern of the descriptivists with mathematising linguistic description. This extension undoubtedly involved a more sophisticated style of mathematics but it did not initially constitute a departure from the goals of the descriptivists. The focus of Chomsky's early work remained that of giving an account of the distributions of linguistic forms. This becomes evident if we look at some of Chomsky's first syntactic work where the close links with the descriptivists show up most clearly. One of the reasons Chomsky's work had the impact it did was that he addressed himself to – and apparently resolved – syntactic problems already acknowledged by them as central. One such problem was that of describing the relations holding across syntactic forms. An example that was classical at the time was the alleged relation holding between sequences of syntactic categories in active sentences and sequences of syntactic categories in passive sentences. While the descriptivists could adequately describe active and passive sentence forms independently, they had no formal means of capturing what seemed an obvious syntactic relation. Chomsky was able, through his more abstract model, to provide a solution to this problem. He proposed a new rule system in addition to those that he had already established formally underlay the constituent structure grammars of the descriptivists. This new rule system was known as transformational analysis.[7] Its details need not concern us here. What is historically significant is that Chomsky accepted without question that accounting for the relations which appeared to hold across sentence forms was an interesting and worthwhile problem to investigate. Indeed, it is this assumption that guided much of his early work, thus setting the course for his linguistics. It was only after a number of years – when the direction of his work was already well-established – that the shortcomings – both formal and substantive – of transformations became obvious. Over time the importance of the transformational level of analysis, which links Chomsky so firmly to the concerns of the descriptivists, has gradually waned. Yet this does not alter the substantial impact which it had on the way his model developed.

Chomsky may at this stage best be described as an important innovator who overcame some of the limitations of his contemporaries' work by putting their analyses on a firmer theoretical footing. Yet even some of his apparent innovations were more in the nature of additions complementing the work of the descriptivists and indeed of 'traditional' grammarians rather than revolutionising it.[8] This sense of a close relation, an almost orderly evolution out of the work of the descriptivists emerges most clearly from an observation that Harris makes at the very end of his *Structural Linguistics*. Harris wrote:

> The work of analysis leads right up to the statements which enable anyone to synthesise or predict utterances in the language. These statements form a deductive system with axiomatically defined initial elements and with theorems concerning the relations among them. The final theorems would indicate the structure of the utterances of the language in terms of the preceding parts of the system. (Harris, 1951:372–3)

Harris did not himself try to convert his analytical procedures into a deductively formulated system. However, with the perspective provided by history, his observations now read like a cue for the entrance of Chomsky on to the linguistic scene. Chomsky, a pupil of Harris', became the 'anyone' who used the analytic work of the descriptivists to develop a formal model which 'synthesised or predicted utterances in the language'.

Nor was Harris alone in recognising that descriptivist grammars should proceed beyond the mere analysis of a corpus, should go further than providing a grammar consisting of lists of constituents and their distribution in texts. Hockett too had found

shortcomings with a model of descriptivist grammar he called
Item and Arrangement. In such grammars, he wrote:

> The pattern of the language is described if we list the mor-
> phemes and the arrangements in which they occur relative to each
> other in utterances – appending statements to cover the phonemic
> shapes which appear in any occurrent combination. (Hockett,
> 1957c:387)

adding that

> The matter is not quite so simple as that.

He looked rather for a model of linguistic description:

> . . . of such a nature that the linguist can account also for
> utterances which are *not* in his corpus at a given time. That is, as a
> result of his examination he must be able to predict what *other*
> utterances the speakers of the language might produce, and, ideal-
> ly, the circumstances under which those other utterances might be
> produced.[9] (Hockett, 1957b:279)

Furthermore, he added in 'Two Models of Grammatical
Description' that:

> A model must be *productive*: when applied to a given language,
> the results must make possible the creation of an indefinite num-
> ber of valid new utterances. (Hockett, 1957c:398)

Whereas Harris and Hockett suggested that grammars should
describe existing forms in such a way as to predict (Harris) or
create (Hockett) an indefinite number of new sentences, it was
Chomsky who was to propose formal machinery for implementing
these ideas.[10] In doing so however he was continuing, if at a
greater level of abstraction, the general style of work of the
descriptivists.

This is particularly evident from the two fundamental assumptions which he shared with the descriptivists. First, that meaning
should be excluded from linguistic analysis. And second, that in
place of meaning, analysis should be based on the distribution of
form.

(i) The exclusion of meaning

In an earlier paper Chomsky stated a theme which was to recur repeatedly in *Syntactic Structures* and *The Logical Structure of Linguistic Theory*:

> Meaning is a notoriously difficult notion to pin down. If it can be shown that meaning and related notions do play a central role in linguistic analysis, then its results and conclusions become subject to all of the doubts and obscurities that plague the study of meaning, and a serious blow is struck at the foundations of linguistic theory. (Chomsky, 1955:141)

This strong and unequivocal exclusion of an appeal to meaning in linguistic analysis provides one of the tightest links between Chomsky and the descriptivists. Both shared the conviction that meaning was a vague and obscure concept. Their commitment to ensuring that linguistics was a rigorous and exact science obliged them to exclude that which could not be reduced to a rigorous and exact form. The difference between Chomsky and the descriptivists on the question of meaning was that as time went on and Chomsky's style of linguistics became more established he did accept the introduction of a semantic component into his model of linguistic structure. But this was done by grafting it on to an existing syntactically-based model without reopening the question of whether deductively formulated theory could deal satifactorily with the 'vague and obscure concept' meaning.

The results of this grafting operation have never been illuminating about problems of word or sentence meaning largely because these problems have been approached in terms of the formal apparatus deemed to be appropriate for the generation of syntactic structure not for an account of meaning. We shall be looking more closely into this question of the relation and dominance of syntax over semantics in a later chapter.

(ii) Distribution as a methodological tool

On the methodological level, Chomsky was in some ways continuing the concerns of the descriptivists in that he was interested in the distributional equivalences and non-equivalences of syntactic form. What was alleged to be significant about his famous pair of sentences:

(i) John is eager to please
(ii) John is easy to please

is that while they appear to have the same structure:

Np   Cop   Adj   V

they can be shown to have different distributional potential. For example, the first Adj + V combination could be nominalised and occur in the structure underlying the sentence:

(iii) John's eagerness to please surprised them

but the second could not:

(iv) ? John's easiness to please surprised them

Similarly, the second Adj could occur in the structure underlying the sentence:

(v) It is easy to please John

while the first could not:

(vi) ? It is eager to please John

Typically Chomsky would make other, generally a few other, observations of this sort about what the descriptivists would have called the freedom of occurrence of constituents with *eager* and *easy*. He would then demonstrate that, to describe these distributions across different sentence forms in a simple and economical way, what was needed was a transformational rule system to supplement the rule systems already proposed as underlying the grammars of the descriptivists. From an historical perspective however what is significant is that once again he took the adequacy of the appeal to distribution of forms, not meanings, wholly for granted. In making no reference to the fact that *eager* and *easy* are different in meaning, Chomsky was continuing the kind of work which had already been characteristic of the descriptivists: the statement of distributional equivalences and non-equivalences of syntactic form.

Despite the underlying similarities, Chomsky's search for a
firmer theoretical basis for the constituent structure grammars of
the descriptivists eventually did lead him to reformulate the goals
of linguistic theory. Recall that Harris had expressed the aims of
the descriptive linguists in the following terms:

> The overall purpose of work in descriptive linguistics is to
> obtain a compact one-one representation of the stock of utterances
> in the corpus.

Chomsky added an apparently new and far-reaching dimension. He wrote:

> We are antecedently interested in developing a theory that will
> shed some light on such facts as the following: A speaker of a
> language has observed a certain limited set of utterances in his
> language. On the basis of this finite linguistic experience he can
> produce an indefinite number of new utterances which are im-
> mediately acceptable to other members of his speech community.
> He can also distinguish a certain set of 'grammatical' utterances,
> among utterances that he has never heard and might never pro-
> duce. He thus projects his past linguistic experience to include
> certain new strings while excluding others. (Chomsky, 1975:61)

The dimension Chomsky added to the concerns of the descriptivists was to link his technical work on the general structure of
grammars to the linguistic behaviour of native speakers. He
claimed that:

> Any grammar of a language will *project* the finite and somewhat
> accidental corpus of observed utterances to a set (presumably
> infinite) of grammatical utterances. In this respect a grammar
> mirrors the behaviour of the speaker who, on the basis of finite and
> accidental experience with language, can produce or understand
> an indefinite number of new sentences. (Chomsky, 1957:15)

It is easy to overlook the fact that these statements of goals,
particularly the first, pick out not one but two very distinct aspects
of linguistic behaviours as being of theoretical interest. The first is
the ability, after limited exposure to language, to produce and
understand an indefinite number of new utterances. It is in the

exercise of this ability, independent of stimulus control, that a native speaker regularly shows what Chomsky calls the creative use of the language.[11] Having laid out this general creative ability, however, he immediately assigns a second much more confined and highly questionable ability to native speakers: that of being able to distinguish the grammatical from the non-grammatical utterances of their language without relying on meaning.[12] The reason for this shift of interest from creativity to the concept 'grammatical in a language' is to be found in the exceedingly limited nature of his technical work. His original model was restricted to the characterisation of syntactic form and was thus far too narrowly-defined to throw any light on the creative use of language in its full sense. Thus in spite of his claims to the contrary his model mirrored not creativity as such but rather the apparent ability of native speakers to distinguish, on grounds other than meaning, grammatical from non-grammatical utterances of their language.

Chomsky has rarely stated this distinction clearly, largely because as a speculative philosopher he has always been drawn to the discussion of broad, far-reaching questions. As a theoretical linguist on the other hand, he was obliged because of the constraints imposed by his syntactically-based model, to introduce a subsidiary and much narrower problem: how do speakers distinguish grammatical from non-grammatical sentences? His technical work was addressed almost entirely to the narrower problem, which we shall show in Chapter 2 was a pseudo-problem. At the same time his speculations suggested that his formal theory did contribute to the solution of the broader question. This has meant that there has been from the outset a tension running through a great deal of his theoretical writing. It is a tension between what we see as the rhetoric and the substance of his linguistics. We call Chomsky's rhetoric those claims and speculations about language which are not backed by or relatable to the formal theory which forms the substance of his work. There can be little doubt that Chomsky's rhetoric has exerted an enormous influence not only on linguists but also on philosophers, psychologists and others interested in language.

The tension lies in the way that Chomsky has implied or allowed it to be inferred that his broad speculative claims are in fact supported by his technical work. This seems to have been the result of a desire on Chomsky's part to invest his otherwise rather restricted technical work with broader significance. In more recent years Chomsky's rhetoric has taken the form of speculations on rationalism and innateness. We shall discuss the discrepancy between the substance of his technical work and his psychological and philosophical claims in Chapter 3.

We conclude the chapter by focusing on an absolute presupposition that Chomsky shared not only with the descriptivists but with many other linguists of the twentieth century. It is the presupposition that language is readily isolatable from its users and characterisable as an independent and self-contained system. In their assumption that there were 'pure facts' of speech to be described, the descriptivists were clearly working within this presupposition, which dates back at least as far as the twentieth century is concerned to Ferdinand de Saussure and Antoine Meillet. In certain respects in shifting the domain of linguistics from language to the knowledge about language held by native speakers, Chomsky appears to be breaking free of this long tradition and concerning himself with language users. However a close look at the substance of his work shows that this is an illusion. Chomsky is still making the same rigid separation but making it in a different place. For Chomsky, users' knowledge of language is separable from other types of knowledge of the world of their experience and is to be characterised distinctly. This assumption is reflected in the distinction he makes between the linguistic competence of speakers, that is their implicit knowledge, and their actual performance in using language. Thus in spite of the theoretical innovations which he introduced into linguistics, Chomsky was – and still is – working very firmly in the tradition of those who view language as an entity which may be isolated for analysis and description. It was the assumption that language could be characterised as an entity separable from its users that appeared to make linguistics a science analogous to an exact science. It is, however, in our view this assumption which caused linguistics to begin to diverge very early on from its subject matter. In keeping within this general tradition, Chomsky was following a long line of linguists. To be genuinely revolutionary, he would have had to abandon it.

Notes

1.   A fuller, more rounded picture of Bloomfield's views would

of course have to begin with his *Introduction to the Study of Language* (1914), especially Chapter 3, and certainly take into account, along with his well-known work *Language*, his contribution to the International Encyclopedia of Unified Science, 'Linguistic Aspects of Science'.

2. The similarities here with Watson's behaviourism will be obvious.

3. Joos also remarked: 'Children want explanations, and there is a child in each of us; descriptivism makes a virtue of not pampering that child.' (Joos, 1957b:96)

4. What is ironic about this comment of Haugen's is that it is almost identical with the kind of comment that was to be made time and time again about the analyses of Chomsky and his co-workers.

5. The subtitle of A. A. Hill's textbook, *Introduction to Linguistic Structures: From Sound to Sentence* reflects this methodological principle.

6. Edward Sapir is an outstanding example of a contemporary North American linguist who was not a descriptivist, and who was able to make illuminating use of the insights of his American Indian informants. See particularly his paper, 'The Psychological Reality of the Phoneme' in *Selected Writings of E. Sapir in Language, Culture and Personality*, ed. D. Mandelbaum.

7. In fact Harris earlier (1952) had proposed using in the context of discourse, rather than sentence, analysis what he called transformations to express equivalence classes between elements in structures. Although Chomsky, along with Lukoff and Brown, had collaborated with Harris in this work, Chomsky's notion of transformation is technically distinct from Harris'.

8. As far as the investigation of language itself is concerned, Chomsky appears to have assumed that recasting the information provided by traditional grammars in formal terms was a worthwhile enterprise. This may help to explain why the content of his theory sometimes appears curiously old fashioned. In *Aspects of the Theory of Syntax*, he wrote: 'The investigation of generative grammar can profitably begin with a careful analysis of the kind of information presented in traditional grammars . . . The main topic I should like to consider is how information of this sort can be formally

presented . . .' (Chomsky, 1965:63-4). What is not an issue
for Chomsky is the adequacy of this information.

9. Hockett added a note characteristic of this scientific temper
of the time. 'Attempts to include predictions of the circumstances (except in terms of preceding utterances) constitute
semantic analysis. Structural analysis can be scientific without being semantic.' (Hockett, 1957b:279)

10. There are differences however reflected in their language, in
the way Harris and Hockett saw the new goal. Harris
appears to have been more of an instrumentalist. While he
wants a theory that will predict new utterances, there is no
suggestion that it need be psychologically plausible. Hockett
on the other hand appears to have been a realist; the grammar is seen as providing a psychological analogue to native
speaker abilities. In this respect, Chomsky is much closer to
Hockett than to Harris.

11. We shall have more to say about the relevance of this aspect
of language to Chomsky's refutation of behavourism in
Chapter 3.

12. There can be little doubt that at the outset Chomsky intended to keep the notion 'grammatical' distinct from the
notion 'meaningful'. He wrote: '. . . grammatical cannot be
identified with meaningful or significant in any semantic
sense.' (Chomsky, 1957:15)

2 Grammar and Explanation

> The significance of a scientific theory, and the security of the results to which it leads depend to a considerable extent on the clarity and operational interpretability of the terms which enter into the theory.
>
> Noam Chomsky

There seems little doubt that Chomsky's work, whatever one's view's of its limitations and ultimate value, constitutes a foundational study in theoretical linguistics. The most significant outcome of that study was the adoption into linguistics of a particular view of what is to count as an explanation. The view of explanation that Chomsky introduced into linguistics is known among philosophers and scientists interested in the nature of explanatory theories as the received view. According to the received view, explanation should be formulated as a deductive chain of reasoning from axioms through rules of particular types to the phenomenon to be explained. One of the major themes of this book is that this type of explanation has turned out to be inappropriate to the subject matter of linguistics: language. The reasons for finding it inappropriate are complex but two stand out. Firstly it has meant that the only aspects of language that could be included within the scope of the explanatory theory were those that appeared to be sufficiently well-defined to be expressible in terms of the type of formal notation that axiomatic theories require. The result has been an exaggerated emphasis on the importance of linguistic form and – initially at least – the total exclusion of meaning from the domain of linguistic theory.

The second reason for the inappropriateness of Chomsky's model of explanation to a human science such as linguistics has been its reductive character. This has imposed on linguists an approach that because of its formal rigour allows insufficient reference to language users' knowledge and intentions, beliefs and expectations. In later chapters we shall be arguing that language is inextricably bound up with language users and their supportive frameworks of knowledge, intentions, beliefs and expectations. Any theory of language that purports to shed light on the way language works but ignores the positive role played by users in its operation is thus bound to be unrevealing.

In arguing that deductively formulated explanatory theories are not appropriate to linguistics, we are not of course suggesting that they have not proved illuminating in certain of the physical sciences. Taking a very simple example, the explanation of a specific phenomenon such as ice floating in water can on the received view very fruitfully be formulated in terms of universal principles and a chain of deductive reasoning. The principles in this case would include those about the relative density of solids and liquids, the Archimedean principle that a fluid buoys up a body immersed in it with a force equal to the weight of the fluid displaced by the body, and further principles about the conditions under which the bodies subjected to forces are in equilibrium. Reasoning from the independent principles using established rules of inference and substituting for the 'variables' implicit in the universal formulations the particular values for ice and water, it is possible to show that ice floating on water is not an isolated phenomenon but a consequence of more general principles.

One of the attractions of theories formulated in this way is that the behaviour of a wide range of disparate phenomena may be related. An account could be given, for example, not only of why ice floats but why solid lead spheres sink in water whereas hollow lead spheres of an appropriate thickness float and why innumerable other observations about the floatation properties of bodies hold. Furthermore, since the principles can be viewed as axioms in the forms of universal conditionals, then by substituting particular values for the 'variables' in the conditionals and by following the appropriate rules of inference, it is possible to predict whether, under the specified conditions, a body will float or not. Experiments can then test the accuracy of the prediction.

An even greater degree of explanatory power is deemed to be achieved if a number of apparently independent universal principles can be shown to be deduced from still more abstract ones. As we understand it, quantum theory can explain findings in the thermal behaviour of solids and gases, in the behaviour of chemical interactions and in many other physical phenomena. Indeed, in the physical sciences one of the major functions of a deductively formulated theory is to establish interconnections between the findings of disparate subject matters. The other major function of such theories is to suggest fresh lines of research that might establish new interconnections.

Deductively formulated theories in some of the physical sciences have fulfilled these two functions often enough to have proved themselves not merely useful but spectacularly successful in solving certain problems. This very success has, however, led to attempts to introduce such theories into other types of scientific enquiry. In this chapter we consider what the effects have been of introducing such theories into linguistics, a human or social science. In order to tackle this question effectively we need to look more closely at the particular form of deductively formulated theory that Chomsky devised to explain aspects of linguistic behaviour. We begin by considering the general form of such theories.

General outline of a deductively formulated theory

For the purpose of exposition, this account will need to be a somewhat stark simplification of a highly complex subject.

A deductively formulated theory can be viewed as having two main components: (i) an abstract calculus and (ii) a set of rules that assign empirical content to the abstract calculus by relating it to the phenomena to be explained.

The first component, the abstract calculus, may be thought of as the framework of the theory. It is based largely upon the syntax and vocabulary of formal logic, elements such as quantifiers, logical connectives, individual and predicate constants and variables with their associated rules of information. In addition there are non-logical terms that receive a definition by virtue of the part they play in the overall logical structure. Some terms are said to be 'implicitly defined' by their place in the calculus. In the case of formal linguistic theory, for example, terms such as noun, verb and adjective, N, V, A, are defined by their position within the overall system. To the question 'What is a noun?', the only answer the formal linguist may give is that nouns, Ns, are those elements that satisfy the conditions formally assigned to them.

The abstract calculus we have sketched is uninterpreted in that it provides merely an account of an abstract relational structure among logical and non-logical expressions. If such a calculus is to be used to explain and predict it must be clearly linked with observable phenomena. To state in formal linguistic theory that every sentence has a noun phrase and a verb phase, $S \rightarrow NP + VP$

is to say little unless it is clear at some level of analysis what NP and VP are related to. In the literature on this subject the rules that connect the abstract uninterpreted calculus with observable, testable phenomena have been given a number of names: epistemic correlations, coordinating definitions, operational definitions, and rules of correspondence. These are the rules that, in establishing the links between abstract calculi and relevant data, give point and substance to a formal theory. The ways in which this is done in any specific case are quite complex, but in general such correspondence rules are best viewed as an interpretative system.[1]

There are two important points to be noted about this very general outline of deductively formulated theories in scientific explanation. The first is that it is not of course a description of how theories are usually devised by working scientists. It is rather a reconstruction of the characteristics of one type of explanatory theory. We draw attention to this point because of a curious feature of Chomsky's first major work *The Logical Structure of Linguistic Theory*. In this work Chomsky discusses in considerable detail what the general character of an explanatory theory in linguistics should be. Actual problems thrown up by the investigation of language receive attention only insofar as they can be incorporated into a deductively formulated theoretical framework. The book appears to have been written by a theoretically sophisticated linguist trying to impose a reconstruction of the canonical form of one type of explanatory theory directly on to a subject matter: language. The titles of some of Chomsky's early papers reinforce the view that he was more interested in the characteristics of explanatory theories than in the problems which these might help to explain. Aside from his first major work, *The Logical Structure of Linguistic Theory*, he wrote 'The Logical Basis of Linguistic Theory', 'Explanatory Models of Linguistics' and 'Problems of Explanation in Linguistics'. We shall be arguing that Chomsky's preoccupation with the form of explanatory theories led him to attempt to mould subject matters to theory rather than develop a theory appropriate to his subject matter. The outcome of this process was the divergence of the science of linguistics as Chomsky practised it, from its subject matter, language.

The other general point to be made about deductively formulated theories is that while they may be productive in some of the physical sciences, there are nevertheless a large number of subject areas in which they play no useful part. Frederick Suppe lists a number of examples ranging from Hoyle's theory on the origins of the universe to most theories in histology, cellular and microbiology and comparative anatomy (Suppe, 1977:65). He concludes that it would be both premature and fruitless to try and introduce deductively formulated theory into such sciences because, in their present state, they are insufficiently developed. For the study of language, however, Chomsky appears to have assumed with very little question that linguistics was a science sufficiently well-developed to move what as we saw earlier Northrop called the third stage of enquiry: the stage of deductively formulated theory.

We shall be arguing that moving to this stage only seemed appropriate in linguistics because of the extraordinarily severe idealisations which Chomsky imposed upon his subject matter. We discuss some of these below. Our general claim is that social scientists, rather than attempting to mimic the more abstract of the physical sciences, should look for modes of explanation appropriate to their own subject matter. The cost of not so doing has been in many cases idealising to irrelevance.

A deductively formulated theory for language

Chomsky's original motive for attempting to devise a deductively formulated theoretical model of language was, as we discussed in Chapter 1, to make explicit the underlying properties of the grammars of the North American descriptivists. These grammars, like traditional grammars, were analytic, that is they were based on the detailed analysis of a corpus or sample of utterances of a particular language. Chomsky introduced a new conception of grammar: a grammar was to be a device not for analysing but for synthesising or generating sentences of a language. These synthesising grammars took the form of sets of formal rules with the capacity to generate or produce the syntactic structures underlying sentences of a language. In mathematical terms these grammars were finite systems with infinite output.

Chomsky's conception of grammars as synthesising or generating devices was not without precedent. To use the term 'generate' of a grammar, while undoubtedly new to linguists, would have been perfectly familiar to logicians, particularly those used to Post's theory of combinatorial systems.[2]

In seeking to devise a formal and rigorous grammar for natural language Chomsky thus had available as a model the rule systems or grammars that formal logicians used to generate the strings of symbols that constitute formal languages. To understand the direction Chomsky moved linguistics it is therefore necessary to understand the ways he adapted formal language theory to natural language characterisation. We shall be arguing subsequently that natural languages have characteristics which are fundamentally different to those of formal or constructed languages. In consequence, attempts to define natural language in terms appropriate to such languages have necessarily led to distortion.

Some characteristics of formal language grammars

Typically a formal language consists of a precisely specifiable set of basic expressions, its alphabet, and a number of syntactic rules for the manipulation and combination of these expressions. In such a language, the alphabet is a finite set of symbols. A sentence of the language is a string of finite length composed of symbols of the alphabet combined in ways that accord with the syntax of the language.[3] The rules which generate the sentences of a formal language may be referred to as a grammar.

Consider a very simple example of such a grammar or synthesising device: suppose that the minimal requirement placed on the grammar is that, with an alphabet of just two letters a and b, it generates sentences of the form: ab, aabb, aaabbb . . . that is, all and only sentences containing n occurrences of a followed by n occurrences of b. If we want to write a mini-grammar to generate this language, we may begin by using S as an initial symbol and → to indicate 'rewrite as' and formulate the first rule as:

$$S \longrightarrow a\ b$$

Applying this rule we could generate the following structure:

Since this 'grammar', consisting of only one rule, generates one ab sentence, it obviously does not meet the specified minimal requirement of generating all and only sentences containing n occurrences of a followed by n occurrences of b. Suppose we modify the first rule to read:

S ⟶ a (S) b

Here we adopt the convention that parentheses around an element mean that the element is optional. In addition to generating an ab sentence, we can now generate:

that is, a sentence: aabb or, if we select the S element again:

i.e. the sentence aaabbb.

Clearly, by repeated selections of S, it is possible for this grammar to meet its minimal requirement. It will generate sentences of the allowed form, and it will generate no sentences that are not allowed. Thus, keeping to the rules and conventions of the grammar, it is not possible for it to generate other combinations of the two letters such as:

aa, bb, abba, baab, aaaa, bbbb, aabbaa

Suppose however we want a grammar that *will* generate just that set of combinations, that is, all sentences consisting of a string X followed by its mirror image, X in reverse, and only those combinations. The grammar could be expressed formally as:

$$S \longrightarrow \begin{Bmatrix} a & (S) & a \\ b & (S) & b \end{Bmatrix}$$

Here we add the convention that braces (or curly brackets) represent disjunction. By this convention, S may be rewritten as:

By repeated applications of the rules of this grammar, and by keeping rigorously to its conventions, it is possible to generate all and only the strings of a's and b's that have been stipulated as well-formed or permissible in the formal language.

This extremely simple example shows how it is possible to devise a finite set of rules which generates an infinite set of sequences conforming to a pre-specified pattern. A slightly more complex grammar or set of rules can make explicit the relations which hold between the elements of the strings generated:

$$S \longrightarrow A \quad B$$
$$A \longrightarrow C \quad E \quad (D)$$
$$B \longrightarrow (F) \quad G \quad \begin{Bmatrix} H \\ I \end{Bmatrix}$$

This set of rules can generate a number of sequences of letters such as:

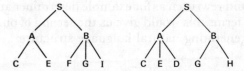

The sequence CEFGI and CEDGH may be assumed to be well-formed sequences. Sequences such as DEFGH or FG which the rules could not generate if they are applied according to the conventions, are assumed to be ill-formed.

This grammar differs from the previous example in that it groups certain letters as higher order units which have their own members. A is one such unit with members C, E and D; F, G and H are members of B. A and B are in turn members of the higher order category S. A set of rules of this type generate structures which show explicitly the relations which hold between for example C and S, or G and B.

The move from formal languages to a model for natural languages

It is important to keep in mind that at the outset at least Chomsky was not, in constructing a synthesising device, attempting to model language in its entirety but rather the syntactic structures underlying the sentences of natural language. Recall that he shared with the North American descriptivists the view that reliance on meaning was to be excluded from linguistic analysis if linguistics was to retain and strengthen its status as a science. If we return to the above rule system with these points in mind, it is reasonably straightforward to see how the various letters or basic elements of the formal language can be replaced by syntactic categories. If we assume that S represents sentence we might then suppose that S could rewrite as noun phrase (NP) and verb phrase (VP) following the traditional view of a sentence as having a subject and a predicate.

This could then provide the first rule of a grammar or synthesising device for the structure of a natural language such as English:

$$S \longrightarrow NP \quad VP$$

In the same way as A and B were subcategorised in the last of the formal language examples, so noun phrase could be subcategorised and rewritten as for example determiner and noun. In more formal terms this would give us the second of our simple set of rules for generating natural language structure:

$$NP \longrightarrow D \quad N$$

We know, however, from traditional grammar that determiners do not always occur with nouns so that we could modify this rule making D an optional constituent:

$$NP \longrightarrow (D) \quad N$$

Similarly VP could be rewritten in a number of different ways e.g. auxiliary and verb:

$$VP \longrightarrow (Aux) \quad V$$

Some subcategories could be further broken down resulting in rules such as:

$$Aux \longrightarrow Tense \quad (Modal)$$

This is only a very rough guide as to the kind of rule system which might generate structures of a natural language using the conventions of formal languages as a model. To make it clearer, consider the following rule system:

S ➝ NP VP

NP ➝ (D) N

D ➝ {Def / Indef}

VP ➝ Aux V (NP)

Aux ➝ T (Modal)

T ➝ {Pres / Past}

The arrow can be thought of as 'has as a member' or 'includes'. A set of rules of this kind would synthesise or generate the structure:

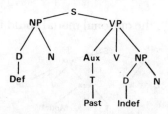

If we then attach words to these categories, it is possible to see more clearly how such a rule system can generate or produce structures which could be said to underlie sentences of English:

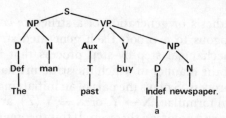

Clearly it is possible to attach a great variety of different words to these same categories in this same configuration:

The dog found a bone
The policeman arrested a burglar
The inquest exposed a discrepancy

Thus this one synthesised or generated structure could be said to underlie a great many English sentences. Variations can be generated by, for example, not selecting the optional D, determiner, category under NP, the noun phrase, and thus generating:

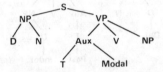

to which a proper noun, not ordinarily requiring a determiner, could be attached:

Max bought a newspaper.

In a reverse way, the optional modal could be selected to yield:

to which the modals *may* or *can* could be attached:

The man may buy a newspaper.

Each synthesis or generation of a structure can be seen as roughly analogous to a proof. Each generated structure is the result of a mechanical step-by-step process that is completely explicit about the manner in which the structure has been generated. In this process, S plays the part of an initial single axiom and the instruction formulae, $X \rightarrow Y$, or $X \rightarrow Y$ (Z), are like rules of inference. The end point is a theorem. If this theorem can be put in correspondence with a grammatical sentence of the language, then it would seem that we could write Q.E.D. against the generated structure. Clearly a crucial question then is: can the link be made between the theorems of sentoids generated by the grammar and a set of grammatical sentences of a language?

As yet we have not included any account of machinery for attaching words to the appropriate syntactic categories generated by the grammar. This is because in our view fundamental questions hang on the presence of words in the final output, a sentoid, of a single top-to-bottom pass through the rule system. While Chomsky undeniably sought to eliminate any appeal to meaning in linguistic analysis, he did not exclude words from his formal grammar. In a later section we shall be arguing that the presence of words led to a covert dependence upon meaning.

Before turning to these fundamental questions, there are a number of points to be noted about the general adequacy of formal grammars of the deductively formulated type that we have so far sketched. The first is that the simple rule system of the sort described above, while adequate to generate a quite complex range of syntactic structures, is certainly not capable as it stands of producing all and only the well-formed syntactic structures of English. It would for example be incapable of generating what traditional grammarians would call complex sentences. Complex sentences are sentences that can be analysed as a sentence containing a sentence. Thus:

Max believed that Alice was doing quite well

can be analysed as a complex sentence containing the sentence – Alice was doing quite well.

Clearly this complex sentence might itself be part of an even more complex sentence such as:

Harry thought that Max believed that Alice was doing quite well.

Extremely common among complex sentences are those involving relative clauses. Thus the sentence:

The man who signed the petition left hurriedly

can be analysed as containing within:

The man left hurriedly

the sentence:

The man signed the petition.

At first glance there appears to be no serious problem for

Chomsky to modify his grammar such that it will generate complex sentences of this type. In the very first example of a grammar generating the sequences of a formal language we illustrated the recursive device necessary to generate such complex sentences. By including the highest level element S as an optional member of a lower element such as NP:

$$NP \longrightarrow \begin{Bmatrix} NP \ (S) \\ (D) \ N \end{Bmatrix}$$

it is possible to generate relative clauses of one type:

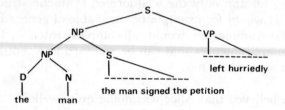

Similarly by including the S within the VP:

$$VP \longrightarrow V \ (NP) \ (S)$$

It is possible to generate:

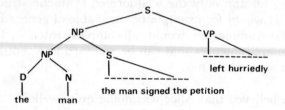

This structure might underlie:

Max believed that Alice was doing quite well.

In fact as anybody who has worked at all with Chomsky's formal rule system knows, the difficulty is not to generate the required structures, but quite the reverse. The problem is that the synthesising devices are all too powerful in that they permit the generation of structures that, while formally quite acceptable, appear never to occur in natural languages.

Another shortcoming of the kind of formal grammars that we have illustrated so far is that they do not in any mechanical or explicit way show the relations between distinct syntactic constructions. As we discussed in Chapter 1, the North American descriptivists had recognised this as a weakness of their own grammars – a weakness which Chomsky was to gain recognition by overcoming. To the rule systems or grammars of the type described above – known as phrase structure or constituent structure grammars – Chomsky added a further level of description, the transformational level, whose function was exactly to state what he saw as regular distributions across syntactic constructions. Thus, setting aside quite complex arguments about the direction of derivation, Chomsky proposed that passive constructions for example should be derived from active ones by a type of conversion rule he called a transform or transformation. Naturally this level of analysis would need its own underlying algebra: a statement of the formal conditions that transformations must meet and further conditions determining their application.

There are of course countless details which could be added to this outline of Chomsky's theoretical approach. These can be found in the numerous textbooks which transformational generative theory has given rise to over the years. Our intention is not to give a detailed account of Chomsky's technical work, but rather to examine the effects which his commitment to deductively formulated theory has had on the general direction of theoretical linguistics over the past two decades.

We argue that the formal requirements of the reductive model of explanation Chomsky introduced into linguistics imposed such strict idealisations that fundamental properties of language had to be excluded from the domain of the theory. In the following section we discuss some of these idealisations, idealisations which have resulted in the divergence of theoretical linguistics from basic characteristics of its subject matter, language.

A deductively formulated theory for language: the question of appropriateness

(i) Idealisation: the necessity for a restricted domain

In order to construct a deductively formulated theory which related to natural language, Chomsky had no choice but to take a highly restricted view of his subject matter. To construct a rule system of the type desired he required a limited number of primitive elements. There was little point in turning to semantics since, as we saw in Chapter 1, Chomsky, like the North American descriptivists, believed that the study of meaning could not provide the kind of restricted and well-defined set of primitives a formal theory would need. Traditional syntactic categories, on the other hand, appeared readily incorporable into a formalised theory. It was thus theoretical necessity that gave syntax its prominence within transformational generative theory. This point is important to understanding the direction of Chomsky's work. He did not investigate in an informal pre-theoretic way language understanding and production, and as a result of his investigation pick out syntactic form as of striking interest – or as presenting special problems which a formalised theory might help to solve. On the contrary, he picked out for inclusion within his explanatory theory just those aspects of language which lent themselves to expression within the terms of a formal theory. Other aspects of language, aspects more central to language in use such as meaning, intonation, user expectations, were not reducible to the required primitives and so could not have been the basis of a formal theory of the type Chomsky was elaborating. The manner in which the domain of enquiry was thus reduced takes on a special significance because of Chomsky's interest in cognitive psychology and in particular because of the claims he was eventually to make for the psychological, not merely formal, validity of his model.

The exclusion of all aspects of language not readily reducible to a formal notation was the first Chomsky's over-strong idealisations which led to a distortion rather than a clarification of his subject matter. Disregarding meaning in particular was felt to be justified by assuming that a clear distinction was possible between form and meaning. It is not too strong to say that an absolute presupposition of Chomsky's work has been that language users have intuitions of linguistic form and that these are quite distinct from their intuitions about meaning. This presupposition allowed him not only to justify restricting his original model to syntax, but also to go further and claim that the model explained the very intuitions of form that in order to have any empirical content it in fact required.

It is often overlooked that Chomsky's early technical work was sharply focused on a highly restricted problem, that of explicating the notion 'grammatical in language'. More generally he has always maintained either strongly that a distinction between form and meaning can be made or at times, more mildly, that the implications of such a distinction are worth pursuing.

As his approach became more established however a new dimension was added when the assumption that meaning had necessarily to be excluded from the domain of analysis came to be questioned. We shall be discussing in the Interlude some of the consequences of attempts to introduce meaning into a deductively formulated model set up to give an explicit characterisation of linguistic form independently of meaning. Here we want simply to point out that it was a strongly idealised version of meaning that was eventually introduced into the deductively formulated model. The variability of meaning, its flexibility and its intimate links with language users all had to be excluded. Thus even in attempting to broaden his domain Chomsky was forced, by the demands of his formal model, to keep to a very restricted view of language. As a result of adopting a reductive model of explanation he was unable to tackle the real mysteries surrounding meaning, mysteries which stem from the variability of individual linguistic units and the different degrees to which language users are able to understand one another. We discuss in more detail in Chapters 4 and 5 some of the fundamental aspects of language in use that Chomsky was forced to disregard.

There were in addition other general restrictions that followed from transposing the requirements of formal language theory to the description of natural languages. Chomsky's view of what constituted a valid scientific explanation obliged him for example, in order to make his approach feasible, to assume that under-laying native speaker use of language there is a body of unchang-ing, independent and uniform linguistic knowledge. He called this body of tacit knowledge: *competence*. In this technical sense of competence, he described the competent user as:

> . . . an ideal speaker-listener, in a completely homogeneous speech community, who knows its language perfectly . . . Chom-sky, 1965:3)

By making this idealisation he was able to disregard the fact that actual language in use is dynamic, involving as it does the complex interaction of language users' knowledge, intentions, beliefs and expectations both of one another and of the world as they individually perceive it. There are compelling reasons for believing that this idealisation has been counter-productive. One such reason is that the assumption of a homogeneous speech community seriously distorts the object of investigation. The language of any speech community is necessarily heterogeneous as a consequence of the variety of knowledge and experience of its users. A theory of language forced by its model of explanation to idealise to a monolithic homogeneity cannot even start to tackle that most puzzling of questions: how is it that language, given its heterogeneity, nevertheless appears to work?[5]

Another consequence of the idealisation to 'an ideal speaker listener in a completely homogeneous speech community' is the accompanying assumption that a native speaker can have 'perfect knowledge' of his language. The difficulty with the idealisation to 'perfect knowledge' is that it encases the language user within a complete system. It then becomes impossible to view him as necessarily having imperfect knowledge that is constantly, and to different degrees, being extended, adapted and refined to meet the exigencies of his experience of the world. The idealisation to 'perfect knowledge' excludes from the domain of investigation what seems to us to be close to the heart of the problem of explaining language, namely, that we are dealing with a subject matter which in its operation appears to be necessarily imperfect, incomplete, open and only admitting of partial regularities.[6]

In the case of each idealisation it was the adoption of a formal model of explanation of a deductively-formulated type that necessitated the exclusion of just those aspects of language that we shall argue are basic to its functioning. It is no accident that these are the aspects of language that reflect the way it is inextricably bound up with language user. Chomsky, in isolating language as an object of study independent of language users, was continuing an inveterate and in our view highly unfortunate idealisation in linguistic theory – an idealisation that dates at least in this century to the work of Ferdinand de Saussure. Saussure argued that language could be separated from local instances of language in use and viewed as a system, self-contained and common to all language users. That system Saussure called 'langue'; the task of the linguist he saw as characterising 'langue' – the linguistic system which language users might be said to share.[7]

In assuming that language exists apart from its use, Saussure set linguistics in a direction which many, including the North American descriptivists, Chomsky and those who have worked in the Chomskyan tradition, have since followed. It is a direction which however has proved largely barren of insights into the way language works; a direction which caused linguistics to diverge very early from its subject matter – a divergence which with the gift of hindsight seems inevitable, since it involved ignoring the contribution made by language users' experience of their world to the successful functioning of their means of communication.

In order then to make deductively formulated theory appear appropriate as a model for an explanatory theory of natural language, Chomsky had to restrict his subject matter in a number of ways. He had to:

(i)   separate form from meaning and concentrate on form.
(ii)   assume counterfactually that speech communities could be homogeneous.
(iii) isolate language as a system from language users.

The result of these severe restrictions on the subject matter is that Chomsky's theory is not in any ordinary sense a theory of language at all, not if language is construed as a means of expression that is dynamic, multipurposed and necessarily, not contingently, heterogeneous. What has confused those reading Chomsky's work – especially those who have come into theoretical linguistics more recently – is the very real difficulty of keeping distinct the terms 'grammar' and 'theory of language'. Chomsky's grammar or generator of labelled and bracketed sequences of symbols takes the form of a deductively formulated theory. It thus became easy to slide from discussing 'a grammar of a language' to 'a theory of language' without recalling clearly that the theory being discussed was restricted to, in its essentials, an account of linguistic form. When Chomsky refers in the early days to his 'theory of language' it is more accurate to construe the expression as 'theory of syntactic form', or as 'a grammar generating syntactic structures' or more briefly as 'a syntactic generator'. It is not that these expressions too are not capable of misconstrual. It is rather that they shift the focus from 'theory of language' to the actual object that provides the substance of Chomsky's original work: providing grammars and meta-grammars for grammars.

As we shall discuss in the Interlude, attempts have been made over the past two decades to break out of the syntactic straitjacket imposed by the formalisms with which Chomsky was working.

One result of these attempts is that his theory might now be more accurately characterised as 'a theory of purely linguistic knowledge'. However, the same difficulties which beset his original efforts to characterise the abstract notion 'grammatical in language' are also evident in his attempts to distinguish 'purely linguistic knowledge' from other kinds of knowledge involved in our use of language.[8]

In sum, our first grounds for questioning the appropriateness of deductively formulated theory to the study of language has been that such theories in enforcing an overly severe set of idealisations upon their subject matter, distort, not explain, the workings of language. We have however other even more serious misgivings about the appropriateness of deductively formulated theory. These arise partly from the nature of the problems that became central for theoretical linguists once it was taken for granted that deductively formulated theory provided an appropriate model of explanation. But partly also from the lack of a satisfying congruence between Chomsky's theory itself and the limited domain of language it purported to explain. Both of these can be thought of as falling under the general heading of the justification of grammars.

(ii) The justification of grammars

Chomsky in his writing has devoted a good deal of space to discussion of the justification of the kinds of grammars he was devising. From the outset he established a distinction between internal and external justification. A grammar was said to be externally justified if it gave an adequate account of the relevant data. Empirical confirmation is of course a minimal but essential requirement for any scientific theory. On the assumption that external justification presented no real problems, Chomsky chose to concentrate his attention on questions of internal justification. Problems of internal justification, while new to theoretical linguists, were an inescapable concomitant of the kind of deductively formulated theory Chomsky was developing. Such problems arise because of the difficulty of justifying the selection of one formulation of a grammar over others equally capable it is believed of generating an equivalent range of grammatical sentences. Put in other words, the problem of internal justification is equivalent to the problem of evaluating the relative merits of different forms of the formalised grammar, or as it was generally expressed, finding an adequate evaluation measure for grammars.

Chomsky argued that if a particular version of formal grammar was constructed exactly according to the same principles as successful grammars for other languages, then such a grammar would be more strongly justified than a generative grammar that was merely adequate for a single language. He called his efforts to establish explicit principles for the construction of successful formal grammars the development of a general theory of linguistic structure. The function of this general theory is then to provide a logical framework for the construction of the grammars of particular languages. The general theory of linguistic structure came to be known as universal grammar. If a grammar, or as we may call it, a local grammar, is the set of rule systems at a number of levels that purport to describe the syntactic structure of a particular language, universal grammar provides the overall framework setting the general conditions for the construction of the local grammars. On this approach the problems tackled by theoretical linguists appeared to be at different levels of abstraction. Chomsky wrote:

> To recapitulate so far, we see that linguistic research has two aspects. It aims to provide for each language a theory of the structure of that language (i.e., a grammar), and at the same time to develop a general theory of linguistic structure of which each of these grammars will present a model. (Chomsky, 1975:80)

The search for internal justification for grammars thus led generative linguists to concentrate on problems far removed from language, problems relating to the development of evaluation measures for formal grammars which led in turn to the elaboration of a general theory of linguistic structure.

Our thesis is that a grave weakness of Chomsky's work arises from his moving to such problems without first ensuring that the grammars under discussion were externally justified, gave that is an adequate account of the relevant data. Chomsky called this fundamental requirement 'the external condition of adequacy' and commented correctly that such a condition:

> ... cannot be eliminated, or there are no constraints whatsoever on grammar construction; ... (Chomsky, 1975:81)

Our chief misgiving about the appropriateness of Chomsky's deductively formulated theory to linguistics is that it has never met this external condition of adequacy, in other words, that he has never provided a satisfactory interpretative system linking his model to an interesting range of data. Much of the rest of this chapter is devoted to cutting through the elaborate theoretical superstructure of the generative grammars that now exist, and looking carefully at the degree to which the original theory was externally justified, that is minimally adequate. We return to the original form of the theory because the subsequent developments, in supplementing and complementing it, have assumed it was empirically adequate, assumed, that is, that it had been tested against relevant data and found satisfactory. The thesis of this section is that it was only in the very early stages when the efforts to be formally rigorous were at their most serious that Chomsky's model had even the semblance of an explanatory linguistic theory. If we can show convincingly that the theory even at its most formal was never securely linked to relevant data and thus was virtually untestable, then the problems of testing for later less rigorous versions of Chomsky's theory are so severe that the model as a deductively formulated explanatory theory diminishes into insignificance.

Taking our cue from Chomsky then we ask how successful the grammars are in meeting the minimal requirement or external condition of adequacy. In the case of Chomsky's original grammar or syntactic generator, the external condition of adequacy would have been satisfied if the sentoids or strings of bracketed symbols generated by the grammar could have been put in correspondence with sentences of English. Since, the argument would run, we have a formal, explicit, rigorous and effectively decidable procedure accounting for the derivation of the well-formed sentoid, then we have an explanation of the grammaticality of the equivalent sentence of English.

For this style of explanation to work it is of course necessary to be able to apply tests to establish the equivalence or correspondence of a well-formed sentoid to a grammatical sentence of English. Establishing this correspondence or, in other words, securing the links between the theory and the data turns out to be a very serious problem indeed. It is a problem moreover whose roots lie not in the nature of natural languages but in the attempt to transpose formal language theory as an explanatory model to natural languages. Because of the fundamental importance of empiral confirmation, it is worth drawing out this distinction between establishing the external condition of adequacy on the one hand for a formal grammar of a formal language and on the other for a formal grammar for a natural language. In formal language theory testing the adequacy of a formal grammar – that is showing it to be minimally justified – cannot constitute a problem, because what is to count as a well-formed expression is specified in advance of constructing the grammar. In terms of our earlier example, if the task is to devise a grammar that will generate the sentoids:

aa, bb, abba, baab, aaaa, bbbb, aabbaa, abbbba, . . .

and in general all sentences consisting of a string X followed by the reverse of X and only these, then clearly the test of the grammar is unambiguously set by the pre-specified conditions. Were the grammar to permit the generation of the sentoid:

abab

we would know that it had failed. Were it to generate:

abba

that it was succeeding.

In the case of natural language, however, unless a limit is arbitrarily imposed, there can be no question of stating in advance what the properties of the set of grammatical sentences of English are. In the set-theoretic sense of set, there is no set of English grammatical sentences, since one cannot define them either by enumeration or by description. The absence of pre-specified conditions as to what is to count as a grammatical sentence leaves the theoretical linguist using formal language theory in a curious position. Unlike the formal language theorist, he has no clear test for the adequacy of his grammar, no way of telling whether his grammar is performing well or badly. One obvious and, for an empirical science, natural conclusion would be that there was little point in elaborating the grammar until some adequate and theory-independent tests of grammaticality had been devised.

There would be little point because there would be no way, apart from intuition, of testing the output of the grammar. What is revealing about Chomsky's methods is that this was not his conclusion. In both *Syntactic Structures* and in *The Logical Structure of Linguistic Theory*, he does consider a number of tests that might be used to provide a check on the output of the grammar. Strikingly, he rejects them all. The total absence of reliable tests for establishing grammaticality did not deter him from continuing to devise and elaborate formal grammars that were supposed to explain judgements of grammaticality. The reason it did not deter him was that he was prepared to substitute for public tests of grammaticality the intuitive judgements of native speakers. Chomsky, at least initially, appears to have been convinced that native speaker judgements on what constituted a grammatical sentence provided a sufficiently secure and accurate gauge against which the output of the grammar could be measured. The rejection of empirical considerations and the reliance on intuitive judgements have been such significant and influential aspects of Chomsky's work that they deserve closer consideration. We turn first to the various tests that Chomsky considered using to separate the grammatical from the non-grammatical sentences of the language, and then take up the reasons for his conviction that intuitive judgements alone would serve as an adequate measure of the success of the theory.

Tests for grammaticality I: identification with a corpus

Bearing in mind Chomsky's roots in the work of the North American descriptivists, it is not surprising that he should first consider whether the set of grammatical sentences in a language can be identified with any particular corpus of actual utterances obtained by the linguist in his fieldwork. Chomsky rejected this test on the grounds that the utterances in a corpus are only an arbitrary selection of the possible utterances of a language. Thus a grammar that merely generated the set of utterances in a corpus was failing to generate the open set of possible utterances of a language. On this line of reasoning it is possible to claim that any corpus of English sentences, let us say the set of sentences in the books in the University Library, Cambridge, is incomplete in that it is always possible to think of a 'new' sentence that it is reasonable to suppose is not contained in any book in the University Library.

It is important to note, however, that this reasoning rests on conflating utterances of a language – an open set – with the set of possible well-formed grammatical constructions of that language which are arguably not an open set. In essence, the problem is the same as we say in Chapter 1 faced the North American descriptivists: what constitutes a representative sample of a language?

The obvious answer – and the only one they gave – is that a sample is representative when no new sample yields constructions not already described. Chomsky, on the other hand, by confusing all and only the utterances of a language with all and only the grammatical sequences of a language is able to disregard the commonsense observation that every new sentence need not be a new grammatical construction. He is thus able to reject a corpus of any size whatsoever as providing an inadequate and unrepresentative test for the adequacy of his grammar.

Underlying this rejection was the awareness that his formal model required recursive devices in order to generate certain types of syntactic construction. The inclusion of such devices meant that the formal rule systems were so powerful that they could generate infinitely many grammatical constructions of any length. This characteristic of his model then led him to claim that, for simplicity of description, languages should be treated as infinite.[9]

Tests for grammaticality II: identification of grammaticality with probability of occurrence

A second possible test Chomsky considers is that of equating the set of grammatical sentences of a language with those that are most likely to occur. He rejects the equation of 'grammatical' with 'high order of statistical approximation to the language' on the grounds that sentences that are equally unlikely to occur can nevertheless in his view be distinguished as to their grammaticality. He takes as an example the context:

I saw a fragile —

and observes that the words *whale* and *of* have:

... equal (i.e., zero) frequency in the past linguistic experience
of a speaker who will immediately recognize that one of these
substitutions, but not the other, gives a grammatical sentence.
(Chomsky, 1957:16)

The question of whether or not what is being recognised as
the result of the substitution is a difference in grammaticality
leads us to the third test.

Tests for grammaticality III: identification of 'grammatical' with 'meaningful'

The third way Chomsky considered of giving some empirical
content to the concept 'grammatical in language' is generally the
best known. It centres round the question of whether the set of
grammatical sentences of a language could be identified with the
set of meaningful sentences. If 'grammatical' were equivalent to
'meaningful', then it would be sufficient to establish whether a
particular sentence made sense to know whether it should be
included in the set of grammatical sentences of the language in
question.

Chomsky firmly and unequivocally rejects this approach. As
evidence he cites the following sentence, which over the years has
become notorious not only within theoretical linguistics:

Colorless green ideas sleep furiously

In Chomsky's view, this sentence is 'thoroughly meaningless
and nonsignificant' yet he would regard it as grammatical. If a
sentence can be meaningless yet grammatical, then this shows, his
argument runs, that grammaticality is independent of meaning.

We shall be examining in some detail the substance of this
crucial argument. Here we only draw attention to its importance
for Chomsky's position. If he had not been able to find an argument for the separation of syntactic form from meaning then his
entire technical work would have been called into question. As we
have argued earlier, syntax was largely imposed upon Chomsky
as a domain of enquiry given the particular formal model he had
adopted. He was well aware that if grammaticality could be
equated with meaningfulness then the floodgates of uncertainty
and user-idiosyncrasy would be opened. Meaning was not, and is

still not, a well-defined phenomenon. In order to demarcate for himself a domain that was sufficiently well-defined, as he thought, to be susceptible to formal representation he had to exclude meaning. We shall be arguing however in the next section that Chomsky was too easily satisfied by his own arguments for the independence of grammar from meaning. Consequently he overlooked certain crucial problems in relating his theory to data and as a result his technical work was never, even at the outset, well-grounded.

We may sum up at this point by noting that Chomsky rejected as inadequate all the tests of grammaticality he considered. Instead of seeking more adequate tests, however, he chose to rely on his belief that we can assume:

> . . . intuitive knowledge of the grammatical sentences of English (Chomsky, 1957:13)

Chomsky's decision to rely on intuitive knowledge of the grammatical sentences of the language is the more surprising since he was aware that:

> . . . intuition . . . is an extremely weak support. (Chomsky, 1975:101)

Since it clearly is a weak support, a strong case could be made for the view that if a grammar is to be viewed as a theory that explained the meaning-independent concept 'grammatical', then the first step would be to establish some theory-independent tests for grammaticality. As Chomsky himself acknowledged:

> The program of linguistic research would be a much clearer one if we could show experimentally that these intuitions have distinct behavioral correlates. (Chomsky, 1975:101)

Yet despite this clear grasp of the importance of establishing firm empirical foundations for his theory, Chomsky appears to have been convinced that intuition would provide it with a sufficiently secure base.

This conviction appears to have been based on the following 'clear cases' argument: there exists, Chomsky claimed, a considerable body of data about which no native speaker could ever have any reasonable doubt as to its status as a sentence of English.

Given, to take an early example:

John ate a sandwich

and some scrambled version, say:

ate John sandwich a

no native speaker will fail to recognise that the first is a sentence of English and the second is not. In Chomsky's terms, this recognition is part of native user's tacit knowledge of the language. It is knowledge of this order that the grammar is then said to 'mirror'. 'Clear-cases' of this sort Chomsky believed made up an 'enormous mass of unquestionable data concerning the linguistic intuition of the native speaker (often, himself); . . .' (Chomsky, 1965:20)

The crucial problem for grammatical theory was as Chomsky saw it the inadequacy of contemporary theories of language to explain what was clear and obvious. Chomsky's view was that:

> Neither the study of grammar nor the attempt to develop useful tests is hampered by lack of evidence with which to check results, for the present. (Chomsky 1965:20)

In a rhetorical way, this might be persuasive. There might appear to exist a considerable body of data about which there is very little disagreement as to whether it is or is not a sentence of English. The existence of such data however is not what is at issue. The question that Chomsky's theory is addressed to is whether a sentence is syntactically well-formed, grammatical, or not. Pointing to sentences which make sense and scrambled versions of them which do not, does not provide any evidence whatsoever as to the character of the crucial notion 'grammatical in language'. This must be particularly the case for a theorist who wants no appeal to meaning in the study of linguistic form.

For Chomsky's position on the existence of 'clear-cases' to be tenable, there needs to be a reliable body of data consisting of clear cases of sentences that have been judged as grammatical regardless of whether they make sense or not. Judging whether a sentence is a sentence of English or not brings in knowledge of a great many different kinds. The onus is clearly on Chomsky to demonstrate, not merely claim, that there is one kind of knowledge that is specifically grammatical in the sense he intends. While this onus is not discharged, observing that there is an 'enormous mass of unquestionable data' does not advance his specific argument.

Chomsky's reliance for testing his model on the meaning-independent intuitions of grammaticality of native speakers gives rise to a crucial question: can native speakers actually perform this task of recognition? Can they in general and without relying on meaning tell whether a sentence of their language is grammatical or not? The importance of this question of whether we are able to recognise grammaticality without relying on meaning cannot be overestimated. If meaning can be shown to play an essential role in intuitions of linguistic form, then the validity of Chomsky's model would be totally undermined since it would be entirely untestable and based on an insecure, user-dependent variable and varying foundation. Once it is so undermined, the elaborate superstructure which has been constructed on the basis of the original model – as well as the psychological analogue which Chomsky has claimed for his technical work – is called into question.

Can native speakers make meaning-independent judgements of grammaticality?

We have argued so far that in order for his model to be testable, Chomsky had to assume that native speakers have intuitions of syntactic form, or as it was more generally known, intuitions of the grammaticality or grammaticalness of sentences. This intuitive knowledge of the grammatical structure of a sentence Chomsky believed was independent of considerations of the meaning of the sentence. The point of Chomsky's early critical pieces of data such as:

> Colorless green ideas sleep furiously

was, as we noted earlier, to establish that a sentence could be meaningless but grammatical. If Chomsky's judgement of what was meaningless but nevertheless grammatical had been generally supported by similar judgements on both counts by native speakers, for a considerable range of cases, then there would have been some reasonable grounds for assuming what was a theoretical necessity, namely a general distinction between an intuition of grammaticality and an intuition of significance.

The importance of this distinction which has remained central to generative theory lies not only in its separation of syntax from semantics, but also in the priority it accords to syntax. To make the first goal of an explanatory linguistic theory that of giving an account of structure is to be convinced, as Chomsky appeared to be, that structure can be shown to have some priority over meaning. It is important to be clear that the kind of priority Chomsky intended was not psychological or temporal priority but what we might call 'logical priority'. In his view structure was logically prior to meaning in the sense that it was required in order to explain meaning, much as in order to explain arithmetical operations, concepts such as 'zero', 'number' and 'successor' are required. The observation that we learn to add, multiply, divide and subtract without first learning these concepts has no bearing on their logical priority in this sense.

Clearly, then underlying the question of whether native speakers can make meaning-independent judgements of grammaticality there is a more fundamental question: was Chomsky's assumption of the logical priority of structure over meaning a valid one?

We begin by noting that structure is a relational term. If we return to Chomsky's early work, it is clear that the structural relations he was concerned with were those holding between the words of a sentence. When, in *The Logical Structure of Linguistic Theory*, he outlined the levels of description his theory would require, it is curious that he excluded a semantic level yet explicitly included a word level. Very little in the book is said about the characteristics of the word beyond the observation that it was to be taken as a prime. Once structure among words in a sentence is accepted as the object of explanation, the first step in formulating the argument that structure is logically prior to meaning would be to show that the structure of a sentence could be recognised without reliance on the meanings of the words. The shortcoming of this argument is that it requires us to be able to identify a sentence as a unit. To do that, however, we need to be able to identify a unit of meaningful words. In natural languages we cannot of course have sentences without words. Chomsky's belief that in discussing sentences we are necessarily discussing structure loses a great deal of its persuasiveness once we recall that structure, as a relational term, refers to structure among words, and that words have meanings. Without words, the structure of a sentence is merely an abstract syntactic form. If Chomsky had genuinely intended to disregard the meanings of words in judging the grammaticalness of sentences, he would have had to exclude a word level altogether from the components of this theory. Its rules would then have generated sequences of syntactic categories in various combinations. But then in order to test the adequacy of the grammar's output, a native speaker would need to be able to judge the grammaticalness of, for example, the string:

D N prep prep D N cop adv adj

To do this he would have to attach words to the categories. This he might do from his own intuitive knowledge of traditional grammar. Thus, for example, he might insert the words:

The man from across the road is always late.

It would then appear to be fairly straightforward to decide by abstracting from the words back to the categories whether the string of categories was well-formed or not. To know whether this judgement is a judgement on the sequence of categories themselves, distinct from a judgement of the categories with those words, inextricably bound up with their meanings, in that combination, we should have to be able to randomly substitute other words of the same syntactic categories and observe whether those sentences too were found to be well-formed. This was not Chomsky's practice. Consider the results of carrying out this small but vital test of the independence of judgements of grammaticalness from meaning.

D	N	prep	prep	D	N	cop	adv	adv
That	function	of	of	a	crumb	is	around	sullen

It seems unlikely that native speakers would have intuitive knowledge of the structure of that sentence. If Chomsky wished to persuade an informant that it contained a permitted sequence of categories, that it was well-formed, he would have to point out that its structure was parallel to that of a sequence of words in a sentence that made sense. This in fact is what he did with the 'Colorless green ideas' sentence. He observed that it was grammatical:

. . . by virtue of such sentences as 'revolutionary new ideas appear infrequently' that might well occur in normal English. (Chomsky, 1975:146)

It should then be clear that it was a sentence with meaning that provided the grounds for determining whether a sequence of syntactic categories was well-formed or not. The difference in response to the two sentences with the same syntactic structure but different words brings out plainly that judgements on sentences are made with reference to the particular words assigned to the categories. The structure without the words is a syntactic form or formula. Without the words it is not the structure of a sentence, merely a formula for a sentence. With the words it may or may not become the structure of a sentence depending upon the relations emerging from the words. Words cannot be dissociated from meaning.

Once that is granted and words are not seen as semantically neutral, it becomes hard to avoid the conclusion that reliance upon meaning is essential to judgements of grammaticalness.

That this is so becomes strikingly obvious if we re-analyse Chomsky's own example:

Colorless green ideas sleep furiously

which he judged to be grammatical, that is syntactically well-formed. The syntactic formula Chomsky assigned to the sentence was:

Adj   adj   N   V   adj   (Chomsky, 1975:146)

Let us once again substitute other words that appear to belong to those syntactic categories. We do this in order to try to determine whether native speakers would judge this sequence of categories to be grammatical whatever words were attached, or whether the same sequence with different words be judged differently. The importance of this simple test is that for Chomsky's position on the independence of judgements of grammaticality from considerations of meaning to be seriously tenable, it should be the case that substituting other words, providing they are of the appropriate syntactic category, should make no difference to the judgement. Suppose that for the first adj we substitute 'antepenultimate', for the second 'idiosyncratic', for the N, 'elocution' for the V, 'paragraphs', and for the adv, 'bright'. This will give the sequence:

adj   adj   N   V   adv
antepenultimate idiosyncratic elocution paragraphs bright

This sentence in our experience is invariably read with the list intonation Chomsky says is characteristic of an ungrammatical sequence of unrelated words. But then that is just what the sentence is – a string of semantically unrelated words each of which may – through our awareness of traditional syntax – be assigned a syntactic category. Note that we have assigned the category verb to 'paragraphs'. We have done this in spite of the fact that it is used much more commonly 'as a noun' to refer to 'a portion of text' than 'as a verb' to refer to the activity of putting into paragraphs. We have done this to illustrate that in a sentence such as:

Antepenultimate idiosyncratic elocution paragraphs bright

which makes no sense at all, there is no way of deciding apart from arbitrarily whether 'paragraphs' 'is' a noun or 'is' a verb since such assignments are partly made on the basis of meaning. If we arbitrarily assign to it the category verb then according to Chomsky's view, the above is a grammatical sentence of English and would be recognised as grammatical by native speakers. If on the other hand, equally arbitrarily, it is assigned the category noun then the above is not, again according to Chomsky's views, a well-formed sentence of English and would be recognised as not being such by native speakers of English. It is our view that native speakers of English would in fact have very little to say either way about the grammaticality of this nonsense sentence since they would have the gravest difficulty in assigning any meaning and thus any category assignment to it at all.

What offers further evidence for the position that grammaticality is inextricably bound up with meaning is a sentence that Chomsky rejected as clearly ungrammatical:

Furiously sleep ideas green colorless

This sentence Chomsky arrived at by simply reversing the order of the original grammatical sentence 'Colorless green ideas sleep furiously' to obtain the apparently ill-formed sequence of categories:

adv V N adj adj

To test whether Chomsky's judgement that this structure was ungrammatical is sound, we should proceed as before and see if, by using our knowledge of traditional grammar to substitute other words of appropriate syntactic categories, we can reverse the judgement. As one candidate sequence of words that fit the categories and would achieve that effect, we suggest:

Always dye shirts greenish blue

which would be likely to be accepted as grammatical by native speakers. There is however a further syntactic reason why Chomsky's judgement on the sentence

Furiously sleep ideas green colorless

is misguided. To arrive at the judgement he has assumed a syntactic analysis of 'sleep' as a verb and 'green' as an adjective. If the assignment of syntactic categories is done without reference to this particular combination of words but only according to their possible categories in isolation, then any dictionary will show that 'sleep' may also be noun and 'green' an adjective, noun or verb. It is possible then to analyse.

Furiously sleep ideas green colorless

as a sequence of:

adv N N V adj

The question of whether this sequence is a grammatical sequence can be tested, just as Chomsky tested the 'Colorless green ideas' sentence, namely by seeing whether a parallel string containing words of those syntactic categories can be devised which native speakers would not read with a list intonation and which they are likely to judge as grammatical. Consider the sentence:

Inevitably newspaper people appear tactless

This sentence can be represented by the string categories:

adv N N V adj

and, at least as clearly as

Colorless green ideas sleep furiously,

is a grammatical sentence of English.

The point again emerges that judgements of grammaticalness are not made independently of the words that occur in the sequence of syntactic categories. The syntactic category that a word is assigned to in a sequence is as much determined by the relations established by the presence of other words in that sequence as the syntactic relations such as subject and object are. No syntactician thinks that the subject and the object of a sentence are properties of units outside a sentence. Similarly assigning a syntactic category of *green* or *sleep* in a sentence in which it occurs depends on understanding its semantic relation with other words in the sentence. Such an assignment is done via intuitions of meaning. Chomsky's approach appears to have assumed that the syntactic categories of words may be pre-specified. Thus, given a sequence of categories established as well-formed, he must assume that any other words belonging to the appropriate categories could be substituted without the grammaticality of the sequence being affected. But given that words may in general be assigned to a number of categories, the result would be that virtually any list of words is potentially grammatical.

If judgements of grammaticalness cannot be made on strings of syntactic categories without assigning words to those categories, then it seems we must recognise that the judgements are not judgements of grammaticalness but judgements on particular sequences of words in a structure. Furthermore that judgements of grammaticalness distinct from judgements on sequences of words and meanings are impossible to obtain. We may conclude that Chomsky imputed to native speakers an ability that they do not possess, the ability to distinguish syntactically well-formed sentences from syntactically ill-formed sentences without relying on meaning. The attachment of words to the syntactic categories of necessity introduced considerations of meaning. It is just these considerations that we think are unavoidable. Words it seems to us have been Chomsky's Achilles heel.

If, as we have shown, meaning does play a determining role in syntactic analysis, then syntax cannot be said logically to precede semantics. Thus, to return to our original question, it seems clear that native speakers cannot make judgements of grammaticality independently of meaning. This seriously weakens the relevance of Chomsky's deductively formulated model in that it depended, in order to be testable at all, on the personal judgements of individuals involving the vague, obscure but nevertheless essential concept, meaning. The absence of adequate tests for grammaticality has meant that even when the theory was apparently at its most rigorous, there was no way of empirically confirming its findings. Chomsky's model has invariably been at the mercy of the conflicting views of native speakers as to the acceptability of its output.

It would we believe be difficult to exaggerate the fundamental importance of this point. Whatever the various elaborations and modifications of Chomsky's theory that are under discussion, the output of each in the end has to be tested against native speaker intuitions. It has, however, always regrettably remained the case that these intuitions have never been subject to rigorous testing. This rather cavalier attitude to external justification was taken early in the development of the theory and set the direction the work was unfortunately to take. Chomsky once wrote:

> Assuming the set of grammatical sentences of English to be given, we now ask what sort of device can produce this set . . . (Chomsky, 1957:18)

It was an assumption that should never have been made. Once made however it allowed the construction of elaborate formal superstructures without any solid empirical foundations.

The lure of the model

In this section we begin to consider the question of how it was that Chomsky's theory, despite the weakness of its empirical foundations and its highly restricted domain, nevertheless continued to occupy the forefront of theoretical linguistics for more than two decades. It has undoubtedly sustained and invigorated a large body of teaching and research within linguistics and, outside the field, stimulated a re-opening of links between linguistics and philosophy on the one hand, and linguistics and psychology on the other.

Naturally, a large number of factors have contributed to this highly complex situation. Of these, two are of particular significance:

(i)   The research programme for linguistics that Chomsky laid out.
(ii) The 'psychological analogue' Chomsky found for his formal model.

In the final section of this chapter we shall discuss the attraction which Chomsky's research programme came to exert among linguistics. The 'psychological analogue' has had such far-reaching consequences that we devote to it the whole of Chapter 3.

A research programme for linguistics

The research programme that resulted in prodigious activity both in the United States and abroad emerged from Chomsky's particular view of the relation between explanation, theory and data in linguistics. The programme centred largely on the internal justification and evaluation of local generative grammars for particular languages and the development of the universal grammar or general rule schema which was to provide the ground rules for writing the local grammars.

If there had been widespread empirical support for the theory, if, that is, it had been externally justified in a clear and unmistakable fashion, this programme would have been not only appropriate but formally essential. The reason for this relates to a general problem which arises with the confirmation or corroboration of deductively formulated theories. Without an adequate evaluation procedure such theories commit the fallacy of affirming the consequent. To see this more clearly, suppose that A is some deductive theory, B a theorem of that theory and empirical verification is possible: consider the argument:

If A, then B

Suppose that B is not the case, then we may say that, since A predicted B and B is not found, A is disconfirmed. In other words when B is not empirically confirmed, A is, at least to some degree, falsified.

Consider however the argument:

If A, then B

Suppose B is the case, what is the status of A?

Curiously enough, while in the first case the falsification of a theorem of a deductively formulated theory is formally valid, the confirmation of such a theorem, as in the second case, is formally invalid. The problem is that the experimental corroboration of B is no proof of the uniqueness of A, the theory from which B is derived. Experimentally confirmed data could not ensure that from some different, possibly only slightly different, deductively formulated theory C, B could not equally well have been derived. In other words, if B is the case; that is, if B is experimentally confirmed, it may be the case that A or C or D or some other theory are all logically possible.

If these observations are transposed to generative theories in linguistics and if empirical verification is possible, then the problem of how to establish which of a number of competing grammars is the correct and thus truly explanatory grammar is a major one. Under Chomsky's influence theoretical linguists either set aside the problem of empirical confirmation or assumed that it could be resolved. In concentrating on the formal properties of grammars, they found themselves for the first time in the history of their field grappling with problems of the formal evaluation of abstract syntactic models.

The way they proceeded was to be found in the second part of the research programme: the development of the meta- or universal grammar which was to provide the overall framework within which local grammars would be written. Chomsky's view of the relation of grammar to meta-grammar is laid out very clearly on the first page of *Syntactic Structures*:

> We can determine the adequacy of a linguistic theory by developing rigorously and precisely the form of grammar corresponding to the set of levels contained within this theory, and then investigating the possibility of constructing simple and revealing grammars of this form for natural languages. (Chomsky, 1957:11)

Researchers working within this general programme had to be professionally astygmatic, keeping one eye on the fragment of the local grammar they were working on, the other on the meta-grammar which would at the same time provide the form of the working grammar and be further enriched by it. One of the attractions of this approach was that linguists working on local generative grammars for particular languages also felt themselves to be contributing to the development of the universal grammar, thus apparently giving their work a double significance.

The difficulty with this research programme is that the problems it tackled would only have been important if the competing grammars had already been shown to account for a significant range of data, in other words that they met the external condition of adequacy. As we have already seen, however, the problem with Chomsky's model is that it has never been empirically corroborated. The progamme has nevertheless been attractive largely because of the prestige of its formalisms. To apply Chomsky's theories linguists had to master methods familiar to mathematicians and to logicians but new to linguists. If the North American descriptivists had tied linguistics to a positivist, classificatory view of science, Chomsky's views of explanation, theory construction and theory validation appeared to bring linguistics up-to-date, to make it a much more sophisticated branch of science, akin to the most respected of the sciences, theoretical physics. It was hardly surprising that this exerted a considerable influence. No longer were linguistics characterised by the extent of their fieldwork or the rigour of their discovery procedures; instead, a new elite was to emerge from those who could master, or appear to master, the complex formalisms necessary for the construction and evaluation of generative grammars.

The papers that have resulted from this research programme have inevitably been highly specialised. They have customarily taken as their starting point specific aspects of a local grammar or of the meta-grammar and examined its capacity to handle some range of data. Such papers are not easily penetrated by those outside the field and this has sometimes added to the prestige of the approach. There are of course many technical fields not easily entered by outsiders. The problem about the introduction of a highly technical and abstract approach into linguistics however has been that the requirements of the model have resulted in such severe idealisations that what is formalised is only a pale shadow of language. We believe that the prestige associated with the technical nature of the approach served to disguise these short-comings. It has also led to the widespread adoption of Chomsky's notations without in some cases a clear understanding of the deductive style of explanation he was attempting to establish.

In time however this notion of explanation in linguistics took on an even more special significance for researchers in this pro-gramme. When Chomsky added a psychological gloss to his for-mal theory, the lure of the model was immediately strengthened. Workers in the field came to see themselves as developing a theory of linguistic structure that was at the same time a contribution to the study of mind. The way in which a linguistic theory devised to generate grammatical sequences came to be seen as a theory of cognitive structure is one of the most curious events in the history of twentieth-century linguistics. It has however resulted in the links between linguistics and psychology and linguistics and phi-losophy being once again re-established. Because of the general significance of Chomsky's 'psychological analogue' for keeping his theory in the forefront of theoretical attention, we turn to examine it in more detail in Chapter 3.

Notes

1. It was the absence of a satisfactory interpretative system for Chomsky's deductively formulated theory of language that first led us to question its validity.
2. Chomsky refers to Post in *Aspects of the Theory of Syntax*. It is worth recalling that Chomsky at Harris' suggestion had begun as a graduate first at the University of Pennsylvania and later at Harvard to study logic, philosophy and the foundations of mathematics.
3. It is customary in referring to formal systems that generate sequences of symbols to use terminology drawn from the description of natural languages, terms such as 'language', 'sentence' and 'syntax'. This can be highly misleading since the resonance of words is such that it may suggest that there are useful parallels between formal systems and natural lan-guages.
4. One example of constructions that were readily derivable using Chomsky's formal apparatus but that appear never to occur in natural languages are self-embedded constructions.

A structure is said to self-embedded when it is generated within a construction of its own type and certain other conditions are met. In for example the self-embedded sentence:

the rabbit the girl the cat ignored pursued dropped a glove

the relative clause (Rel.S) *the cat ignored the girl* is embedded within another relative clause *the girl pursued the rabbit*. Diagrammatically self-embedded constructions may be represented as follows:

$$[\ldots \quad [X \quad [\quad\quad] \quad Y] \quad \ldots]$$
$$\text{S} \quad \text{Rel.S} \quad \text{Rel.S} \quad \text{Rel.S} \quad \text{Rel.S} \quad \text{S}$$

The recursive devices contained within grammars of Chomsky's type make it easy to multiply instances of self-embedding to any degree of depth. However, even self-embedding at the first or lowest degree of depth such as that underlying the example above generates constructions that have no counterpart in natural languages. Ian Watson's science fiction story, *The Embedding,* which makes use of such constructions, is not as the story is developed a counter-example.

5. Weinreich, Labov and Herzog in an extremely interesting paper being finally revised at the time of Weinreich's death, have emphasised that for an adequate theory of language change it is necessary to view language not as homogeneous but as 'an object possessing orderly heterogeneity' (Weinreich *et al.*, 1968:100).
6. The procedures for deriving sentences in a formal grammar are not intended in any way to represent the dynamic processes involved in language understanding and production. Although from time to time he has been misinterpreted, Chomsky has always been clear that he never intended the initial axiom S in his formal grammar to be construed as the starting symbol for the production of a sentence in a natural language. He never held the absurd view that speakers in speaking begin with an S and work their way through the various sets of rules. The procedures of derivations in a formal grammar are outside constraints of time.
7. Saussure was aware that, in identifying 'language' as the object of study, he was excluding 'everything that is outside its

organism or system – in a word, . . . everything known as external linguistics. But external linguistics deals with many important things – the very ones that we think of when we begin the study of speech' (Saussure, 1959:20). The important aspects of language that Saussure set aside were the relations of language to the history of a race or civilisation, the relations between language and all sorts of institutions; the growth of literary languages and their dialect splitting. Despite his view that 'This schematic simplification seems to go against reality . . .' (Saussure, 1959:196) he continued to insist on a distinction between internal and external linguistics. The posthumously published *Course in General Linguistics* concludes with the characteristically Saussurean sentence: '. . . the true and unique object of linguistics is language studied in and for itself' (Saussure, 1959:232).

8. Chomsky has made confusing and at times seemingly contradictory remarks about the difficulties of distinguishing 'purely linguistic knowledge' from other types of knowledge However he is on record as saying that linguistic knowledge is 'easily distinguishable . . . from other factors that enter into linguistic behaviour' (Chomsky, 1979:150).

9. Chomsky wrote:

In general, the assumption that languages are infinite is made in order to simplify the description of these languages. If a grammar does not have recursive devices . . . it will be prohibitively complex. If it does . . . it will produce infinitely many sentences. (Chomsky, 1957:23–4)

3 Grammar and Mind

... we do not really learn language; rather, grammar grows in the mind.
Noam Chomsky

There can be little doubt about the prestige that attached to Chomsky's formal approach to linguistics, yet this alone is insufficient to account for the sustained impact of his work. Reinforcing that prestige have been Chomsky's claims that his study of language was at the same time a contribution to the study of mind. His psychological speculations have exerted an enormous influence not only in linguistics, but also in psychology and philosophy, and they account, it seems to us, very largely for his continuing reputation. In this chapter we set out to show that the psychological gloss that Chomsky added to his deductively formulated mode of explanation shares, in spite of its attractions for those outside the field, the weaknesses and limitations of his technical work.

The view of a linguistic theory as a contribution to the study of mind did not, in North America, originate with Chomsky. Some at least of the North American descriptivists believed their work had psychological significance. Indeed, a recurrent issue dividing the North American descriptivists concerned the status of the models of linguistic description then being developed. On the one hand, there were those characterised as 'hocus-pocus' or 'games' linguists, and on the other, there were the 'God's truth' linguists. It was held that the 'hocus-pocus' linguist looked on his grammar as merely a convenient way of describing utterances in a corpus, whereas the 'God's truth' linguist believed his grammars were also descriptions of language processes going on in the speaker's head.[1] Hockett wrote:

> The analytical process of the linguist thus parallels what goes on in the nervous system of a language learner, particularly, perhaps, that of a child learning his first language. (Hockett, 1957b:279)

Chomsky's position on this issue appears quite straightforward. While agreeing with those linguists who looked for some psychological gloss to linguistic work, he firmly rejected the specific psychological claims of the descriptivists as being inadequate and totally unfounded. He argued that the methodological requirements the descriptivists had imposed upon themselves as a consequence of their view of science were at obvious variance with whatever processes the child draws on to acquire knowledge of its language. There was no reason to suppose, for example, that a descriptivist principle such as the separation of levels was strictly followed by the child, and indeed every reason to suppose that it was not. Chomsky commented on Hockett's analogy of the linguists' 'discovery procedures' and the child's process of language acquisition:

> But clearly the child does not master the phonology before proceeding to the syntax, . . . there is no possible justification for the principle of separation of levels from considerations of this sort.[2] (Chomsky, 1964a:108)

Here Chomsky is insisting that the methodological requirements the descriptivist places upon himself should not be taken as equivalent to descriptions of processes in language acquisition and use.[3] This is an important observation and one that we shall return to in considering Chomsky's psychological analogue to his own linguistic model.

There were, however, deeper reasons for Chomsky's turning away from psychological claims made by some North American descriptivists. These centred on the links he saw connecting them with the then prevailing school of psychology, behaviourism.

In an early and extended review of Skinner's *Verbal Behaviour* Chomsky had argued forcefully against the behaviourist view that verbal behaviour is under the control of stimuli and that it is acquired and maintained by contingencies of reinforcement. He was quite ready to believe that Pavlovian and operant conditioning were processes well understood by behaviourists. But he could not accept the extrapolation of these processes of conditioning from the strict control that obtained in the experimental laboratory to the looser uncontrolled situations in which the acquisition of language took place. In particular, the notion of reinforcement, which can be given content in the context of carefully controlled schedules of some reinforcer such as food pellets, becomes virtually meaningless outside the laboratory and thus useless to explain the acquisition of language. The evidence, Chomsky wrote elsewhere:

> . . . shows clearly that knowledge of language cannot arise by application of step-by-step inductive operations (segmentation, classification, substitution procedures, 'analogy', association, conditioning, and so on) of any sort that have been developed or discussed within linguistics, psychology, or philosophy.[4] (Chomsky, 1967:11)

The main reason for Chomsky's strong, and at times abrasive, attack on such views was that they virtually discounted the role, both in learning and actual behaviour, of the internal structure of the organism itself. Like Lashley, he was convinced that internal structure was the key to understanding behaviour. This led him to attempt to relate his formal theory of linguistic structure to the linguistic knowledge assumed to underlie language acquisition and use.

Chomsky's view of the relation of theories of grammar to theories of mind seems to us to represent an extraordinarily intricate intertwining of different strands of his thought. Attempting to disentangle those strands is necessary, however, because of the enormous influence Chomsky's speculative psychology has exerted on the interrelation of linguistics, psychology and philosophy over the last quarter of a century. Unfortunately, in our view, that influence, while it has undoubtedly served to initiate and strengthen contact between the three fields, has been largely unproductive of insight and explanation. For all the general interest it has aroused in highly abstract conceptions of structures and rules, it has not resulted in light being shed on the processes involved in language learning, production or understanding.

We begin our attempt to unravel the intricate web Chomsky has spun by recalling that he was dissatisfied both with prevailing linguistic theory *and* prevailing psychological theory. He had attempted to overcome some of the insufficiencies of current linguistic theory by developing formal grammars which were sufficiently explicit, rigorous and comprehensive to provide a firmer theoretical basis for the North American descriptivists' syntactic work. He attempted to overcome some of the insufficiencies of current psychological theory – at least insofar as it bore on language acquisition and use – by focusing attention on the internal structure of the behaving organism, in this case, the language user. This he did by asking how the linguistic knowledge used in the task of producing and understanding language might be organised.

What is significant is that he found a possible answer in the abstract grammars that as a technical linguist he was already developing, grammars as we saw earlier, based on the rule systems of formal language theory. These suggested to Chomsky an intriguing hypothesis: linguistic knowledge might itself be organised in the form of generative rule systems – in mathematical terms, finite systems with infinite output – of the sort he was independently developing.

Despite its serious limitations, the power and beauty of this hypothesis that linguistic knowledge was organised in the form of generative rule systems was that at one stroke it appeared to destroy both the descriptivist and the behaviourist approaches to the analysis and description of language. The power and beauty lay in a single, simple and apparently conclusive argument. If knowledge of a language did take the form of rule systems of the type that Chomsky was devising, then it would be impossible to claim that such rule systems were directly relatable to stimuli or that they could be characterised by procedures of segmentation, classification, substitution and so on. While the proposed rule systems would certainly interact with relevant stimuli, they were in no sense determined by, or indeed directly derived from them. In the course of developing this hypothesis, the conviction that grammars, not languages, were the proper subject matter of linguistics came to dominate Chomsky's work.

Chomsky's hypothesis that linguistic knowledge took the form of a finite rule system with infinite output in its turn raised a further question: how was such a rule system acquired? Chomsky came to propose a second and even more seductive hypothesis that claimed both to answer that question and give psychological substance to his highly technical work. This second hypothesis was that humans, but not animals, are innately equipped with what he has called a specific 'faculté de langage'. This hypothesis that humans are genetically endowed with the capacity to learn language – Chomsky's innateness hypothesis – has provided a great deal of the motivation for work in generative linguistics. It has caused Chomsky to concentrate more and more on using his technical work as a basis for developing the linguistic universal rule schemas, or universal grammar, that he claims characterise this species-specific innate linguistic faculty.

It has not been easy in the subsequent debate that Chomsky's psychological speculations have aroused to keep distinct general arguments about innateness from specific arguments about the plausibility of versions of Chomsky's theory of grammar as a model of the alleged innate linguistic faculty. Our conviction is that two questions need to be kept firmly apart. First:

Are human beings innately equipped to acquire language?

Second

Is Chomsky's theory of grammar a plausible model of that innate faculty?

In arguing that his formalised grammar provides some account of the rule schemas that allow humans to acquire and use language, Chomsky has frequently, it seems to us, assumed that general arguments in favour of innateness *in some form*, the first question, were also arguments supporting his particular grammatical theory as a model of innateness, the second question. This style of argument has led to considerable confusion over the status of Chomsky's technical work, both within linguistics and outside. In assessing the psychological claims of generative linguists, it is important to keep in mind that in rejecting Chomsky's model as a plausible account of innateness, one is not at the same time rejecting the view that innate programming of some sort is likely to explain language acquisition and use.

There are a number of reasons for thinking it unlikely that Chomsky's grammars could be seen as a plausible model of innate programming of any sort. Foremost among these is their origins and motivation. Chomsky's grammar was originally set up, as we saw earlier, to provide a rigorous theoretical account of the restricted concept, 'grammatical in language'. It did not – quite naturally given its aims – involve any investigation of language acquisition, language production or language understanding. The psychological gloss that was subsequently added to the theory was thus an attempt to justify and give relevance to an already-existing, highly restricted formal theory.

If we look more closely at Chomsky's arguments in favour of
his psychological hypotheses they turn out to be interesting more
for what they reveal about his anti-descriptivist and anti-
behaviourist views than for any support they lend to the psychological plausibility of his own linguistic model. Broadly, these arguments can be grouped under two heads: linguistic creativity and
the abstractness and universality of linguistic structure.

Linguistic creativity

The significance of creativity in Chomsky's sense was that, at the
time, it seemed a perfect stick with which to beat behaviourists. A
great deal of confusion has arisen however over Chomsky's use of
the term, linguistic creativity. In part this is no more serious than
the difficulties that regularly arise with the use of an expression
from ordinary language in a technical sense. In this case Chomsky
has chosen an expression that in its non-technical sense has
distinct resonances when used of language, referring as it so often
does to artistic, poetic creativity, the power of the imagination to
create something original and valuable.

The real confusion arises however when it comes to understanding Chomsky's technical use of 'creativity', which appeared
to vary, sometimes quite subtly, depending on whether he was
writing as an anti-behaviourist psychologist or as a technical
linguist. In an attempt to lessen the confusion we want to distinguish between a fuller technical sense and a narrower technical
sense. The fuller technical sense emerged most clearly when
Chomsky was criticising behaviourism; the narrower technical
sense when he was developing aspects of his formal theory of
linguistic structure.

Chomsky's fuller technical sense of 'the creative aspect of
language use' has to be set in the context of his criticism of
Skinner. In *Verbal Behavior* Skinner had sought to show that the
utterances an individual makes are under the control of stimuli
and thus determinable by manipulation of those stimuli. In
his review of *Verbal Behavior*, Chomsky countered Skinner's argument.

A typical example of *stimulus control* for Skinner would be the
response to a piece of music with the utterance 'Mozart' or to a
painting with the response 'Dutch'. These responses are asserted

to be 'under the control of extremely subtle properties' of the physical object or event. Suppose instead of saying 'Dutch' we had said 'Clashes with wallpaper, I thought you like abstract work, Never saw it before, Tilted, Hanging too low, Beautiful, Hideous, Remember our camping trip last summer', or whatever else might come into our minds . . . (Chomsky, 1964b:552)

His point being that while verbal responses may be related to stimuli they are not under their control:

> We cannot predict verbal behavior in terms of the stimuli in the speaker's environment, since we do not know what the current stimuli are until he responds. (Chomsky, 1964b:553)

If we cannot know until after the event what current stimuli are, it is difficult to see how one could manipulate stimuli to determine responses. It would be easy to multiply examples of utterances speakers make that do not depend on any stimuli objectively identifiable independently of the resulting behaviour. Chomsky is thus able to argue that language is not stimulus-bound as Skinner believed but stimulus-free.

Chomsky called the native speaker's ability to innovate in freedom from stimulus control 'the creative aspect of language use'. Thus his full sense of creativity emerged directly from his antipathy to the behaviourist view of language as stimulus-bound. He wrote that by the phrase he meant the ability:

> . . . to produce and interpret new sentences in independence from 'stimulus control' . . . (Chomsky, 1967:4)

More generally, without reference to behaviourism, linguistic creativity was frequently described as the capacity to:

> . . . produce or understand an indefinite number of new sentences. (Chomsky, 1957:15)

It would be difficult to overestimate the importance Chomsky attached in the early days to this creative aspect of language as he defined it. Insofar as it was a central aspect of linguistic behaviour that behaviourism was not able to explain, creativity seemed to offer conclusive evidence against the behaviourist approach. Chomsky wrote:

> It is a crucial fact about language that a person is quite capable of using and understanding sentences that have no physical similarity – no point-by-point relationship – to any that he has come across in his linguistic experience or has produced earlier. This creative aspect of language is quite incompatible with the idea that language is a habit-structure. Whatever a habit-structure is, it is clear that you cannot innovate by habit . . . (Chomsky, 1968:687)

It is incidentally the creative, stimulus-free use of language that provides a crucial distinction for Chomsky between human and animal systems of communication.[5]

> This creative aspect of normal language use is one fundamental factor that distinguishes human language from any known system of animal communication. (Chomsky, 1972:100)

For Chomsky, the ability of native speakers to use language innovatively, independently of stimulus control showed quite clearly that behaviourist and descriptivist approaches to the analysis and description of language, concentrating as they did on external conditions rather than internal structure, were inadequate to explain verbal behaviour.

It is important to note however that this was an argument *against* the behaviourists and the descriptivists rather than *for* the correctness of his own hypotheses. The onus was still on Chomsky to show that linguistic knowledge did in fact take the form of rule systems of the sort he proposed, and that we are innately equipped to acquire such rule systems.

Obvious as this must seem, the persuasiveness of Chomsky's arguments against the descriptivists and the behaviourists appears to have lent a spurious credibility to his own hypotheses. Clearly proving one set of ideas to be wrong is not the same as proving another set to be right. To establish that innate mechanisms are required of a kind undreamt of in Skinner's psychology does not establish the adequacy of Chomsky's formal theory as an account of those innate mechanisms.

This becomes even more apparent once a further complicating factor is taken into account. When Chomsky was writing as a technical linguist, concerned with describing and justifying his formal theory of linguistic structure, he used the term creativity in a different and considerably narrower sense. The reason for this has directly to do with particular formal properties of his model. It was, as he once noted, the incorporation of recursive devices into his grammar that made it formally possible to generate an unbounded number of hierarchically bracketed structures. Chomsky wrote of the significance of incorporating such devices into a grammar in the following terms:

> Although it was well understood that linguistic processes are in some sense 'creative', the technical devices for expressing a system of recursive processes were simply not available until much more recently. In fact, a real understanding of how a language can (in Humboldt's words) 'make infinite use of finite means' has developed only within the last thirty years, in the course of studies in the foundations of mathematics. Now that these insights are readily available it is possible to return to the problems that were raised, but not solved, in traditional linguistic theory, and to attempt an explicit formulation of the 'creative' processes of language. There is, in short, no longer a technical barrier to the full-scale study of generative grammars. (Chomsky, 1965:8)

This is not an easy passage to interpret. We understand Chomsky to be saying that the development within mathematics of recursive devices had made it possible to devise formal systems which could model creative processes in language. The problem here is that the 'technical devices for expressing a system of recursive processes' which Chomsky incorporated into his model applied only to syntactic form. They were formal devices that made it possible for an unbounded number of syntactic structures to be generated independently of meaning. There was thus a clear shortfall between the notion of creativity taken in its full sense – the ability to produce and understand an indefinite number of new utterances in freedom from stimulus control – and the narrower technical version of creativity incorporated into Chomsky's formal model.[6] The existence of this shortfall casts considerable doubt on his claim that his formal grammars constitute an explicit formulation of the 'creative' processes of language. As we noted in Chapter 1, Chomsky undoubtedly saw the importance of the creative processes of language, and recognised that current psychological and linguistic theory were too narrowly-based to account for them. Yet, in his own technical work he was forced, by his commitment to deductively formulated theory, to take a very narrow view of creative processes as limited to syntactic form. What has confused readers over the years is that this distinction between creativity in its full sense and the narrower version incorporated into Chomsky's technical work is frequently blurred in his writings. It has thus been easy for the unwary outsider to assume – wrongly – that Chomsky's technical work provides a model of creativity in its full sense and, in so doing, lends support to his psychological hypotheses.

Despite impressions to the contrary the North American descriptivists did in fact also recognise creativity in its full sense to be a fundamental characteristic of language. They invariably explained it in terms of analogy. Bloomfield was aware that:

> . . . the possibilities of combination are practically infinite. (Bloomfield, 1935:275)

To explain how it was that a native speaker could produce and understand sentences he had never previously heard, Bloomfield proposed:

> . . . we say that he utters them *on the analogy* of similar forms which he has heard. (Bloomfield, 1935:275)

In a similar vein, Hockett wrote:

> When we hear a fairly long and involved utterance which is evidently not a direct quotation, we can be reasonably certain that analogy is at work. (Hockett, 1958:425)

It is significant that Chomsky invariably reacted strongly and scornfully both to descriptivist and more traditionalist invocations of analogy. Indeed some of his harshest invective is directed against appeals to analogy as an explanation of creativity. Chomsky wrote:

> To attribute the creative aspect of language use to 'analogy' or 'grammatical patterns' is to use these terms in a completely metaphorical way, with no clear sense and with no relation to the technical usage of linguistic theory. It is no less empty than Ryle's description of intelligent behavior as an exercise of 'powers' and 'dispositions' of some mysterious sort, or the attempt to account for

the normal, creative use of language in terms of 'generalisation' or 'habit' or 'conditioning'. (Chomsky, 1966:12–13)

It is not difficult to see why he should feel so strongly. On the face of it analogy offers a different explanation for the creative aspect of language use and a rival to his own hypothesis. It is however an explanation that Chomsky sees as inherently vague and untestable. Given his commitment to explanation in the form of a rigorous and explicit deductively formulated theory, he would be unlikely to accept informal appeals to analogy as explanatory. Analogy necessarily involves speakers' and hearers' perception of the world and as such does not lend itself to explanation in terms of the kinds of formalisation Chomsky was using.[7]

Thus while it is true that the descriptivists and the behaviourists were not able to give any rigorous account of the creative use of language, it is also true, although for different reasons, that Chomsky was unable to offer any illuminating account of it. The reason in Chomsky's case was that his commitment to explanation in the form of deductively formulated theory required him to concentrate on structure at the expense of meaning. This was particularly so at the outset when the foundations of his approach were being laid.[8] Between his interest in creativity in its full sense and his need, in order to construct a deductively formulated theory, to separate out form for special attention, there was a fundamental inconsistency, an inconsistency masked by the implications in much of his writing that his technical work dealt with broader questions. It should have been obvious that the full creative processes of language could not be explained in any revealing way by concentrating predominantly on linguistic form. No doubt it would have been obvious to Chomsky had he not already become committed to explanation in the form of a deductively formulated theory.

Abstractness and universality of linguistic structure

The other important argument which Chomsky advanced against descriptivist and behaviourist theories of language was from what he claimed to be the abstract and universal character of linguistic structure. His analysis of a wide range of sentences led him as we saw in Chapter 1 to the conviction that syntactic relations among sentences could only be accounted for by postulating abstract levels of structure related by complex sets of rules – levels such as deep and surface structure, and rules such as transformational rules – none of which had any simple and direct relation to the physical linguistic signal. This enabled him to argue that descriptivist and behaviourist theories of language, concentrating as they do on the surface forms, cannot but be inadequate. According to Chomsky, in order to explain syntactic relations between sentences:

> We are led to postulate highly abstract structures, structures which have no direct connection with the physical facts, which are related to the physical facts only by a long chain of operations of a very specific and unique and highly abstract character . . . This abstractness is of a sort which cannot be represented as an associative net. (Chomsky, 1968:687)

These arguments from abstractness, like those from creativity, supported Chomsky's rejection of descriptivists and behaviourist approaches to the analysis and description of language. They did not however at the same time support Chomsky's own hypothesis that the internal organisation of linguistic knowledge is in the form of a rule system of a specific type and that we are innately equipped to acquire such rule systems. Support for that hypothesis might have come from the work of those psycholinguistics who, in the mid-sixties and early seventies, sought psychological correlates to Chomsky's theoretical constructs such as 'transformation' and 'deep structure' in subjects' responses to sentences. However, as is well-known in the field, no such support for the technical apparatus of Chomsky's model was ever reliably found.

Chomsky further claimed that since the formal grammars he proposed were adequate to describe the structures of a wide range of languages, this suggested that languages themselves, like the grammars, must be organised in highly specific ways.

> Deep structures seem to be very similar from language to language, and the rules that manipulate and interpret them also seem to be drawn from a very narrow class of conceivable formal operations . . . Furthermore, the underlying abstract structures and the rules that apply to them have highly restricted properties that seem to be uniform over languages and over different individuals speaking the same language, and that seem to be largely invariant with respect to intelligence and specific experience. (Chomsky, 1967:7)

In effect he is claiming that there are constraints on the way formal grammars are constructed across languages, constraints which may be just those that are to be found in the universal grammar or rule schema with which children learning language are genetically endowed. He assumes without question that the apparent universality of formal grammars bears directly on the way linguistic knowledge is organised within language users, and on the conditions under which language is acquired. Chomsky's conviction that the structure of a linguistic theory reflected the structure of linguistic knowledge allowed him to conflate the terms 'grammar' and 'language'. When for example he states that:

> There is no a priori necessity for a language to be organised in this highly specific and most peculiar way. (Chomsky, 1967:7)

the 'highly specific and most peculiar way' to which he is referring is actually the form of his own particular rule system or grammar. He would have been less open to contradiction had he said that there was no *a priori* necessity why a *grammar* should be organised in the highly specific way which he – in order to construct a deductively formulated system – had elected to organise it. Similarly, when he observes that the underlying abstract structures and the rules that apply to them seem to be 'uniform over languages and over different individuals speaking the same language . . .', he appears to be assuming that if the rules are uniform over grammars, they must be uniform over languages – a totally unfounded assumption. When the distinction between grammar and language is clearly drawn, then there can be nothing remarkable in the fact that generative rule systems for providing description of limited aspects of language are similar across a number of languages. Certainly nothing illuminating follows from this observation either about the organisation of linguistic knowledge in humans, or about any innate language learning mechanisms they may be equipped with. If Chomsky's formal system could be shown to represent a more complex range of structures more elegantly than a simpler constituent structure grammar then one might want to argue that of the two it was the more adequate. Any such argument would still leave the question of the psychological plausibility of either type of representation as completely unproven.

Thus the arguments which Chomsky used most frequently to justify his own hypotheses are better taken as arguments against descriptivist and behaviourist views of language. Such arguments undoubtedly serve to bring out the complexity of the problems of the creative use of language and of the problems of how the ability to use language creatively is acquired in the first place. Yet they offer little support to Chomsky's own hypotheses that linguistic knowledge is internally organised in the form of rule systems of his type and that the child is innately equipped to acquire just such rule systems.

The failure to test

The reasons for Chomsky's concentration on attacking descriptivism and behaviourism and his failure to support his own hypotheses lie in the constantly recurring and deep-seated confusion of his psychological and philosophical views with his formal theory of linguistic structure. Chomsky was not a psychologist but a linguist of a very specialist type, concerned with an extremely idealised view of language as a user-independent ordered system in which structures could be characterised independently of meaning. His technical work on linguistic systems had suggested to him important hypotheses about the way knowledge of linguistic form might be organised and acquired. As we showed in the last section, these hypotheses flew in the face of prevailing psychological theory. It was moreover the psychological theory to which the principles and procedures of the North American descriptivists had been linked. If Chomsky had been a working cognitive psychologist, the next stage of enquiry would most naturally have been an attempt to investigate these hypotheses empirically. This would not have been easy since psycholinguistic experiments are notoriously difficult to devise and execute. Chomsky however made no attempt to do this. Indeed he has on occasion revealed considerable distaste for experimental work. On the contrary, he made a move that has been peculiarly characteristic of his work. He argued that the best way of exploring these hypotheses further was not to investigate the behaviour of language learners and language users to see whether certain regularities in it were subsumable within a rule system, but rather to embark upon:

> . . . a deeper investigation of the nature of grammars. (Chomsky, 1967:5)

In other words, instead of testing formally inspired hypotheses about the cognitive organisation of certain kinds of highly restricted linguistic knowledge, he proposed to develop his psychological claim by further elaborating formal, mathematised grammars. Yet the most such a move could have achieved would have been to suggest fresh hypotheses that would themselves have required empirical testing.

In moving to the further elaboration of the nature of formal grammars, Chomsky was in effect – without a shred of positive evidence – assuming his psychological hypotheses to be plausible. In making this move, however, in keeping his psychological claims so closely in line with his technical work, he transposed the limitations of his formal linguistics into his psychology. These limitations, as we showed in Chapter 2, sprang from the strict idealisations imposed on him by the adoption of a deductively formulated model.

Such limitations would not have mattered, we must emphasise, had he simply used his technical work as a source of ideas, a springboard to the formulation and testing of hypotheses. But that was not Chomsky's way. By setting aside the problem of empirical confirmation, by carrying on with the elaboration of his formal model, he put his work into a curious limbo of unsubstantiated hypotheses and ill-grounded mathematical models for highly restricted aspects of linguistic behaviour.

Chomsky's approach however is entirely in line with his view of science and of what constitutes an explanatory theory. Recall that he adhered to the received view of science, according to which explanatory theories should take the form of deductively formulated systems. Chomsky had devised such a formal system or grammar, claimed initially to explain a very limited aspect of language: the notion 'grammatical in a language'. This formal system, devises for reasons independent of psychology, had nevertheless given rise to psychological hypotheses. Historically there is an interesting parallel here with the psychological claims of the descriptivists. We saw earlier that Hockett had assumed that their 'discovery procedures', the separation of levels, the bottom-to-top ordering principle, and so on, paralleled the processes by which the child acquired its first language. Chomsky's attack on this assumption was that it emerged from a commitment to a certain methodological procedure, not from empirical investigation. This reflects our reservations about Chomsky's own psychological

claims. They too emerge not so much from a commitment to
methodological practices as from a commitment to a model of
explanation in the form of deductively formulated theory. Conspicuously absent from both Chomsky's and Hockett's work is any
justification for the psychological claims from empirical work. For
Chomsky however the question of psychological justification of
his linguistic work has turned out to be crucial. Putting it strongly,
he *required* his work to have such significance in order to make it
worthwhile. It is clear from remarks he has made that he has never
taken an instrumentalist but always a realist view of theories.[9] It is
this realist interpretation that has provided the enormous attraction of his theory and yet it has been at the same time the source of
considerable misunderstanding. We saw earlier the way in which
Chomsky conflated the terms 'grammar' and 'language'. Much
more confusing over the years has been his conflation of the
structure of his model with the structure of the mind.

The conflation of mind and model: Chomsky's misleading analogy

Chomsky, like Hockett, drew an analogy between the linguist and
the child. He wrote:

> The construction of a grammar of a language by a linguist is in
> some respects analogous to the acquisition of language by the
> child. The linguist has a corpus of data; the child is presented with
> unanalysed data of language use. The linguist tries to formulate
> the rules of the language; the child constructs a mental representa-
> tion of the language. The linguist applies certain principles,
> and assumptions to select grammar among the many possible
> candidates compatible with his data; the child must also select
> among the grammars compatible with the data. (Chomsky,
> 1975:11)

To many in psychology, linguistics and philosophy, the analo-
gising of the task of the linguist constructing a generative grammar with the task of the child has appeared plausible. Certainly at
first sight it may seem that there are interesting parallels. Given
the far-reaching importance of the issue, however, it is worth
considering the analogy more closely. The first link is said to
concern the data:

The linguist has a corpus of data; the child is presented with unanalysed data of language use. The linguist tries to formulate the rules of the language; the child constructs a mental representation of the grammar of the language.

The analogy begins to be misleading because Chomsky fails to make an important distinction between the linguist's and the child's activities. The linguist has conciously set about his task whereas children learning language act quite unself-consciously. The linguist's self-consciousness cannot but affect both the task he sets himself and the way he goes about fulfilling it. His task is to construct a grammar of a language, which, if he is a generative linguist, he sees for reasons quite unrelated to psychology as a rule system. If he is constructing a grammar for a language he knows well, then in order to achieve his aim, he will idealise his subject matter, isolate those restricted aspects of language which do appear to lend themselves to systematic expression in the form of rule systems – and set aside all other aspects of language even though the aspects he sets aside may be central to actual language in use. The child acts quite differently. He makes no idealisations. He has no need to. He is exposed to language in the context of everyday use, and brings into play his own needs, his relations with others, his developing beliefs and his rapidly expanding experience. We have no reason to assume that he does not use all this other information in the course of language learning, information which the generative linguist, as deviser of rule systems, is obliged by the constraints of his model to set aside. The linguist, in picking out for special attention, as he does, only those aspects of linguistic activity which are regular and thus susceptible to formalisation, is therefore carrying out a much more limited task than the child – and conceivably a very trivial task if it turns out that the apparently systematic elements of language are its most peripheral ones.

If the linguist is constructing a grammar of a language he does not know well, then he appears to be in a much more similar position to the child. Yet even here the analogy still does not really hold. The linguist can do little more than extract from the data that which is systematic and therefore characterisable. In doing this he is bound to be affected by his existing linguistic knowledge. The child presented with 'unanalysed data of language use' on the other hand actually learns the language.

It is interesting that Hockett, who, like Chomsky, drew psychological parallels between linguistic work and the acquisition of language, nevertheless saw the essential difference between the task of the linguist and the task of the child.

> The essential difference between the process in the child and the procedure of the linguist is this: the linguist has to make his analysis overtly, in communicable form, in the shape of a set of statements which can be understood by any properly trained person, who in turn can predict utterances not yet observed with the same degree of accuracy as can the original analyst. The child's 'analysis' consists, on the other hand, of the mass of varying synaptic potentials in his central nervous system. The child in time comes to *behave* the language; the linguist must come to *state* it. (Hockett, 1957:208)

Chomsky, unlike Hockett, seems to have assumed that because linguists choose, influenced by a particular view of science, to construct grammars in the form of rule systems, children in the course of language learning also construct mental representations of such grammars and furthermore that children will have the same theoretical problems as linguists. This seems to be a confusion between a theorist's account of a phenomenon and the phenomenon itself.

Perhaps one of the clearest examples of how misleading is Chomsky's presentation of his work is provided by his conclusion to the analogy:

> General linguistic theory, which is concerned with discovering and exhibiting the principles, conditions, and procedures that the child brings to bear in attaining his knowledge of language, can also be construed as an account of the methodology of linguistic investigation, the methods by which a linguist arrives at a grammar. (Chomsky, 1975:11)

By implying that 'general linguistic theory' (or universal grammar) is concerned directly with discovering the capacities involved in language acquisition and is only also an account of the structure of a linguistic theory, Chomsky has rather deftly depicted himself as one concerned primarily with psychology, and only secondarily with formal language models. But for this to be plausible the linguistic claims would have to have some psychological backing. Otherwise there is no substantive basis for the claim that linguists are concerned with 'the principles, conditions and procedures that the child brings to bear in attaining his knowledge of language'. Looked at more closely, the principles, conditions and procedures that the linguist appeals to are the results of his idealisation of natural language to just those aspects that lend themselves to the adopted formalisation.[10] Why should this separate activity, except fortuitously, reveal anything illuminating about the infinitely richer, subtler and more complex task of the child learning to speak?

The nub of this question was expressed some years ago by Max Black:

> A transformational grammar, . . .can be regarded as a piece of mathematics, suggested grammatical verdicts of qualified informants. So, Chomsky's main premises . . . look to me like mathematical ones, having the form: such-and-such will just suffice to generative such-and-such a class of sentences (abstract structures, suggested by utterances that competent speakers would certify as 'correct'). Yet Chomsky ends with *psychological* and *epistemological* conclusions. If his reasoning is sound, some psychological and epistemological premises must have been introduced in order to warrant the transition: I am unclear as to what these additional premises are. (Black, 1970:456–7)

In fact the additional premises Black is seeking to warrant psychological and epistemological conclusions may be reduced to a single one: Chomsky's assumption of a realist interpretation of his theory. This he introduced through an elusive but characteristic play on the term 'grammar'. In *Aspects of the Theory of Syntax* he wrote:

> Using the term grammar with a systematic ambiguity (to refer, first, to the native speaker's internally represented 'theory of his language' and, second, to the linguist's account of this), we can say that the child has developed and internally represented a generative grammar, . . . (Chomsky, 1965:25)

This is a key passage for understanding how Chomsky succeeded in transforming himself from a technical linguist into a cognitive psychologist. In it two entirely distinct constructs are merged. Grammar is used to refer to processes of unknown complexity by which native speakers come to understand utterances of their language. Grammar is also used to refer to a type of rule system or generative grammar devised as we saw in Chapter 2 to account for highly restricted and debatable aspects of language. Chomsky's 'systematic ambiguity' allows him to claim without further justification that the child develops a rule system of the linguist's sort.

At its most extreme this has led Chomsky to attribute to the child learning language very specific problems that arise rather from his particular type of model. He claims, for example, that:

> The linguist applies certain principles and assumptions to select a grammar among the many possible candidates compatible with his data; the child must also select among grammars compatible with the data.

Generative theorists, as we saw in Chapter 2, faced the problem of evaluating different formulations of the grammars they were devising, grammars for – we must emphasise – limited aspects of linguistic form. Chomsky here equates the child's problems with those of the meta-linguist. This however is a hugely unbalanced equation. Chomsky attempts to sustain it by insisting that a child attempting to devise a grammar for the language he first encounters would be faced with an intractable problem if there were no constraints on the form that the grammar could take. His own general rule schema or universal grammar provides constraints on the form of generative grammars – therefore, he claimed, it may be said to contribute to our understanding of the constraints within which the child comes to formulate grammars and thus learn his language. Note however that his view is only plausible as long as the ambiguity of the term 'grammar' is sustained. Once the two senses are clearly separated, it is clear that there are no necessary explanatory links between the constraints the linguist requires on a particular type of insecurely based formal model and the complex processes involved in language acquisition.

Underlying Chomsky's claims appears to have been a constant and pressing need to justify the highly formal model of explanation he had introduced into linguistics. Chomsky wrote:

> The problem of . . . explanatory adequacy . . . is essentially the problem of constructing a theory of language acquisition, an account of the specific innate abilities that make this achievement possible. (Chomsky, 1965:27)

In other words, the formally required universal grammar will be justified and have much broader significance if it can be shown to be part of an account of the child's specific innate capacities. The point that it is easy to overlook is the direction in which the motivation and justification for work in generative linguistics has flowed. Chomsky first introduced into linguistics a deductively formulated theoretical model in order to provide a firmer theoretical basis for the syntactic work of the North American descriptivists. Thus what existed from the outset, if in a primitive form, was a formal theory of grammar. This theory suggested to Chomsky hypotheses about the cognitive organisation and acquisition of linguistic knowledge. But these psychological claims for which Chomsky has since become well-known stemmed initially from his drive to justify an already existing formal theory. This formal theory however was never devised as a tentative, testable theory that might provide a firmer basis for empirical findings in child language acquisition. Its origins are quite different. Its primary motivation was to provide a deductively formulated theory sufficiently rigorous to count as an explanation of linguistic structure with no reference at all to actual cognitive processes. Yet Chomsky's writings often suggest quite a different view of the relation of his study of language to the study of mind. In, for example, the passage quoted above on the ambiguous use of the term 'grammar', the order in which the 'systematic ambiguity' is presented is highly significant. The native speaker's internally represented 'theory of his language' has become the primary sense of grammar. The linguist is now seen as giving an account of this. Yet it was in fact the linguist's formal theory which provided the basis for the psychological claim that speakers of a language had internally represented a generative grammar. It has been moreover Chomsky's theory of grammar, limited in scope though it necessarily was, that has provided the only solid, non-speculative aspect of his 'theory of language'.

Chomsky's psychological claims for his theory are, it seems to us, important in two ways. First, they matter to Chomsky himself insofar as they have provided for many years now what he sees as justification for work on elaborating formal meta-grammars or universal grammar. Second, they were important in calling into question the basis of the behaviourist psychology that was flourishing at the time Chomsky was originally developing his formal linguistic model. However, because his psychological claims have taken insufficient account of empirical work in the area, they are neither illuminating nor suggestive in the way, for example, Bruner's work is, of what may actually be happening when a child moves from pre-linguistic modes of communication to the use of language proper. We conclude that Chomsky's innateness cannot count as a positive contribution from linguistics to psychology but should rather be seen as a reflection of his antagonism to behaviourists psychology.

Chomsky's anti-behaviourism has been significant in other ways however. In particular it has had an insidious effect on attitudes within generative linguistics towards the very real problems inherent both in establishing relevant data and in finding empirical confirmation for linguistic hypotheses. Quine has described behaviourism as a name for the method a materialist follows when doing psychology. On that account, it is not unreasonable to see Chomsky's rejection of behaviourism as part of a more general rejection of materialism. Simplifying considerably, it can be said that, in the history of thought, the flight from materialism has almost invariably led to some form or other of idealism. For the purpose of this exposition, we construe a materialist as roughly one whose view it is that reality consists of material objects in spatial and temporal relationships that exist independently of anyone's experience of them. An idealist, on the other hand, may be thought of as one who sees reality as a reflection of a rational system, a system so constructed that the nature of its separate elements is intelligible only insofar as the system as a whole is understood. For the idealist furthermore, the system is one that is not extracted from a body of facts that is somehow given to us, but is conceived as to some extent dependent on a contribution made by the mind. Given Kant's mind-dependent view of reality, it is perhaps not surprising that philosophers have sometimes seen Chomsky's innatist views as Kantian ideas in a linguistic coat.

Chomsky himself refers less often to Kant than to the work of Descartes and the Cambridge Platonists.[11] In *Cartesian Linguistics* in a general criticism of empirical views of language acquisition,

Chomsky cites George Herbert of Cherbury, who had developed the notion that there are certain:

> ... principles or notions implanted in our minds that we bring to objects from ourselves ... as ... a direct gift of Nature, a precept of natural instinct. (Chomsky, 1966:60)

Lord George Herbert goes on to observe that although these common notions are 'stimulated by objects ... no one, however wild his views, imagines that they are conveyed by objects themselves.' (Chomsky, 1966:60)

Elsewhere Chomsky notes Descartes' observation:

> Could anything be imagined more preposterous than that all common notions which are inherent in our mind should arise from these corporeal movements, and should be incapable of existing without them? (Chomsky, 1966:67)

It is not within our competence to do justice to the many, varied and subtle positions that have been taken down the centuries on the rationalist/empiricist and idealist/materialist issues.[12] It is nevertheless crucial to understanding Chomsky's position to be aware of just how much his approach to the study of language reflects the preoccupations of the rationalist and idealist and how little the 'resourceful empiricist'.[13] It is extremely difficult without improper simplification to give an effective illustration of the way in which Chomsky's rationalism and idealism show up in his approach to specific linguistic questions. However, the following passage is representative of a style of argument he has used consistently over many years. In this passage, he is discussing the principles underlying the formulation of questions:

> Consider ... the process of forming questions in English. Roughly speaking, wherever a sentence has a name in it, you can question that name. If I say 'I saw John', we have the corresponding question, 'Who did I see?' Similarly, corresponding to the assertion 'He thinks that he saw John', we have the question 'Who does he think he saw?' And so on. So a plausible rule for English would be, say, at a first approximation: 'To form a question, take the position in which a name can appear, put in that position a

word like "Who" or "Whom" or "What", and move it in front of the sentence (and do a few other minor things).' When we try to implement that rule we quickly find that although it works over a substantial range, it fails in some interesting cases. Suppose, for example, I say 'He wonders who saw John' and I try to question 'John'. The resulting sentence; by the rule I proposed, would be: 'Who does he wonder who saw?'. We know at once that that's not a sentence. You may say it's not a sentence because it fails to be meaningful, but it seems quite wrong. In fact the pseudo-sentence is perfectly meaningful. If it *were* a sentence, we'd know exactly what it would mean. 'Who is such that he wonders who saw him?': that is what it would mean – but we don't say it. It's just not one of the allowable sentences of English. So there must be some principle, part of English grammar, that prevents us from saying it. Yet it's extraordinarily unlikely that any such principle was ever taught to anyone . . . in fact nobody knew the principle until recently and we are far from sure that we know it even today . . . If we can discover what that principle is, or formulate a plausible hypothesis as to what it is, it is reasonable to attribute it to a genetic endowment. (Magee, 1978:211)

The general importance of this passage is to be found not in the particular example that Chomsky discusses but rather in the mode of argument he employs, a mode that has become characteristic of generative theorists. In this passage he is explaining to his interviewer, Bryan Magee, why a particular type of sentence does not occur in English. The purpose of his illustration is to argue that non-occurrence of this sentence-type may be attributed to some universal syntactic constraint forming part of a rational system with which language users are genetically endowed.

Suppose we consider in more detail the nature of the argument that leads to the conclusion that some universal and formal principle is attributed to innate properties of the mind.

The argument begins with an assumption that there will be a general rule for the process of forming questions in English. It is furthermore assumed that the rule will be formal in character, that is, that it will not be sensitive to the function of questions in English, nor will it be affected by other constituents in questions – words such as 'wonders', 'doubts', 'asks himself' and so on – but will instead take into account only the distribution and arrangement of forms. The general rule is:

> To form a question in [English], take the position in which a
> name can appear, put in that position like 'Who' or 'Whom' or
> 'What', and move it to the front of the sentence . . .

The next characteristic move is to point to examples such a rule
will *not* account for. In this case, Chomsky chooses sentences of the
type:

> He wonders who saw John.

The mechanical application of the hypothesised general rule
results in a syntactically ill-formed sentence:

> Who does he wonder who saw?

The next stage is typically to raise the question of why such
forms do not occur, and to dismiss, as Chomsky does here, as
'quite wrong' the suggestion that meaning is a crucial factor. This
is an important part of Chomsky's argument since if it could be
shown that the reasons for the non-occurrence of this type of
sentence were semantic, then this would establish that meaning
considerations played a vital role in the formation of questions. If
that were the case, it would be more difficult for him to claim that a
genetically determined *syntactic* principle were at work. It is important to keep in mind that for Chomsky's style of argument to
hold, he requires that the non-occurring sentences although non-
grammatical should nevertheless be meaningful. It is therefore
not surprising to find him claiming in this case that the syntactically ill-formed 'Who does he wonder who saw?' is 'perfectly
meaningful'. He adds moreover that if this question were to occur
it would be easily understood. It would mean, he writes:

> Who is such that he wonders who saw him?

Our difficulty, and we have found that we are not alone, is that
we do not find:

> Who does he wonder who saw?

at all meaningful.

This disagreement over the meaningfulness of the pseudo-
sentence is not trivial. It is a crucial part of Chomsky's case for

genetic endowment with universal syntactic principles that non-occurring forms such as the pseudo-sentence he quotes should be meaningful. For if they were not then their meaninglessness would be sufficient to explain their unacceptability. If however they are meaningful, as he alleges, then the way is open for him to claim that some syntactic, not semantic, principle is needed to explain why they do not actually occur.

Before considering what such a syntactic principle might be let us suppose that we are right in our view that:

Who does he wonder who saw?

is meaningless but that unlike Chomsky we are not committed to an explanation in terms of the distribution of forms. A number of reasons then suggest themselves as to why Chomsky's roughly formulated rule does not apply in this case. These reasons, it is important to emphasise, are not restricted solely to forms and their distribution *vis-à-vis* other forms but include the function and use of questions in exchanges between users of a language interested in understanding each other. For example, among the reasons one would not question 'John' in the manner proposed in the combination:

He wonders who saw John

is that in this case 'John' is already both a constituent of an indirect question – 'who saw John' – and a constituent that would already have been identified for that question to make sense. An analysis of questions would surely show that we ordinarily ask questions about something that counts as known between us and our interlocutor. Without some such presuppositions about shared knowledge, expectations and beliefs, it is difficult to see how questions would arise.[14]

We are not trying to solve the problem which Chomsky raises, but rather to give some idea of the range of factors relating to the role of questions in meaningful exchanges, which he, from his rationalist and idealist standpoint, firmly sets to one side.

Setting them to one side leaves him free to see the non-occurence of sentences such as:

Who does he wonder who saw?

as a problem which he solves by claiming that the original general rule must be constrained in its application. The final move is then to claim that the constraint or condition on the applicability of the rule may be attributed to some innate property of the mind.

The relevant principle, which Chomsky comes to attribute to genetic endowment, was originally known as the A-over-A principle, although it has since been extensively elaborated and now forms part of the more general study of constraints on transformations. The details of the various modifications are not significant since what matters is the general character of such allegedly explanatory principles. What Chomsky does is to establish conditions of the generative power of rules. These conditions which prevent the derivation of non-occurring forms then figure as part of the universal grammar with which language users are said to be genetically endowed.

Apart from the lack of concern for empirical confirmation, what is striking about this style of argument is that it involves problems which are clearly artefacts of a particular approach to theory construction. Typically, Chomsky observes that certain distributions of forms rarely or never occur. He then seeks an explanation for non-occurring distributions of form in constraints on formal devices for generating related forms. What he conspicuously does not do is a further analysis of the use and meaning of the forms – in this case the processes of question formation – in actual exchanges. What appears to have happened is that Chomsky's commitment to a particular style of theory construction and validation has forced him and his co-workers into a style of argument that sees as problematic that which would not be if the aim was not to elaborate a formal model of a specified kind – within an essentially idealist framework.

Our general thesis is that linguistics under Chomsky and those who have worked within his framework, has diverged far from its subject matter: language. This style of argument provides an illustration of that divergence. Chomsky's commitment to a hypothesis that language users are genetically endowed with a universal grammar – a hypothesis originally inspired by his initial formal model devised in response to the work of the descriptivists – has caused him to fabricate problems where none exist. If the scope of theoretical linguistics were enlarged to include a thorough and systematic investigation of the use and function of language as a purposive activity, involving a recognition of the essential role played by speakers'/hearers' knowledge, beliefs and – most important – expectations in the functioning of language, then problems such as the non-occurrence of:

Who does he wonder who saw?

would be explicable in quite different terms.

This is not to say, however, that we want to disregard the contribution of form and structure to language in use. On the contrary, we would want to continue to study form and structure as one factor interacting with a number of others that together contribute to the understanding of utterances. The interesting problem, however, is not whether semantics is dependent upon or determined by syntax, or vice versa, but what the weighting of the relevant interacting factors in typical cases generally is.

Establishing this weighting is not a straightforward task. One point which has become increasingly clear is that an approach which assumes that linguistic problems must be couched in terms which lend themselves to modelling in the form of a deductive system is likely to be counter-productive since it demands idealisations which distort the object of enquiry. This means that linguists would have to distance themselves from the view of explanation which Chomsky had introduced into linguistics from the physical sciences. They would have to seek another style of explanation more suited to their subject matter. An approach which seeks to explore the weighting of interacting factors precludes a central thesis of Chomsky's work, the autonomy of syntax. The idea that syntax constitutes a system that is independent of meaning and, standing further back, the related idea that language can only be studied as a system independent of language users' beliefs and expectations, are reflections of an essentially rationalist and idealist temper that would need to be abandoned. Our own view is that language is an epiphenomenon on the world as language users perceive it, and that therefore a study of language that seeks to be explanatory will need to take into account the knowledge, beliefs, expectations and purposes of those language users. This is a view we explore in Chapters 4 and 5, where we attempt to extricate ourselves from the intricate web of assumptions that have come to dominate much of linguistics over the past two or three decades. We look for a return to what Northrop called the analysis of the problem stage and suggest that linguistics as a human science will need to find a form of explanation that takes into account the special character of its subject matter, language.

Notes

1. Looked at from a broader perspective, the linguistic controversy had some similarities to a more long-standing debate in the philosophy of science over realist and instrumentalist views of the status of scientific theories. These matters can become immensely complicated and may, it has been suggested, be merely a difference in 'preferred modes of speech' (Nagel, 1961:152). In the linguistic literature of the descriptivists, 'God's truth' linguistics were closer to a realist view, while the 'hocus-pocus' linguists approached the instrumentalists. Chomsky 'however' indicates, significantly, that in his work '. . . the "realist" position is taken for granted' (Chomsky, 1975:37).

2. Strictly Chomsky's comments bear not so much on the principle of separation of levels as on the bottom-to-top ordering principle.

3. Chomsky argues that whatever a particular linguist's theoretical and methodological commitments, in practice in coming to understand a fragment of language: '. . . the hearer will bring to bear the full grammatical apparatus that determines the space of possibilities from which this utterance is drawn . . .' (Chomsky, 1964a:106) we shall be arguing that what the hearer actually brings to bear is a great deal more complex than 'the full grammatical apparatus'.

4. Chomsky's rejection to behaviourism may have had other, deeper roots.   It may have sprung from a natural repugnance for the blandly inhuman, blithely optimistic and deeply arrogant view of the potential for human engineering expressed in some behaviourist passage such as the following from the Watson:

Give me a dozen healthy infants, well-formed and my own special world to bring them up in, and I will guarantee to take any one of at random and train him to become any type of specialist I might select – doctor, lawyer, artist, merchant chief – and yes – even beggar and thief, regardless of his talents, penchants, tendencies, abilities, vocations or race or his ancestors. (Watson, 1925:82)

5. This is one of the aspects of Chomsky's work that has found its way well outside the domain of linguistics. We think it worth mentioning here, although it is somewhat in the nature of an aside, that Chomsky's insistence on the distinction between human and animal languages led him to formulate a particularly striking hypothesis. As he sees it, man's use of language represents an evolutionary leap of some kind. This bold hypothesis is perhaps best seen as an extreme consequence of his anti-behaviourist psychology. He has provided no evidence in support of the view that the creative use of language represents an evolutionary leap in the development of man. The state of studies of animal communication is too uncertain to draw any firm conclusions.

6. When Humboldt characterised language as making 'infinite use of finite means' he was referring to creativity in its full sence. As Chomsky himself points out, Humboldt saw the lexicon or vocabulary as itself based on 'certain organising generative principles that produce the appropriate items on given occasions' (Chomsky, 1966:20).

7. This has often led Chomsky to a curious, almost wilful blindness, a failure, because of theoretical preoccupations, to note obvious connections and a concomitant surprise about a relation which if seen from another perspective is not surprising at all. For example, Chomsky analyses the sentence pair:

John's friends appeared to their wives to hate one another
John's friends appealed to their wives to hate one another

and finds them: '. . . very similar – they differ only in one phonological feature, hence minimally – nevertheless, speakers of the language understand them in very different ways, ignoring the obvious analogies' (Chomsky, 1976:142). The really difficult concept here is 'similarity'. What Chomsky appears not to have seen is that these examples constitute a problem only if analogy is restricted to similarities of form. Once the dimension of meaning is admitted, then these sentence pairs could not be 'typical examples that would lead S [the scientist] to reject the idea that an account of language can be based on notions of analogy and generalisation . . .' (Chomsky, 1976:142). On the contrary, they would show that phonological similarities would not take us very far in establishing significant relations between meaningful sentences. If sentences can be so nearly phonologically identical but so different in meaning this tells us simply that analogy is not a profitable line to pursue *when it is restricted to form*. It says nothing about analogy once meaning is admitted.

8. Subsequently we shall be considering the way limited aspects of meaning were eventually introduced into his theory.

9. See, for example, Chomsky, 1975:37 passim.

10. One striking consequence of this idealisations has been Chomsky's description of the data the child is presented with in aquiring language, data which in the early years he regularly described as 'meagre and degenerate'. From the perspective of a developmental psychologist this would probably seem unreasonable since it is not difficult to argue that the data provided by those surrounding a child learning language is rich and tacitly well-structured in relation to the child's needs and experience. It is important to note however that in describing it as 'meagre and degenerate' Chomsky was essentially strengthening his own position. If the language-learning child could have been shown to be provided by his environment with only very limited material then this would have lent support to the view that the complexly-structured universal grammar with which the child is said to be generally endowed is of major importance to the language-learning process.

   Recently in Chomsky's writings there had been a noticeable and notable shift in terminolgy. In *Reflections on Language* the data surrounding the child is for the first time and without comment on the change characterised as 'a fair adequate sample of the language. This would seem to reflect Chomsky's shift of interest from the details of his formal model – now assumed to be soundly based – to more speculative questions in psychology and philosophy.

11. As Passmore noted, before the nineteenth century idealism had flourished in England on two occasions, both times as a defence against materialism.

   On the first occasion the Cambridge Platonists, with help from Descartes and Plato, fought against the mechanically-atheistic philosophies to which seventeenth century scientific developments gave birth; on the second occasion, Berkeley was alarmed into philosophy by the materialism and the Deism which Newtonian science had unwittingly engendered. (Passmore, 1968:52)

It is rare that Chomsky refers to the writings of Plato yet as some have noticed there are Platonic strains in his thought: 'When Chomsky talks about a child being born with perfect knowledge of universal grammar . . . what is this but a revival of the Platonic doctrine of knowledge as a form of reminiscence?' (Hook, 1969:162)

12.   For an interesting and perceptive discussion of problems of idealism and materialism in linguistics, see Peter Eland Jones' forthcoming dissertation 'Materialism and the Structure of Language' Cambridge.

13.   Chomsky has dismissed the approach of 'resourceful empiricism' as too permissive to be of any value. It '. . .includes any specific empirical proposal that anyone can formulate . . . Having no content, the approach is of no interest.' (Chomsky, 1969:158–9). It does, however, as Quine has insisted, while allowing an appeal to innate dispositions, require such dispositions to be made sense of in terms of external observation. With the caveat, as Quine neurophysiologically rather oddly remarks, '. . . the behaviourist is knowingly and cheerfully up to his neck in innate mechanisms of learning-readiness' (Quine, 1969:95–6).

14.   If the name of the person the unknown person saw were not properly understood, then we could ask with an appropriate intonation what is sometimes called an echo question:

He wonders who saw whom?

The question 'who saw whom' is, however, a question in this case about something that has been said rather than a question about the way some event is perceived.

Interlude

In the first part of this book we have portrayed Chomsky's work as a foundational study in theoretical linguistics. We have argued that a profound dissatisfaction with the limited goals and methods of his contemporaries – limitations that sprang from a view of science that was essentially positivist in temper – led him to seek a linguistic theory that would not only describe but also explain aspects of language. The result was the adoption into linguistics of a mode of explanation that had been successful in some of the physical sciences, deductively formulated theory. Unfortunately the only aspects of language that seemed sufficiently well defined to lend themselves to rigorous formalisation of the sort required by such theory were aspects of form, particularly syntactic form.

By an unhappy paradox, the theoretical freedom that Chomsky won by cutting free from the positivist and behaviourist shackles of the North American descriptivists led him, because of the model of explanation he adopted, to forge in his technical work new but equally limiting chains of his own devising. Nowhere is this clearer than in his early views on the role of meaning in linguistic analysis:

> Meaning is a notoriously difficult notion to pin down. If it can be shown that meaning and related notions do play a central role in linguistic analysis, then its results and conclusions become subject to all of the doubts and obscurities that plague the study of meaning, and a serious blow is struck at the foundations of linguistic theory. (Chomsky, 1955:141)

Looking back after a quarter of a century, this passage seems to have set the direction for the place of meaning within Chomsky's style of linguistics. It begins by starting a point of view and closes with a prediction. The point of view is that since meaning, elsewhere described as 'vague' and 'obscure', is 'a notoriously difficult notion to pin down', the analysis of language should not rely centrally on it. If it were to, its 'results and conclusions' would 'become subject to all the doubts and obscurities that plague the study of meaning'. The passage ends with the prediction that if

121

once linguistic analysis does come to rely on meaning, 'a serious blow is struck at the foundations of linguistic theory'.

With one caveat, the developments in linguistic theory over the last two decades seem to us to have shown this prediction to have been remarkably prescient. Since the publication in 1955 of 'Semantic Considerations in Grammar', a number of attempts have been made to incorporate aspects of meaning into Chomsky's theory of linguistic structure. These attempts to introduce a semantic component into a model expressly set up to account for linguistic form have indeed proved the accuracy of Chomsky's prediction.[1] Each attempt has seriously weakened the foundations of linguistic theory of the type Chomsky first proposed. The caveat is that, since each proposal was an attempt to expand the domain of Chomsky's own model, the blow that was struck was not of course at the general foundations of any linguistic theory, but specifically at the foundations of deductively formulated linguistic theories of the type generative linguists had adopted.

The reasons for this were the grounds for Chomsky's original prediction. As we saw in Chapter 2, the conditions that make deductively formulated theory appropriate as a model of explanation are that the phenomenon to be explained must be at least well understood and well-defined and, moreover, be one that lends itself reasonably easily to expression in the terms of a formal notation. Syntax, with its restricted number of categories, appeared to be such a phenomenon. Semantics was clearly not. If meaning is seen as 'vague' and 'inherently untestable', and the study of meaning 'plagued with doubts and obscurities', then it is obviously not susceptible to explanation in terms of a deductively formulated theory. It is in this sense that, insofar as meaning considerations do turn out to be vital for linguistic analysis, the foundations of deductively formulated linguistic theory are seriously threatened. If meaning and a linguistic theory of that sort are not compatible, then either an attempt has to be made to dispel the obscurity surrounding meaning, or a deductively formulated linguistic theory embracing meaning as part of its domain has to be abandoned.

As it has turned out, despite Chomsky's dire prediction, considerations of meaning have come to play an increasingly important part in the subsequent development of his theory. Indeed a large part of the history of Chomsky's approach from the mid-sixties onwards could be written in terms of the problems that arose from attempts to introduce aspects of meaning into the formal model. Theoretical linguists have tackled these problems in ways that have led to an immense fragmentation of the field. The fragmentation resulted in a number of small but active groups resolutely pursuing their own particular adaptation of the theory and just as resolutely denouncing alternative proposals. A detailed account of the various adaptations of the basic model would be immensely complex. Each version is highly ingenious and intensely parochial over some allegedly crucial pieces of data. Because, in our view, the various adaptations have been more noteworthy for their ingenuity than for the insight they have shown into problems of meaning, we shall not attempt to give a detailed account of the internecine and sometimes bitter struggles between apparently opposing versions of the theory. Instead we outline the general picture.

The most plausible apologia for the direction the study of meaning took in the theoretical linguistics inspired by Chomsky's work is probably something along the following lines:

Once a reasonably adequate model for syntactic description is available, then that model – set up, we must emphasise, allegedly without reliance on meaning – could then provide a secure base from which to attack the problems of meaning. At a very general level of discussion, one might hold that since the problems of meaning had effectively resisted frontal assault, they might be successfully overcome by a more indirect approach. In the case of Chomsky's theory this more indirect approach was from the formalisation of syntactic description. Again at a most general level, there is considerable scientific warrant for an approach that appears to make a start on a large and intractable problem by first breaking it down into manageable smaller chunks. Chomsky's otherwise obscure and barely credible remark in *Language and Responsibility* that 'a large part of *Syntactic Structures* and *The Logical Structure of Linguistic Theory* was devoted to the study of meaning' fits well within an interpetation of this sort. On this view, the study of syntax is a prelude to a firmer, more rigorously based study of semantics.

The most striking characteristic of the work generated by this oblique approach to meaning was its emphasis on a syntax-based attack on problems of semantics. Indeed a keynote of later work in transformational generative linguistics has been the way syntactic considerations determined investigation of aspects of meaning. In the literature of the late sixties and seventies the crucial recurring issues revolved around the relations of structure and meaning. For many workers, research has consisted either in seeking some piece of syntactically required formal apparatus that could apparently be shown to provide a basis for semantic interpretation, or in extending some apparatus for syntactic description to provide a representation of meaning itself.

A clear example is provided by the changing fortunes of the syntactic constructs deep structure and surface structure once meaning considerations were introduced into the model. The initial justification for these two levels of representation had been to characterise syntactic not semantic relations. Some sentence constructions could be said to be alike at surface structure but different at deep structure, others alike at deep structure but different at surface structure. A standard example of the first phenomenon is the pair: *John is easy to please* and *John is eager to please*, two sentences with apparently identical syntactic constituents:

   NP   Cop   Adj   V

but which, as we saw in Chapter 1, have different distributional potential. In Chomsky's model this difference of distribution was captured by giving them distinct syntactic representations at one level – deep structure – the same representation at another level – surface structure – the two levels being related by transformational rules.

A familiar example of similar deep structures but distinct surface structures was the relation between active and passive sentences which could be provided with similar deep structures but, as the result of transformational rules, obviously distinct surface structures.

Granting for the moment that these levels of structure did throw light on the relations between similar sentence constructions, what is more striking is the claims that were made for their semantic relevance once a semantic component was added to the syntactic model. Initially it was suggested that deep, not surface, structure formalised those aspects of sentence structure relevant to the semantic component. This was succeeded by the view that deep and surface structure both contributed, but differently, to semantic interpretation. Chomsky's present view is that a suitably enriched version of surface structure alone is sufficient to determine semantic interpretation. The point is not that changes were being made; if new insights were being thrown up, this would simply have been evidence of the productivity of the model. The point is that semantic considerations were subordinated to the framework of a syntactic theory already set up on distributional not semantic grounds. As a result, the complexities of the debate in the linguistic literature over the relations of syntax and semantics have to do not with fundamental questions about the nature of structure and meaning but about how syntactic apparatus modelled on the rule systems of formal language theory could be given semantic significance.

In outline, the general picture of research during the late sixties and seventies is something like the following. It is widely assumed that the syntactic model is securely based. Attempts to graft aspects of meaning on to that model however require continual modifications both of the relations of the various rule systems to each other and of the syntactic component as a whole to the new semantic component. But this new semantic component which is much more loosely defined than the syntactic rule systems is assumed to be able to take in a plethora of issues from traditional semantics – issues such as the representation of aspects of word meaning, presupposition and focus and the scope of negation and quantification – within the framework of a model that was explicitly set up to account for structure without reliance on meaning. The result has been, as Chomsky predicted, that the less well-defined semantic notions have brought about the loss of the apparent rigour, explicitness and formality that had been one of the strengths of the theory in its original form. The syntactic model itself began to disintegrate. The additions, modifications, elaborations and revisions of the theory of linguistic form make it no longer describable as a deductively formulated theory. The trappings of formal theory remain, however, particularly in Chomsky's various presentations of the general outline of the model. But in substance the theoretical apparatus has gradually become no more than a sketch of a deductively formulated theory. At the same time, a commitment to explanation of this sort still prevents the investigation of problems of meaning in a way that is unconfined by the limitations of the syntactic model. Thus, despite what might have been expected from the opening up of semantic considerations, in the reality of actual research the divergence of linguistics from its subject matter has not been effectively reduced. The discussion of semantic data is still related to the formal wraith but never in the rigorous, precise and formal way that had marked Chomsky's early work on the logical structure of linguistic theory.

There are a number of reasons for this weakening of the theory but two stand out. First, semantic notions such as presupposition and focus are not sufficiently well defined or well understood to be introduced into a formal model. Second, as a consequence of the relative obscurity of meaning there is no reasonably comprehensive meta-language or set of categories in terms of which meaning may be formally represented.

This second point is particularly important in attempting to understand the development of generative linguistics. Semantic categories are not given by tradition the way syntactic ones are. In Chapter 2 we argued that syntax was in a sense imposed upon Chomsky – given his commitment to deductively formulated theory as a form of explanation – in that it appeared to be reasonably well defined and, perhaps even more importantly, suitable categories were available. When semantic considerations *were* finally introduced, linguists failed to take seriously enough the question of whether meaning could be formalised along lines that had seemed appropriate for syntax.

This is not to say that attempts had not been made by linguists working in a number of different traditions to devise more or less formal categories in terms of which to represent the meaning of words. Broadly speaking, these attempts have been either *classificatory* or *decompositional*. Under the heading classificatory we include efforts to establish relations among lexical items, whether of a hierarchical nature as is the case for hyponomy (hyponomous relations are of the type dog, cat: animal; or daisy, buttercup: flower) or of a more loosely-defined kind to be found in work on the characterisation of semantic fields or the setting up of semantic classes. Much of the work on semantic classes has been done on verbs which perhaps more easily than other categories lend themselves to being grouped under heads such as MOTION (Come, go, skip, jump) or SURFACE CONTACT (strike, hit, beat, etc.).[2]

We call decompositional those attempts to break down the meaning of individual lexical items into complexes of 'semantic features' or markers. The complex of features characterising the lexical item 'man', for example, would include HUMAN, MALE,

ADULT; to characterise 'bachelor', one would add NEVER MARRIED. This approach was inspired by methods devised by anthropologists, under the label of componential analysis, to describe in an economical and convenient manner the highly elaborate kinship systems existing in some communities. Among linguists it is also referred to as lexical decomposition.

The distinction between classificatory and decompositional approaches to the representation of word meaning in explicit terms is not a clear-cut one. This is particularly the case if the establishment of relations between lexical items is carried out between items already broken down into complexes of features, such that the relation is established on the basis of the occurrence or non-occurrence of particular features in the complex. There is, however, a broad distinction to be made between approaches to the representation of meaning which aim to eliminate some of the finer distinctions which language users are able to make and those which aim to make such distinctions explicit. In the first of these approaches, for example:

John went into town
The man drove into the city

might be given the same semantic representation in which go/drive might be telescoped under the semantic class heading GO or MOVE and similarly town/city might initially be considered to fall into the category PLACE. This reduction of the complexity of meaning distinctions is both useful and generally necessary for computer analyses of natural language. The second approach formed part of the basis of the relatively short-lived linguistic theory, generative semantics. Within this approach the distinction between 'kill' and 'injure' in, for example:

John killed Bill
John injured Bill

would not be blurred, but rather brought out in that 'kill' might be further broken down in CAUSE BECOME DEAD and 'injure' CAUSE BECOME HURT. Furthermore the occurrence of CAUSE and BECOME in both representations enables the extent to which the two items involve similar basic concepts to be made explicit.

Underlying the various approaches to the systematic characterisation of word meaning have been two misleading assumptions:

(i) that words have clearly definable meanings, and that if they have more than one meaning, then each meaning is easily distinguishable from the others.

(ii) if it can be shown to be possible to represent a small selection of simple lexical items in terms of a limited number of semantic features, then a comprehensive set of features covering the entire language could be devised.

Both the clear meaning assumption and the comprehensiveness of features assumption are evident in the Katz and Fodor paper, 'The Structure of a Semantic Theory', the first serious attempt to mark out a domain for semantics within Chomsky's theory. The importance of both assumptions has increased as the lexicon has come to play a more and more dominant role in the recent developments of the theory. Both assumptions, however, while they remain unquestioned, allow linguists to underestimate the problems inherent in integrating a semantic component into a formal model. To see this more clearly, consider each of the assumptions in turn:

(i) Word meaning is clearly definable

If we recall the conditions which are required for a deductively formulated theory to be appropriate, they include the requirement that the phenomenon under investigation must be well understood and sufficiently clearly defined to be expressible in terms of a formal notation. Thus, if word meaning, or rather some limited characterisation of word meaning, is to be included within a deductively formulated model, it too must be assumed to be clearly definable.

This assumption constitutes essentially a 'dictionary view' of word meaning. It is not surprising, then, that Katz and Fodor should have claimed that:

> It is widely acknowledged and certainly true that one component of a semantic theory of a natural language is a dictionary of that language. (Katz and Fodor, 1964:491–2)

They made this claim presumably on the assumption that language users know the meanings of the words of their language, that a dictionary is a list of words and their meanings so that a language user has effectively at his disposal a dictionary. Adding a 'meaning component' to the model being developed by Chomsky to account for native speaker knowledge of syntactic processes thus came to involve the devising of a 'theoretical dictionary', which became known among generative linguists as 'the lexicon'. It was in this lexicon that words were listed[3] – as in an ordinary dictionary – with certain of their phonological, syntactic and semantic features.

Katz and Fodor appear to have assumed without question that speakers use 'dictionary knowledge' in interpreting language. They argue:

> Given an accurate dictionary of English, *which he applies by using his linguistic ability,* the fluent speaker can semantically interpret any sentence . . .under any of its grammatical derivations. (Katz and Fodor, 1964:492)

What is particularly striking is that neither they nor those who have since worked on the lexicon have considered whether it is really plausible to assume an 'accurate dictionary of English'. An 'accurate dictionary' is presumably one in which the words and their meaning are in some ill-defined sense, correct. The assumption that a speaker of a language could have at his disposal a correct list of words and their meanings is, however, to espouse very firmly a view of language whereby words are objects that contain meanings, meanings moreover that may be best studied independently of the knowledge, experience and expectations of language users. We shall discuss this deep-seated and seemingly ineradicable view, a view we call the container view, at some length in Chapter 4. Only under such a view would it be reasonable to assume that language users have as part of their linguistic knowledge an 'accurate dictionary' of their language.

Imputing an 'accurate dictionary' to the linguistic knowledge of native speakers implies that they mean the same thing by the same words. Yet our experience forces us to acknowledge that this is not so. Colour is one of many areas in which individual differences often come to light. Frequently what one person 'calls' green

another may 'call' blue. How could an 'accurate dictionary' help?
A very fallible dictionary[4] defines *blue* and *green as follows:*

> green: of the colour usual in leaves, between blue and yellow
> in the spectrum:
> blue: of the colour of the unclouded sky, or that of wood-
> smoke, skim-milk, lead:

It does, of course, all that it can do, it calls upon the dictionary
user to consult his own experience, giving him only the most
imprecise of guidelines, which would in no way help him to
identify by name colours near the borders of the categories which
are themselves particular to his culture. This he does for himself
and the results are not likely to be identical with those of any other
language user.

Dictionaries are notoriously weak when it comes to areas of
overlap between words relating to the same general area. This is
not surprising, since it is here that individual differences are likely
to be most marked. Consider the pair: sullen, sulky. In one
dictionary, 'sullen' is defined as 'gloomily angry and silent: malignant, baleful', 'sulky' as 'sullen, inclined to sulk', 'sulk' as 'to be
sullen', i.e. gloomily angry and silent: malignant, baleful. In other
words, a real dictionary (as opposed to a theoretical lexicon) tells
us that both words may mean the same, whereas at least some
speakers of English make some, difficult to define, distinction
between them. If we add 'moody' to this set, we find it defined as
'indulging in moods, sullen', 'moods' being 'state of gloom or
sullenness'. Thus on the basis of a dictionary, 'moody' may also
mean the same as 'sulky' and 'sullen'. An informal survey among a
group of native speakers indicated that speakers quite firmly
distinguish between 'moody' and 'sulky' and, further, that they
disagree as to the meaning they associate with 'moody' rather
more than they disagree on 'sulky'. A dictionary, like language
itself, is an extremely rough and ready instrument which relies, to
be useful at all, on language users already having considerable
experience of their language and their environment. It is not clear
that Katz and Fodor, or those who subsequently worked on 'the
lexicon', took the necessarily imprecise nature aspect of 'dictionary knowledge' into account. If they had, on the other hand, this
would have meant recognising that word meaning did not satisfy

the conditions necessary for it to be integrated into a deductively formulated theoretical model.

Katz and Fodor's 'dictionary view' of meaning as clearly definable is further reflected in their account of an entry in the 'theoretical dictionary':

> . . . a dictionary entry is a characterisation of *every* sense a lexical item can bear in any sentence.[5] (Katz and Fodor, 1964:493)

in other words, they held the view that dictionary entries are exhaustive. This seems to be a reflection of a still widely-held view that dictionary writers are omniscient. Such an approach assumes that meaning is an essentially uniform phenomenon, that one lexical item may indeed have more meanings than another, but that this difference would be reflected simply in that one item would have a longer dictionary entry. As an illustration, one might compare their own, well-worn example, 'bachelor', which may have amongst other meanings:

(i)   man who has never married
(ii) young knight serving under the standard of another knight
(iii) one who has the first or lowest academic degree
(iv) young fur seal when without a mate during the breeding time

with an item such as 'heron', which would normally have only a single entry: 'The name of a large natural group of long-necked, long-legged wading birds, belonging to the genus Ardea or family, Ardeidae; esp. the common or Grey Heron of Europe, A.cinerea.'[6] Thus, on a 'dictionary view' of native speaker knowledge, a speaker of English would have at his disposal those lexical items with in one case a number of distinct meanings, and in the other a single meaning.

Suppose, however, we consider other lexical items such as 'do' or 'have'. The difficulty that arises is that while 'do' or 'have' may occur in a variety of different combinations whose meanings are widely divergent, it is not at all obvious that 'do' or 'have' in themselves should be thought of as having a large number of distinct meanings. While 'do' occurs regularly in some combinations:

Max did the dishes/the bed/the job/his hair

and less regularly in others:

Max did the elephant (clipped its tail)/
the frog (exam question on frogs)

It is arguably the case that it *could* occur with almost any noun, since one could 'do' anything where 'do' indicates no more than 'act appropriately in relation to'. What is appropriate depends on the characteristics of the object of the doing, the particular context of utterance and the experience and expectations of the language users. It is thus difficult to see how a dictionary entry could be devised for an item such as 'do' which could be said to characterise *every* sense it may bear.

Composers of real – as opposed to theoretical – dictionaries nevertheless try to list the meanings of items as 'do' just as they list the meanings of 'bachelor': 'do' can mean, for example, 'perform, effect, execute; complete; produce, make; operate on, deal with; cook; (colloq.), provide (food etc.) for; tour, visit as a tourist; swindle'.[7] Generative linguists interested in 'the lexicon', on the other hand, have tended to avoid difficult lexical items such as these by selecting ones which did appear to be reducible to a fixed set of meanings.

The problems raised by lexical items such as 'do' are compounded if we consider another of Katz and Fodor's claims:

The basic fact that a semantic theory must explain is that a fluent speaker can determine the meaning of a sentence in terms of the meanings of its constituent lexical items. (Katz and Fodor, 1964:493)

On this view, understanding a sentence such as:

Max did the dishes

would involve combining knowledge of the meaning 'Max' and 'do' and 'the' and 'dishes'.

An additional difficulty would be arriving at the 'correct' meaning of 'do' and to a lesser extent 'dishes', in this combination. If we consult the above dictionary entry for 'do' we might select 'operate on' or 'deal with' as appropriate for this case. We might then be said to understand from 'Max did the dishes' used in an ordinary domestic context that a specific individual 'dealt with' or 'operated on' a set of objects used in the preparing of food. On this view 'Max did the dishes' would have to be seen as giving only a very imprecise idea of what Max actually did. And yet, since language users have experience of familiar everyday activities, they know not only what 'dishes' are but what one might reasonably be expected to 'do' with them; consequently, they would in fact be likely to understand in fairly precise terms the actual series of operations which Max carried out on the dishes. But they would know this not because they are able to access a 'mental lexicon' wherein they store a long list of possible meanings of 'do' but because of the complex interaction of the various units with one another and with the knowledge and experience of the interlocutors. This is borne out if one considers that in a different context, say an exhibition of pottery, the utterance 'Max did the dishes' would be likely to have distinct, yet equally precise, interpretation.

It seems unlikely furthermore that the processing of all the items of an utterance is of the same type. It may well be, for example, that items such as 'dishes' or 'heron' do enable us to pick out particular types of entity from the set of possible entities; it may be that we do store some kind of representation of characteristics of 'dishes' or 'herons'. It is difficult to see how the same would be true of items such as 'do' or 'have' which, it would seem, interact with other types of item to enable us to access areas of experience appropriate to the interpretation of the utterance as a whole. A dictionary approach by adopting the same strategy for representing the senses of every word blurs an important distinction. It would thus fail to take into account the interaction taking place between items of different types. We shall return to this in Chapter 5. The error which Katz and Fodor and those who have subsequently worked on the lexicon made in basing a component of their semantic theory on a traditional dictionary was in failing to recognise that a dictionary, far from being authoritative, is little more than the best one can do with as unwieldy a phenomenon as word meaning. A dictionary is not a store of word meanings but rather a list of words with guides as to the area of experience to which they may refer, enabling users to confirm or not their already-existing impressions as to the way in which particular words are generally used in their culture. It is rare that we actually learn the meaning of a word from a dictionary. Looked at in this way, it seems odd to use as part of a theoretical description of the 'meaning component' of a speaker's linguistic knowledge what is little more than a makeshift tool. Katz and Fodor were, of course, obliged to assume that one can impose, as the dictionary writer does, clarity and precision on word meaning in order to integrate aspects of word meaning into the existing deductively formulated model. Such an idealisation has, however, been a distorting one.

(ii) Semantic markers can be comprehensive

No less widespread than the first assumption, that words have clearly definable meanings, is the second assumption we noted earlier, namely that since some small selection of lexical items appear to be representable in terms of limited sets of features, then it follows that a comprehensive set of features covering the entire language could be devised. This assumption has meant that the very real difficulties inherent in devising semantic categories appropriate for a reasonably broad sample of language have been overlooked. In fairness to the approach originally developed by Katz and Fodor, it is important to note that they did not see semantic markers or features as entirely representing meaning. They considered that:

> ... the primary motivation for representing lexical information
> by semantic markers will be to permit a theory to express those
> semantic relations which determine selection and thereby to arrive
> at the correct set of readings for each sentence. (Katz and Fodor,
> 1964:498)

In other words, markers were to provide information on the salient semantic characteristics of lexical items with a wide range of use, information which would then be available to the formal system for selecting the appropriate meaning in any given case.[8] As a simple illustration, consider once again their own example: bachelor. In their representation, two senses of 'bachelor'

   (i)   man who has never married
   (ii) young knight serving under the standard of another knight

share the markers MALE and HUMAN. If a further marker

YOUNG is added to the representation of (ii), then the presence of this marker would rule out the selection of (ii) as the meaning of 'bachelor' in:

The old bachelor finally died,

enabling the semantic rules to select the correct sense of bachelor and thus the 'correct reading' of the sentence.

Katz and Fodor's work is interesting in that they glimpse an important problem yet fail to bring out the extent of its significance. What they glimpsed is the essential variability of word meaning. Because they separated language off from language users, however, they convert the complex problem of variability into a much simpler problem of words having a number of distinguishable senses. This enabled them to view language users as simply having to select among the various senses of multiply ambiguous words. In taking this view however, they failed to take into account the flexibility of language which is constantly being adapted to novel experience.[9] In their approach this fundamental characteristic is assumed to be covered by the assumption that words have a number of distinct, specifiable senses. As the 'do' example shows however, such an assumption does not reflect the way in which individual items interact with one another and with the knowledge and expectations of language users. This is particularly significant in that Katz and Fodor, like Chomsky, took a realist view of the status of their theory, proposing that the inclusion of semantic markers within the formal model permitted 'a reconstruction of the operation of the mechanism of selection' carried out by speakers in interpreting sentences containing multiply ambiguous items. They evidently believed that markers could be added into their model of language until the time came when:

> . . . increasing the complexity of a semantic theory by adding
> new markers no longer yields enough of an advantage in precision
> or scope to warrant the increase. (Katz and Fodor, 1964:500)

In other words, there would come a time when the entire vocabulary of a language was represented in terms which included sufficient markers to distinguish all the different senses of all multiply ambiguous items. This they envisaged on the basis of a very small number of examples covering no more than a dozen lexical items. In retrospect, they may be said to have shown extraordinary optimism.

There is furthermore another difficulty with adopting this view arising from the fact that variability of meaning is not confined to a small selection of lexical items, but is characteristic, to varying degrees of most words. Thus, if understanding did involve selection on the basis of semantic features of some sort, and if say four out of the six words in a sentence had several meanings, then the processing mechanisms would have to go through a vast range of possible combinations to arrive at the correct reading of the sentence. In some cases, the result could well be a combinatorial explosion. In Chapter 5 we shall argue that this nest of problems arises from treating language not as epiphenomenal on the experience of users, but as an autonomous object of study.

To see more clearly the problems which arise with the assumption that semantic markers can be comprehensive, consider a further example, that of 'cut', and some of the various combinations in which it may occur. It is difficult to see how markers could explain how it is that 'cut' may occur in numerous different combinations, apparently making a different contribution in each case to the interpretation to the whole this interpretation depending both on the other items in the combination and on the knowledge and expectations of the language users involved in the exchange. Since the sense of 'cut' differs in the following examples:

Max cut his finger/his nails/the flowers/the cake/the sandwiches

and since the 'mechanism of selection' requires, on the Katz and Fodor view, the psychological equivalent of markers attached to the nouns to enable the appropriate sense to be selected in each case, then to devise a set of such markers one has to ask what it is about 'finger' which makes 'cut + finger' mean what it does (make incision causing pain and bleeding) and what it is about 'nails' which makes 'cut + nails' mean something quite different (shorten length of, using appropriate implement), what it is about 'flowers' which makes 'cut + flowers' mean something yet different again (remove from growing place) and what it is about 'sandwiches' which makes 'cut + sandwiches' different from 'cut + cake' in that it is able to refer to a complex operation involving not only producing sandwiches but also gathering together the necessary ingredients beforehand. In each case the marker would have to encapsulate the difficult to define 'what it is' which makes these activities different. 'Cut' is just one lexical item: Katz and Fodor envisaged the entire vocabulary being treated in this way. Like many linguists in recent years, they extrapolated wildly from an extremely meagre and unrepresentative amount of data.

The work of Katz and Fodor and those who have subsequently worked on the lexicon illustrates some of the problems of approaching aspects of meaning within the formal framework that had seemed appropriate for syntax. There were, however, more directly destructive effects of the expansion of generative linguistics into considerations of semantic questions, effects that bore on the formal rigour of the syntactic model itself.

A striking example of the disintegration of the formal character of Chomsky's own work occurs in 'Deep Structure, Surface Structure and Semantic Interpretation', one of the milestone papers marking the introduction into his by then widely accepted theory of the hypothesis that surface structure as well as deep structure contributed information relevant to semantic interpretation. The background to the discussion in the paper is that in the purely syntactic model various syntactic constructions had been freely generated by transformational rules from underlying deep structures. Thus from the structure underlying declarative sentences such as 'John wrote poetry in the garden', transformational rules would freely generate related constructions such as those underlying:

> it was John who read poetry in the garden
> it was poetry John read in the garden
> it was in the garden John read poetry

Once, however, an attempt was made to incorporate within the syntactic model the observation that these three sentences, while they may be syntactically related, are nevertheless distinct in terms of what they presuppose and what, in each case, is in focus, the question arises as to which level of syntactic description such semantic observations should be related. For various reasons that are largely technical, Chomsky decided that the relevant syntactic level was that of surface structure.[10] The result was that at this stage of the elaboration of the theory, both deep and surface structure were deemed to be semantically relevant. Clearly the extension of the model now required a new rule system able to combine from each level of syntactic representation the information relevant to semantic interpretation. Yet nowhere in the paper did Chomsky give any formal account of the nature of such a rule system.

The lack of rigour in this paper is all the more remarkable because of the expectations Chomsky's earliest work had aroused. On closer examination, on the other hand, the lack of precise and explicit procedures only became more obvious when semantic considerations were introduced into the syntactic model. Opponents of Chomsky's theory might have earlier picked on certain elements of the syntactic model itself as being glaringly vague. For example, while the formal properties of the rewriting systems that provided the early phrase structure grammars were very carefully constrained, no such comparable attention was paid to the formal nature of transformational rules. It was the function, very generally, of transformational rules to convert one structure into another of a different form. Since some transformational rules operated on the output of other transformational rules, it was clearly essential that the output of any one transformational rule should be precisely specified. Without this it is difficult to see how to write the description of any transformational rule that applied to a transformationally derived structure. In short, a rigorous syntactic theory of Chomsky's sort required an algorithm not only for phrase structure rules but also for the derived constituent structure of transformational rules. Chomsky however never provided an algorithm for derived constituent structure. To that extent, even before the problems of adequately formalising semantic notions such as focus and presupposition ever arose, the syntactic theory itself was already insufficiently explicit and lacking in rigour.[11]

More generally, the result of attempts to incorporate ill-defined semantic notions into a formally insecure syntactic model was that linguists working within this framework had the worst of both worlds. They had neither the advantage of working with a highly rigorous theory on an admittedly limited domain, syntactic structure, nor the freedom to explore semantic questions untrammelled by syntactic preoccupations imposed by commitment to a deductively formulated style of explanation. Furthermore, since the theory itself has less and less the rigour required of a formal system, it is no longer reasonable to claim that it is an adequate explanatory theory of a deductively formulated type.

What has been lost in this theoretically unhappy state is productive research into problems of language understanding and language production. Despite the apparent broadening of the domain, linguistics has come no nearer to converging on its proper subject matter. Instead of the move to semantics opening up research on language problems, it had led to theoretical linguistics becoming a more and more fragmented field.

It is our view that the time is more than ripe for a return to what Northrop called the analysis of the problem stage. If it can be agreed that meaning is central to linguistic analysis, then however vague and obscure it is, an attempt must be made to dispel that vagueness and lighten that obscurity. In the second part of the book we take some tentative steps in that direction. We do so starting from two firm presuppositions. First, linguistics is not at a stage where deductively formulated theory is an appropriate mode of explanation. Second, it is counter-productive to assume that language or linguistic knowledge is best viewed as a self-contained entity divorced from the other knowledge, beliefs, expectations and experience of language users. We begin with the conviction that language is an epiphenomenon and, in analysing problems of language in operation, we make central the individual language user's perception of the world.

Notes

1. The first proposal for a semantic component intended to be integrated with Chomsky's theory of syntactic structure was Katz and Fodor's 'The Structure of a Semantic Theory' (1963). Chomsky broadly accepted Katz and Fodor's work, incorporating it into the model outlined in *Aspects of the Theory of Syntax* (1965). This model, which became known as the Standard Theory, included for the first time syntactic, semantic and phonological components. The syntactic component remained the base component, generating through the filtering operations of the transformational rules well-formed surface and deep structures. The semantic and the phonological components were both viewed as purely interpretative. The semantic component was said to use information available at the derivatively defined deep structure to assign semantic interpretations. Put at its simplest, its role was to assign meanings, known as readings, to the structures generated by

the syntactic base component. The phonological component was said to assign phonetic interpretations to well-formed surface structures.

2. Some of those working on the computer analysis of natural language have made use of such groupings in order to devise sets of primitives in terms of which an initial computer semantic analysis of a sentence might be made.

3. As is well known, the lexicon has never been extensively implemented. There is certainly no accepted list of lexical entries being systematically extended. Linguists have simply tended to assume that the lexicon was potentially realisable. Such detailed work as there is, is to be found scattered throughout the linguistic literature.

4. Chambers Twentieth Century Dictionary.

5. We shall return to the serious limitations of this view in Chapter 5, where we discuss the claim that a grammar providing a full account of linguistic knowledge 'will simply have to list in the lexicon for each word of the language the sum total of its syntactic, semantic and phonological properties' (Smith and Wilson, 1979:53).

6. The Shorter Oxford English Dictionary.

7. Oxford Illustrated Dictionary.

8. On the limitations of markers for representing aspects of meaning, see Karen Sparck Jones's paper, 'Semantic Markers'; also Dwight Bolinger, 'The Atomization of Meaning'.

9. The flexibility is a corollary of the necessary indeterminacy of word meaning. It is because word meanings are, to different degrees, indeterminate that words may be applied to new experiences or fresh versions of familiar experiences. By entirely idealising away from the necessary indeterminacy of word meaning in favour of a lexicon of fixed meanings, Katz and Fodor were obliged to set aside the problem of creativity in its full sense.

10. Technically, it was in fact a phonologically interpreted surface structure that was held to be semantically relevant.

11. The significance of this formal insufficiency was increased when transformations, besides relating one construction to another, were further required to act as filtering devices to remove ill-formed phrase markers. It was in this function that they came to be essential for identifying 'deep structures'. Despite popular accounts deep structure was not directly

defined by the basic phrase structure rules. Its definition depended derivatively on the notion 'well-formed surface structure'. This is a somewhat technical point, but what it is important to note is that transformations remained the key to defining surface structure and thus indirectly deep structure so that while they remained inexplicit, the levels of both deep and surface structure were necessarily only vaguely defined. This of course has serious drawbacks for any version of formal semantic theory that needs to refer to either level of representation. The fact that in recent years the role of deep structure in semantic interpretation has been taken over apparently by a suitably modified version of surface structure has not overcome this problem of insufficient rigour, only shifted it from the deep to the surface level of representation.

Part II

Towards a Post-Chomskyan Linguistics

We are in the position where discovering exactly what we need to explain is itself a major problem.

Part II

Towards a Post-Chomskyan
Linguistics

4 Prerequisites for Understanding Language

> . . . the mind of the hearer is just as active in transforming and creating as the mind of the speaker.
>
> Wilhelm Wundt

Understanding language processes: the general framework

On a mundane level, language understanding is something we tend to take for granted. When we go into a shop, or stop at a garage, it rarely occurs to us to wonder whether the shop or garage assistant will understand us when we ask for a packet of cigarettes or four gallons of petrol. The fact that we receive the cigarettes or the petrol is confirmation that our requests have been understood. Not many instances of language use are as straightforward as this however. What is significant in the shop or garage case is that here language is used as part of a familiar transaction in which the range of likely exchanges is fairly limited. Language plays an ancillary role. Indeed, the widespread existence of supermarkets and self-service garages shows that language need play no part at all in these transactions. When it does play some part, then the degree of precision of understanding is likely to be high since the exchanges are heavily backed by seeing what is being talked about and by familiarity with the kind of situation involved. Another way of putting it is that the participants in the exchange share a supportive framework of knowledge and experience and it is this which enables their language to operate successfully.

Consider, however, another kind of everyday occurrence, one in which a stranger to your home town asks for directions to the town hall or art gallery, or to a street you know well. Suppose that the way involves, among other things, crossing a piece of waste ground, going along a narrow lane beside a church-yard and eventually cutting through a shopping arcade. You are confronted with the task of translating into language a fairly convoluted route

145

in such a way as to distinguish it from all other routes. Suppose that you manage to do this, the stranger now has the task of matching your words with what he sees around him, of picking out from all the possible turns the particular ones that you have attempted to characterise using language. He has been told to look out for a piece of waste ground on his right and he comes to an open space with a few tree trunks and pieces of what looks to him like scrap metal. Now you know, because you know the town, that this is an adventure playground, so that if you had meant him to cross the adventure playground, then you would have used that term and not waste ground. What you were calling waste ground is in fact a few hundred yards further on. He, on the other hand understands waste ground to be something very like this adventure playground, particularly since, coming from a rural area, he has no experience of such things. So either he makes an error and crosses the adventure playground or remains in doubt until he reaches the waste ground you actually meant. He has been told he will be turning left along a narrow lane beside a church-yard. He sees, on his left, a Methodist chapel with a smallish area of land around it. There is a narrow street going alongside of the land next to the chapel. To the stranger, this tiny street may count as a narrow lane. What he does not know – and you are no longer there to advise him – is whether for you a chapel is the same thing as a church, and whether the street he sees is really small enough to count as a lane. What he does not know, in addition, is that round the next bend is a large Catholic church with an alley running alongside the church-yard. If the stranger survives all this and reaches the centre of the town, he will then have to decide which part of the traffic-free shopping precinct you were referring to by the term 'shopping arcade'. He may be particularly puzzled by a part which is covered, with shops on either side, for only about thirty yards before opening into a square with a fountain. Does thirty yards count as an arcade or were you referring to something else?

We have gone through this example in some detail because it appears, in contrast to the shop or garage situation, to be a case in which language is of central rather than ancillary importance. In the absence of a map, or of a guide, the stranger asks a random individual – whose background may be very different from his own – to translate part of his experience of the physical world into words. The degree to which the interlocutors share a common supportive framework is more limited in this type of exchange. As a result, in spite of their sharing a common language, there were a number of areas in which confusion may have arisen. We take a first step in understanding language use to be a grasp of the notion of language as dependent upon a supportive framework of knowledge and experience. The degree to which on any occasion language works is closely related to the degree to which the supportive frameworks of each interlocutor overlap.

This may be further illustrated by the following experiment. A short text was recorded and then played back to two groups of high school student volunteer subjects, who were asked to rate the passage for comprehensibility, and then to recall as much of it as they could in writing. Additionally, one group was allowed 30 seconds before hearing the passage to study an appropriate context picture; the other group was not given a picture but heard the passage twice whereas the group that also saw the picture heard the passage only once. The passage was the following:

> If the balloons popped, the sound wouldn't be able to carry since everything would be too far away from the correct floor. A closed window would also prevent the sound from carrying, since most buildings tend to be well-insulated. Since the whole operation depends on a steady flow of electricity, a break in the middle of the wire would also cause problems. Of course, the fellow could shout, but the human voice is not loud enough to carry that far. An additional problem is that a string could break on the instrument. Then there could be no accompaniment to the message. It is clear that the best situation would involve less distance. Then there would be fewer potential problems. With face to face contact, the least number of things could go wrong. (Bransford & Johnson, 1972:719)

Note that the passage contains no erudite, obscure or unusually technical vocabulary, nor is the syntax especially involved. Thus the subjects being asked to rate a passage for comprehensibility were faced with a test that in terms of vocabulary and structure should have been quite straightforward. Using a seven point numerical scale, the mean rating of the group that had not seen the picture was 2.3 after the first hearing, indicating 'difficult to comprehend'. This went up to 3.6 after the second hearing, indicating 'more than moderately difficult to comprehend'. The mean rating for the group that saw the picture, on the other hand, was

6.1, 'easy to comprehend', after hearing the text only once. The no-picture group can be thought of as being in a situation in which language is virtually unsupported. This is the case both because in an experimental situation the cues and clues present in ordinary instances of language use are missing, and because no contextual information in any other form is provided. In this extreme situation we should expect the degree of understanding to be low and this is borne out by the ratings. These ratings are further supported by the results of the recall test which followed. Of the fourteen ideas which Bransford and Johnson identified in the passage, the no-picture group recalled an average of only 3.6; this rose to 3.8 after the second reading. The picture-group, on the other hand, had a mean score of 8 after only one reading. This is what one would expect on the basis of their subjective comprehensibility rating and on the fact that they were placed in a situation in which language was backed by 'support'. This 'support' is incidentally difficult to characterise because of the artificiality of the experimental situation. It is not, in spite of being a picture, straightforwardly simple visual support. It is rather that seeing the picture gave the picture-group information which provided the grounds for constructing a supportive framework that enabled them to understand the passage.

As a final example, consider the following extract from a newspaper report:

> At the 7th and 8th his ball lay behind old holes which the referee could not smooth satisfactorily, and so they were declared ground under repair and Nicklaus was given relief. (*Observer*, 16.7.78)

It is highly likely that this extract would be given a very low comprehensibility rating by someone who was familiar with all the words used but who had had no contact whatsoever with golf. There would furthermore be a considerable difference between the degree of understanding by a golfer and by someone whose knowledge of golf was confined to having driven on a number of occasions past a golf course. The difference would have nothing to do with the linguistic skills of the understanders but would be related to the extent to which they are able to bring to bear appropriate support to their interpretation of the text. The golfer, because he has experience of the game, is familiar with the kinds of activities associated with expressions such as: smooth old holes,

declare ground under repair, and give relief. Understanding for
him would involve using language to access areas of knowledge
about golf which, in some generalised form, he has 'stored'. The
non-golfer on the other hand would have to work much harder for
less return. If he reads the extract quickly, he is likely to understand very little, since he is not familiar with the activities associated with the words and would thus be unable to access relevant
knowledge or experience. If he goes back and reads more slowly,
he could attempt to use his limited knowledge of the game to
formulate hypotheses about activities that 'smooth old holes' and
'declare ground under repair' and so on, may refer to. But they
would remain hypotheses; his understanding of 'give relief' for
example, could not, on the basis of the words alone, be more than
very imprecise. So, whereas he could certainly use language to
attempt to supplement an inadequate supportive framework, this
is still not going to enable him to understand with the same degree
of precision as the golfer whose supportive framework for this area
of experience is detailed and comprehensive.

These observations backed by examples about the extent to
which language use is intimately bound up with the knowledge
and experience of language users are, we believe, reasonable ones,
neither particularly new or especially revolutionary. What we do
find striking however is the extent to which the symbiotic relationship between the workings of language and the supportive
frameworks of language users has been largely ignored by those
who see themselves as developing explanatory linguistic theories.
This appears to have occurred as a result of the idealisation we
have argued is widespread in linguistics, the idealisation that
abstracts language from its users and views it as an object that
may be characterised as a self-contained entity. One of the consequences of this idealisation is that linguists have been led to
concentrate a disproportionate amount of energy on form and
structure at the expense of the still largely unresolved question of
how language actually works. Linguists have not by and large
attempted to characterise language in such a way as to explain
how it is that strings of sounds emitted by one individual are, or
appear to be, understood by another.

The idealisation which views language as a self-contained
entity has appeared plausible even when extended to meaning
because of a fundamental assumption that nearly all of us appear
to make, namely that in some way the words and sentences that we

use 'contain' meanings, and that in using words and sentences we are able to 'convey' these meanings to other individuals. It is customary and in many ways convenient – perhaps it would not have become customary were it not so convenient – to speak of words and sentences as 'having' or bearing meaning and of sentences as transmitting, imparting or conveying meaning. Indeed, metaphors of containment and transport are ubiquitous in formal as well as informal discussions of meaning. At times we appear to recognise that these expressions of containment and transport are metaphors, or even, only metaphors. Yet such is the power of metaphor that theories of meaning of various sorts have been devised on the assumption that the metaphors are descriptions of what is the case. There is for example a long tradition going back at least to Plato of believing that words contain meaning. This container view is clearly reflected in the ways we ordinarily discuss word meanings. If we come across some new word, say, *opsimath,* and ask the apparently natural question, what does *opsimath* mean?, the response is likely to be either to give examples of what the word refers to or picks out in the world, or to give some set of properties or attributes that we believe are criterial for defining the class of objects that would satisfy or meet the requirements of being an *opsimath.* Yet this apparently natural response rests on a number of assumptions that we need to draw out in order to assess whether the container approach to the study of word meaning is likely to be revealing.

Theories of meaning: some reflections on the container view

The container view of meaning, a view that underlies both formal and informal theories of word meaning, presupposes that meaning can be studied independently of language users. On the container view, people do not mean something by words, rather words themselves have meanings. From this starting point, a three-term relation appears to have been assumed. It is supposed that there are:

(i)   words.
(ii) the various classes of objects, events, situations, etc. in the world which the words refer to or pick out.
(iii) the meanings of words.

On this view, characterising word meaning may be thought of as characterising a relation believed to exist between language and the 'world'. It is further implied that the world to which language may be related can be assumed to be independent of language users' perception of it. The difficulty with such a view is that it ignores the crucial *active* role of language users in relating the words they process or produce each to their own experience of the world. Denoting, as Polanyi once remarked, is an art, and the individual using words in combination is engaged in a necessarily inexact, personal, highly subjective activity. The container view that words 'have' meanings, however, assumes – misleadingly – that speakers and hearers are no more than passive users of a system which may be revealingly characterised independently of them. It sees language as an object or entity rather than a means whereby one language user is able to cause complex processing mechanisms to come into play within another language user. An alternative view, which we call 'epiphenomenalist', will be developed later in the chapter.

Arising from the three-term relation is the assumption that the meanings of words may be specified – as in a dictionary – objectively and definitively. Furthermore, once the three-term relation of the container view is assumed and thus unquestioned, then in the minds of thinking people certain kinds of question almost inevitably arise and, just as importantly, others almost as inevitably do not. As in all types of enquiry, the absolute presupposition – and the three-term relation has something of the nature of an absolute presupposition – has had a determining affect on the type of enquiry undertaken.[1]

One obvious question is whether all the words and expressions of a language do in fact fall readily within the idealisation assumed by the three-term relation. Clearly some words and expressions cannot easily be thought of as containing their meaning without reference to speakers and hearers and, in a broad sense of context, the context of utterance. Typical cases of these have been held to be words such as *here, now, today*, and personal pronouns such as *I, you, she, we* and *they*. Such terms have been labelled indexical or deictic terms.

There have been many philosophers and linguists concerned with meaning who at least as an initial idealisation have wanted to exclude the problems they see aroused by indexical or deictic terms from an account of meaning.[2] Idealising away from these expressions allowed aspects of meaning which more obviously do depend on the knowledge, beliefs, circumstances and expectations of language users to be excluded from the domain of semantic theory. The move to viewing indexical or deictic expressions as a special sub-class of words and expressions that would need to be treated differently was itself however a consequence of adopting a container view. Once the container view is abandoned the now traditional distinction between deictic and non-deictic expressions may prove to be of little significance.

Once expressions that did not fit obviously within the three-term relation were excluded, then a number of other questions arose. Foremost among these was the question of the third term – the meaning of the word – and its relation with the other two terms. About this question there has been an unbroken history of controversy leading up to the present day. A history of semantics might be written setting out the various views that have been adopted towards this question.

Perhaps the simplest of these views has been that the meaning of a word can be understood as being the relation between that word and the object or objects in the world which the word picks out or to which it refers. On this view, the relationship between word and object has been called the relationship of reference. There is a long tradition in semantics of equating the problem of word meaning with the problem of reference. Thus in the most transparent case a proper name like *Max* or *Cambridge* refers to a particular individual or entity. Just as proper names may refer to individuals, common nouns to classes of objects, verbs may be said to refer to classes of action, adjectives to properties of individuals and adverbs to properties of actions.

This view of the reference relation is sometimes known as extensionalism. It treats word meaning in terms of the objects, called extensions, or members of an extension set, to which the words of the language are said to refer. A number of problems have arisen with this approach to word meaning in terms of extensions. A piece of data that is believed to provide a refutation of the simple extensionalist approach was given as long ago as the end of the last century by Frege. Consider the problem: if examples of expressions can be found that have the same extension set, that is, appear to refer to the same set of objects, but those expressions are not understood in the same way, then an account of word meaning in terms of extension must be inadequate. Frege took the two expressions, 'the morning star' and 'the evening star', both of which refer to the same object, the planet Venus, and showed that they did not have the same meaning. If they did, the sentences:

the morning star is the evening star

would be understood in the same way as

the morning star is the morning star.

Yet the first sentence is informative, the second uninformative. Identity of reference he thus showed is not a sufficient condition for identity of meaning.

Examples of this sort have led philosophers and linguists to distinguish, but not always uniformly, between sense and reference, between the meaning of a word and its referents, or in earlier times between the connotation of a word and its denotation, or more recently between the intension of a term and its extension. The point that the distinction in its various forms makes is that between a word or a term and its extension set or its denotation range there must be something the grasp of which enables us to know what does or does not fall within the extension or denotation of the term. This something is the set of conditions for applying the term successfully. It is known in one of the oppositions as the intension of the term, in another as its connotation, in another its meaning. To take just one of the pairs, the intension of a term, put more simply than would probably be allowed in the philosophical literature, is the set of criterial properties which determine the applicability of the word. Thus the Fregean distinction between the sense of an expression and its referents could be restated as a distinction between the intension of a term and its extension. To know the meaning of a word, in this view, is to know its intension.

The prevalence of the three-term relation of the container view has meant that philosophers and linguists interested in word meaning have focused a great deal of attention on the relation between intension and extension – which in many respects brings us back to the relation we mentioned earlier between words and the 'world'. These efforts have concealed an absolute presupposition, namely that between a word and some object or class of objects to which it may be said to refer, there is a one-to-one relation which may be uniquely specified. Some words may refer to a number of distinct objects or classes of object; in these cases a number of distinct, separately specifiable relations may be established. We shall be challenging this view of word meaning by looking more closely at other types of 'linguistic unit' – items such as 'in', 'cut', 'round', 'have', 'do' – where no clear cut relation with 'the world' may be established. These items we call 'variable units'. The significance of data of this sort is not so much that container theories cannot account for it, but more broadly that it gives us grounds for calling into question attempts to establish a one-to-one relation between language and the 'world'. In its place we focus attention on a different relation: that holding between language and the world as perceived by individual language users, this being reflected in the 'knowledge stores' or 'data bases' they call upon in producing and understanding language. We give some substance to this approach in the remainder of the book.

The view we are calling the container view, the view that language somehow contains its meaning and speaks for itself, is reflected not only in theories of word meaning but also in theories of sentence meaning. As with the assumptions underlying container approaches to word meaning, it is possible that some at least of the problems that have long preoccupied philosophers and, more recently, linguists interested in the nature of sentence meaning are unresolved not because they are especially abstruse, but because the fundamental assumptions about language which cause them to arise are misguided.

Approaches to theories of sentence meaning assuming a container view appear, like those of word meaning, to presuppose a three-term relation. There are:

(i)   sentences.
(ii)   the objects, events or situations about which sentences are asserted or denied.
(iii) the meaning of sentences.

On this assumption the problem become that of characterising the meaning of sentences – the third term in the three-term relation – in terms of the relation between the other two, between sentences and the objects, events, situations etc. in the world or 'reality'.[3]

Some philosophers working within the assumptions of the container view have attempted to characterise meaning by invoking the notion of truth. At its simplest this has amounted to a claim that the meaning of a sentence may be expressed in terms of the conditions that would need to hold for that sentence to be true. A true sentence is characterised as one whose statement about the world corresponds to the way the world, or some possible world, is.

Anyone entirely unfamiliar with the conventions of formal logic would be likely to find this approach to the characterisation of meaning somewhat strange. To understand why philosophers interested in the nature of meaning should turn to truth, one needs to appreciate that it enabled them to draw from work in formal logic – work that had the substantial weight of a long tradition behind it – notions such as truth value and truth condition. It has seemed to some philosophers and recently to some linguists that these notions could be usefully incorporated into the study of the meanings of sentences of natural language. One reason why this appeared to represent a step forward is that in logics terms such as truth value and truth condition are formally defined. It was believed that if these same terms could be made to apply to natural language, then the result would be a formal and rigorous account of natural language meaning.

However plausible this approach may seem, there are, for the student of natural language, a number of severe drawbacks. We shall not try to assess the arguments for and against various proposals that have been made to overcome these drawbacks since we believe the enterprise itself is fundamentally misconceived. The grounds for this belief are only partly that in order to apply logics to the semantics of natural language, some of the essential properties of meaning have to be either omitted or distorted.[4] It is as important that the kind of semantic analysis provided by formal semantics is only indirectly related to ordinary language. The relation is indirect because the procedures of formal semantics may be applied only after ordinary language has been converted or translated into the kind of representation required by the formal logic. That however presupposes that suitable translation procedures exist. The drawback here is that there has never been any rigorous procedure for effecting such a conversion for an interesting range of natural language utterances.[5] Jardine has made a similar point:

It is increasingly fashionable for linguists to claim that substantial fragments of natural languages may be captured by formal languages . . . As a minimum adequacy criterion for such capture we may require that effective translation rules be specified which take into account contextual information to transform sentences of NL (natural language) into well-formed formulae of the formal language, and do so in such a way that the entailments which hold amongst NL sentences are preserved by the consequence operation defined on the formal language . . . by this minimal criterion of adequacy no substantial fragment of NL has yet been captured. (Jardine, 1975:493)

It should have been clear to linguists that if they were genuinely interested in the semantics of natural languages, then the absence of conversion procedures made approaches using formal logics highly suspect.

Unfortunately the prestige of formalisms coupled with the 'container' assumption that language may be treated as an object of study independent of language users appear to have prevented linguists from realising that propositional and predicate logics are not suitable tools for investigating the semantics of natural language sentences.[6]

In propositional logic, for example, sentences are treated as unanalysed wholes, entities without a syntax. On a very simple level a sentence such as:

Max has a dog

may be represented by the symbol s, the proposition it expresses as p. If we assume a world in which Max has a dog and if p is tested against that world then s is a true sentence. If the meaning of a sentence is said to be the conditions that need to hold for it to be true, and if, furthermore, s is true if and only if p corresponds to reality, it can then be said, on some approaches to meaning, that:

s means p

i.e. a sentence 'means' the proposition underlying it. If we follow a similar procedure with another sentence, r:

Alice has a cat

and assume that in this same world Alice does have a cat, then p does not correspond to the way the world is and therefore r is false. If the two sentences are conjoined:

Max has a dog and Alice has a cat

or:

s and r

the first being true, the second false, then the truth tables or rules for assigning truth values that hold for conjunction of atomic true and false sentences decree that the whole conjunction is false. The rules would give the same result if both conjuncts were false.[7]

Philosophers interested in tackling the study of meaning from this point of view have not been primarily concerned with devising ways of converting different types of sentence of a natural language into formal language formulae, nor have they seriously considered how one should test the atomic sentences against the world.[8] Both these procedures were simply assumed to be possible. Their interest has been rather with the manipulation of formulae containing truth-functional logical connectives, in other words, in the manipulation of structures already converted from natural language. For those outside philosophy interested in the meaning of the natural language sentences that are converted into the logical variables that form the components of the complex formulae, this truth-based approach can often seem difficult to justify, apparently trivial and largely unilluminating.[9] The reason it has nevertheless attracted some workers in linguistics is that it appeared to represent a way of providing a formal account of a notoriously vague and obscure concept, meaning.

While propositional logics treat atomic sentences as unanalysed units, predicate logics, concerned as they are with relations that hold between the elements of a sentence, might seem more relevant to the linguist interested in meaning. In practice, however, this is not the case. Logicians use predicate logics to overcome certain limitations in drawing valid inferences in propositional logics. There is thus no need for such logics to correspond very closely to the syntax of natural language. It would for example be possible for a predicate logician to analyse:

Max read the review

as

P (a,b)

that is, a predicate, P, with two arguments, 'a' and 'b'; where read, is assigned to the predicate costant, or simply predicate, P and 'Max' and 'review' to the individual constants, 'a' and 'b' respectively. It would also however be just as possible for the same sentence to be analysed as:

P (a)

where P would represent the entire phrase 'read the review'. In predicate logic, even complex expressions such as 'drives to the station five mornings a week between 7.30 and 8' are reducible to a simple predicate, P. As with propositional logics, there is a problem for the linguist, although not for the logician, with procedures for uniformly converting sentences of natural language into the formulae of predicate logic.

We make no attempt to do justice to the problems and controversies involved in formal semantics because we believe that efforts to apply the techniques of formal logic to natural language are misdirected. To argue this in any further detail would take us too far from our main theme. We draw some support for this position, however, from the writings of Tarski who, somewhat paradoxically, is sometimes seen as the father, as the phrase goes, of attempts to give an account of meaning in terms of a theory of truth. Tarski expressed serious reservations about the adequacy of formal language approaches to meaning in everyday language. In a paper that appears to have been taken as seminal, entitled 'The Concept of Truth in Formalized Languages', he set himself the task of constructing 'a materially adequate and formally correct definition of the term true sentence'. In the first section of that paper, sub-titled 'The Concept of True Sentence in Everyday or Colloquial Language', he argued that it seemed to be 'impossible' to construct an account of the expression 'true sentence' for everyday language. Part of the reason for this impossibility was what Tarski called the 'universality' of language. By universality he meant that the 'open texture' of language permitted paradoxes such as the paradox of the liar. Such paradoxes, he wrote:

> . . . provide a proof that every language which is universal in above sense, and for which normal laws of logic hold, must be inconsistent.

He concluded that:

> . . . the very possibility of a consistent use of the expression 'true sentence' which is in harmony with the laws of logic and the spirit of everyday language seems to be very questionable, and consequently the same doubt attaches to the possibility of constructing a correct definition of this expression. (Tarski, 1956:165)

The second section, entitled 'Formalised Languages, especially the Language of the Calculus of Classes', opens with the observation:

> For the reasons given in the preceding section I now abandon the attempt to solve our problem [define 'true sentence'] for the language of everyday life and restrict myself henceforth entirely to *formalised languages*.[10] (Tarski, 1965:165)

Much of the reason for our reluctance to consider further the relevance of formal semantics to natural language meaning is parallel in many ways to the case we made in Chapter 2 against Chomsky's attempt to devise a formal model for linguistic structure. It is that attempts to fit natural language meaning to formal logics have necessitated severe and unrevealing idealisations. It has meant for example that undue prominence has been given to one form of sentence, the declarative sentence in the indicative mood. This is because such sentences may be most easily related to propositions which may in turn be seen as true or false.

As a result different sentence types have been either excluded altogether or treated as peripheral. A consequence of this has been that other philosophers, in recent history first Austin and then Searle, interested in the meanings of these sentence types, have had to make room for them by devising supplements or additions to the formal theory. These include what came to be known as speech acts. Speech acts are certain non-proposition-making uses of sentences, such as promising, ordering and naming. Speech

acts are seen however as forces added to the essential propositional character of sentences and thus do not constitute an alternative
to the basic formal approach.

Another consequence of the idealisation imposed by adopting
formal semantics as a model for natural language meaning has
been the enshrining of an absolute distinction between words, or
phrases, and complete sentences. The standard view on these
approaches is that words may have meanings but that only sentences can express propositions which are true or false. A consequence of accepting this distiction is that whenever a single word or
an isolated phrase appears to express a proposition, it will have to
be regarded, in order to maintain the theory, as being an ellipsis
for a syntactically complete sentence of which only a part has been
uttered. Acceptance of the distinction requires then a theory of
ellipsis. It is true that it is usually necessary to combine words and
phrases according to certain conventions. But there are innumerable cases, many of them very far from simple and many of them in
spoken language, where the intended effect can be produced by
words in looser patterns or even by a single word. An isolated
word or phrase may lead or not lead our interlocutor to understand what we have in mind no more or no less adequately than a
syntactically complete and well-formed sentence. The difference
in effectiveness of the word against the sentence does not depend
upon one being structurally 'incomplete' and the other 'complete'. Rather it depends almost wholly upon the precise configuration of the knowledge, beliefs and expectations of our interlocutor at the moment of hearing or reading. It is this rather than
the distinction between words having meanings and sentences
expressing true or false propositions that will largely decide the
degree to which our utterances are understood.

We have given this brief sketch of approaches to theories of
sentence meaning to bring out the prevalence of the container
view, with its assumption that the relation which needs to be
characterised in order to understand the nature of meaning is that
holding between language and the 'world'. In the next section we
outline an alternative to this view.

An epiphenomenalist view

A container view of language gives rise to preoccupations about
the relation between language and what is loosely known as the

world, or sometimes, as 'reality'. In the last section we suggested that the absence of real progress in resolving the problems arising from these preoccupations implies a serious inadequacy in the general framework of enquiry, the container view itself. At the heart of the container view we have singled out its absolute presupposition that meaning is an inherent property of words and sentences. Accompanying this view has been an idealisation widespread in theoretical work on meaning in linguistics and philosophy away from the speaker and the hearer, the writer and the reader, and, in general, the users of the language with their supportive frameworks of expectations, beliefs and categorised experience. Insofar as complex matters of this sort can be at all adequately summed up, we might say that, despite the different guises they come in, container theorists have assumed that language is best studied as a self-contained, largely autonomous system used by members of a language community to convey meaning.

In our alternative approach to the study of language, an approach we call epiphenomenalist, we look at language as necessarily dependent upon language users and their individual 'states'.

We begin, then, with language users rather than language itself. We observe that they are familiar with their environment, that they have experienced or otherwise learnt about a range of phenomena and that this knowledge and experience has somehow been assimilated. Within this perspective, language may be thought of as a medium whereby one language user can cause another to access his own 'store' of accumulated and generalised knowledge and experience, to locate what appears to make sense of the sounds he hears. Looked at this way, nothing is *conveyed* from one language user to another. Language enables people to communicate – with different degrees of success – by enabling speakers to initiate within understanders a complex series of processing mechanisms which are intimately bound up with their states at the time of processing.

As well as the individual language user achieving a degree of understanding, his 'store' of accumulated and generalised experience is also likely to undergo modification. The modification may be totally insignificant as with the processing of well-worn phrases, or it may be considerable if the utterance involves unusual paths for the processing mechanisms. In this respect a fragment of language has some of the characteristics of a catalyst.

The perspective that sees language as a catalyst or trigger serving to initiate a complex series of processing mechanisms has an important consequence. Unlike the container view, there is no longer a relation to be established between language and the world, or between the structure of language and the structure of the world. In place of that relation there is a new problem: the relation between language and the accumulated and generalised experience of language users? What, to put it another way, is the relation between language and what we might call the 'data stores' of individual language users?

What to call the knowledge and experience that language users draw upon in both production and understanding is a problem. 'Store' is in part a misleading term, since it suggests something fixed or static. It is more likely to be the case that an individual user's accumulated and generalised knowledge of the world is constantly being modified through continuing experience, both linguistic and non-linguistic. It is possible that a better metaphor is to see the seat of the complex processing mechanisms as in a continuous state of excitation. If we think of what we grossly call 'knowledge' as traces of some kind in the brain, the entire mesh of such traces can be thought of as in varying states of excitation. Language input can be seen as causing modifications in this mesh of traces. Knowledge of language makes it possible for aural signals to engage or hook up with certain traces. The 'hooking up' process must be a highly complex one in which at least some traces may be well-defined, while others only become defined in the course of processing. It is possible that this is a more helpful metaphor, but no more than a metaphor. In the present state of knowledge very little is known about what actually goes on. The way in which language users 'store' the knowledge that using language enables them to access, that is the structure of the 'store', is also mysterious.

At this point, three conclusions emerge. First, language does not, indeed cannot, convey meaning. From the epiphenomenalist perspective, language acts as a locating medium enabling one individual to cause another to gain access to knowledge, or to draw inferences from knowledge that he already has. On this view of language, meaning does not inhere in utterances but emerges from them. For the epiphenomenalist, meaning is not an inherent but an emergent property of language. We shall attempt to give more substance to this view in Chapter 5.

The second point, and it is a corollary of the view that meaning is an emergent property, is that users and their supportive frameworks of expectations, beliefs and knowledge cannot be excluded from the study of language and, in particular, from the study of meaning. Meaning, what is understood as a result of an utterance being processed, only emerges from the complex interaction of the sounds constituting the utterance, the environment and the current state of the understander's constantly shifting 'data store'.

The efforts of linguists and philosophers during this century have been to idealise away from this view of language to something they have seen as less intractable – essentially a container view in which language is explicitly separated from language users and analysed as an entity in itself. Our claim is that this idealisation, while apparently a legitimate effort to reduce the complexity of the problem of understanding language to manageable proportions, has not led to insights into its workings.

Abandoning the container view and recognising the central importance to the functioning of language of language users and their 'data stores' has a profound effect on the type of explanatory theory which can be achieved. There is clearly little point in attempting to construct a deductively formulated theory for a phenomenon which is at this stage ill-defined and irreducible without gross distortion to a formal notation. While this appears self-evident, we should like to argue that the climate of opinion within theoretical linguistics and some branches of philosophy over the past two decades has made it difficult to take this commonsense view. The prestige of the deductively formulated model which we discussed in Chapter 2 has meant that to gain respectability within linguistics and other social sciences, problems have had to be reduced to terms which appeared to be expressible in at least relatively formal terms. The fact that this made them unilluminating took second place.

The absence of insights into the workings of language as a result of that approach strongly suggests that it should be abandoned. In our attempts in Chapter 5 to give substance to our emergence view of meaning, we are concerned to be systematic rather than formal. Our approach to science, which we see as very similar to the practice adopted in many of the physical sciences, is to start from a set of problems, aspects of language in use we do not understand. We devise informal working concepts on the basis of which to tackle the problems, and test the validity of the concepts against the aspects of language under investigation as we proceed. This enables us to remain open to the characteristics of what we are analysing rather than being trammelled by an over-rigid theoretical framework.

The third point that follows from adopting an epiphenomenalist perspective on language is that the question of the relation between language and the world, or reality, or between the structure of language and the structure of the world, simply does not arise. Simple as this observation appears to be, it turns out to be an extremely difficult one to keep in mind. One of the reasons that the view of meaning as somehow an entity in itself is so pervasive and difficult to shake off may arise from the fact that language may be used metalinguistically. We are accustomed to use language to talk about language, to talk about the meaning of words, the structure of sentences, the articulation of sounds. This convenient, everyday custom may well reinforce the view that language is an object or entity which may be isolated and studied in itself. It requires a great deal of determination to keep always in mind the extent to which we are all trapped within our own heads; to recognise the way in which utterances – combinations of linguistic units – far from conveying messages or information from A to B, do no more than enable A to cause B to attempt to locate within his own 'store' of accumulated and generalised experience that which appears to him to make most sense of A's words.

It does not follow from looking at language from this perspective that we are no longer interested in the characteristics of the combinations of linguistic units which make up utterances. We do, however, accord them a different status. If they are seen as instrumental in causing complex processing mechanisms to come into play, then a new set of problems will emerge. Questions will arise concerning the structure of the data store given that the 'same' utterance, i.e. the same combination of words, may be understood differently, that is enable the same user to access different 'areas of his store' in different circumstances. Using our alternative metaphor the 'same' utterance does not always cause the same variation in the states of excitation within the brain, does not always cause the same patterns to be formed. What consequence does this have for the characterisation of linguistic units? On the container view, it was possible to assume that words make a regular contribution to the combinations in which they occur. On the epiphenomenalist view, that idealisation would have to be abandoned. On that view the fact that the 'same' word is understood differently in different combinations is a puzzle, a mystery which highlights the complexity of the processing mechanisms involved in language production and understanding.

One of the consequences of the epiphenomenalist view is that it becomes considerably easier to call into question the rather special status accorded to language, especially written language, in literate cultures. On the epiphenomenalist view, language is one among a number of devices that, from the earliest times, people have used in their attempts to cause others to access their 'data stores'. Bodily movements, facial expressions and gestures are other such devices. Some peoples, in some cultures, particularly those that are predominantly oral rather than literate, have at times developed movements and gestures into communicative systems of considerable complexity. In first semi-literate, then literate communities, however, the development and slow diffusion of writing systems came to endow language with an apparent permanence. This permanence not only made it seem an appropriate object for analysis and study, but also at various times and in varying degrees transformed the written word into an object whose possession and use reflected, it was believed, higher powers and greater prestige. J. Goody and I. Watt have begun to tell the complex story of the social effects of the different kinds of writing systems that gradually evolved in various parts of the world. They describe the wide gaps that existed in Egypt, Mesopotamia and China between an esoteric literate culture and an exoteric oral one; a gap they comment, that 'the literate were interested in maintaining'. (Goody and Watt, 1972:323). Among the Sumerians and Akkadians, writing was preserved as 'a mystery', 'a secret treasure'. Gordon Childe is quoted as observing, 'The scribe is released from manual labour, it is he who commands'.

In our own culture the influence and prestige of written language has had complex and, for the study of language, in some ways insidious effects. Most linguists are academics whose education has centred upon books contained within universities whose *raison d'être* has been in large part the possession of storehouses of these written records. A consequence has been that the analysis of written language has tended to take precedence over spoken language. It would be misleading to say that analysis was concentrated upon written language as a deliberate choice. It is rather that it has been tacitly assumed that written language is the proper object for study. As a result it has seemed quite natural to isolate language, that is written language, from the overall process of communication in which other factors, gestures, postures, vocal noises other than spoken sound, play a part. This is all the more understandable since, as these other factors are not present in written language, ignoring them seems justified.

What is rarely justified however is the covert assumption that the characteristics of written and spoken language are sufficiently similar to ensure that the analysis of the written will throw light on the spoken. There are important differences between spoken and written language such that each requires an independent analysis in terms of its strengths and limitations as an instrument for enabling one speaker to cause another to access his 'data store'.[11] Written language may be studied in its own right. It would on the other hand be a confusion of categories if the analysis of written language were to be treated as equivalent to the analysis of language in its entirety.[12]

Given this special status that literate cultures accord to language, and in particular written language, it is easy to overlook the fact that language is only one of a number of devices individuals use to cause others to access their own 'data stores', thus enabling communication to take place. It may help to place language more clearly amongst other systems of communication if we take one of the most common of our gestures and consider the complex sets of conditions which must in fact hold if it is to be used successfully and understood. Consider the case where, in order to direct our interlocutor's attention to an object, we point to it. For this to be successful certain conditions must be satisfied. One such condition is that we share a framework of knowledge and attitudes about pointing. If we do not share that framework, then the pointing is best described as a bodily act, extending the forefinger, and will not be successful in directing attention. Indeed, extending the forefinger is an apter description of what we do if we try and direct a cat's attention to its bowl of milk. The most likely result, however hard we point, is that the cat will inspect our fingertips. Equally we may fail in directing attention by pointing with the finger within a culture, as was the case among certain of the North American Indians, where pointing is done with the lips.[13]

Pointing does not speak for itself. When we point, we are not making an isolated gesture to a person in a state of total ignorance. On the contrary, the person for whom we are pointing has, in the course of his life, accumulated and generalised experience of his environment. If he is a member of the same culture as ourselves, then a tiny part of that experience will have related to pointing. Some version of this sub-part of his experiences will form an element of his 'data store': understanding a fresh occurrence of pointing will involve his locating this area of his 'store'. This is an extremely gross account of enormously subtle and complex mechanisms. The account is gross partly for ease of exposition, but much more importantly because the brain's storing and accessing strategies are as yet ill-known. What is nevertheless clear is that if we are to characterise something even as simple as pointing, or at least apparently simple, then in order to do so we must take into account the whole situation in which gestures are made and have their effect. Gestures do not, any more than words and sentences, contain their meaning within themselves.

We have given some attention to gesture in order to illustrate another device other than language whereby we may cause others to locate appropriate items in their own 'data stores'. We have done this not, of course, to deny that language is one of the more useful and effective of all the communicative devices that men have contrived or, more likely, stumbled upon, or to deny that it is the most widely employed in the cultures we know. Our point is that language, especially written language, is only one such device and, what is more, is not in all cases the most effective, as is likely to be agreed by teachers, artists, mathematicians and lovers, who find it inadequate for their special purposes. It may be that, since these are early days in the development of mankind, in the future some further device may be contrived or stumbled upon which will be even more effective and will, after a time of supplementing language as we know it, perhaps supersede language as our primary means of communication as language has largely superseded gestures.

If, for a gesture to be effective, individuals must share a common framework of experience and expectations in relation to gestures, then for language to be effective, it is likely to be the case that much more complex conditions must hold. In the following section, we discuss the nature of some of those conditions.

Conditions for language functioning

It is a sub-theme of this book that language should be seen as a necessarily imperfect instrument by means of which interlocutors, each with their own supportive frameworks of knowledge, beliefs and expectations, are able to set in motion within one another complex processing mechanisms. As a result of the workings of these mechanisms, interlocutors feel, to a greater or lesser degree, that they have understood one another. Understanding is possible whenever one speaker is able to use the sounds uttered by another to locate some appropriate area within his own 'store' of accumulated and generalised experience.

The reasons for our conviction that language is an instrument which is necessarily imperfect lie in the conditions we see as needing to hold if understanding of some sort is to take place. In discussing these conditions we find we have to move away from language to the more general conditions for knowing itself. If language cannot operate without the supportive frameworks of language users, then it follows that to understand language functioning we need to sharpen this notion of support. If language enables its users to gain access in part to what they already know, however imperfectly, then knowing more about what they know is clearly relevant to the study of language.

This move may seem ill-advised for reasons perhaps linked to the way knowledge is pursued in our culture. The way specialist fields of enquiry have developed make it especially hard to follow through lines of thought which take the investigator into areas where he is not, and cannot be, an expert. Awareness as a specialist in one's own small sub-area of where the interloper can apparently 'go wrong' leads easily to the conviction backed by scholarly caution – and academics are not noticeably bold – that one should stay in one's own parish. However, on this occasion we have resisted this conviction, largely in the end because the subject of enquiry appeared to require it. In this section we briefly discuss non-linguistic matters which seem to us essential as background to gaining some understanding of how fragments of language are understood.

We have argued that the traditional efforts of linguists and philosophers to characterise meaning as a relation between language and the world have been misdirected. The relation which should be characterised is that which holds between language and language users' perception of the world as reflected in the 'store' of accumulated and generalised experience they call upon in language use. Language users' perception of the world is, on the other hand, extremely difficult to characterise. Partly as a result of the structure of their sense organs and partly as a result of the effects of various attention-directing mechanisms, they do not straightforwardly perceive or experience 'the world' but only select fragments of it. We want first therefore to draw attention to the diverse mechanisms involved in perception in order to give some indication of the complexity of the conditions which need to hold for language to operate.

Consider as an example of sense perception, seeing. A commonsense notion about the eye once was that it was a kind of window on to the world. This turned out to be not a happy metaphor. It is better to see the eye as a hole in the head that lets in a few light rays. In the front of the eye, in the pupil, there is a lens much like the lens of a camera. There is an iris around the pupil which functions like the aperture control in a camera to allow in more light on a dull day and less on a sunny day, by adjusting the size of the aperture in the middle of the lens. When light rays from the sun or some other source fall on objects around us they are reflected or bounce off the objects and some of them fall on the lens of the eye. The lens focuses these light rays, that is it binds them into little cone-shaped bundles and directs them to the retina. The retina is a small surface about the size of a one penny piece on the inside of the back of the eyeball. The retina is sensitive to light in much the same way as a camera film is, in that when light falls on it, certain chemical and other changes take place in it. As a result of these changes in the retina, impulses start to move along the nerves from the eye to the brain. These nerves incidentally do not go to the front of the brain as we might expect, but to the back. After the nerve impulses have reached the brain, and only then, do we have the experience we call 'seeing'.

'Seeing', therefore, is not as simple and direct as commonsense might have us believe. The simple assumption that things exist 'out there' and that we see them directly is not supported by investigations of the neurophysiology of sight. Many complex and intricate reactions have to take place before we have the experience we call 'seeing'. Curiously, owing to the time-lag in the passing of the nerve impulses from eye to brain, what we see is not what is affecting the eye now but what affected the eye a fraction of a second ago. We never see, and never can see, the present. All we can ever see is the very recent past.

Not all light waves, that is electro-magnetic vibrations, affect the retina enabling us to have the experience we call 'seeing'. The only ones that do are those between roughly 1/60,000th and 1/30,000th of an inch in length. Only when waves between these upper and lower limits are reflected by objects and fall on the eye, do they cause changes in the retina, which in turn cause changes in the nerves behind the eye which in turn cause changes in the brain. There are many other waves we do not detect because they are longer than those to which our sense organs react; there are also waves such as ultra-violet rays and gamma rays we do not detect because they are shorter. Putting it only apparently para-doxically, our eyes are blind to very nearly everything that is around us. More significantly, the way the world appears is conditioned by our physiology. If our eyes were physically differ-ent, we would have a different experience of the world.

The observations that hold for the eye can be extended and repeated for another organ, in some respects closer to the interests of the linguist, the ear. The difference is that for the ear the waves that matter are not electro-magnetic waves but air pressure waves. There are air waves of all sorts of length around us. If these air waves are longer than an upper limit of about 35 feet or shorter than about 7/8ths of an inch, they are not, to human ears, detect-able. Waves between those upper and lower limits pass down a hole in the head we call the ear, and press upon the ear drum, a thin skin stretched across the hole like a drum head. The waves of air pressure make this skin vibrate at their own rate of vibration. On the inner side of this drum is an arrangement of three small levers of bone which transmit and amplify the movement to another piece of thin skin stretched across a window still further inside the head. This window opens into a chamber – the cochlea – filled with liquid which in consequence vibrates in time to the original air waves. Little nerve endings like hairs project inside this chamber into the inner liquid so that when it moves to and fro these nerve endings are bent. These impulses travel along the bundle of nerves leading to the brain. When the impulses reach the brain, we have the experience we call 'hearing'. As with the eye, there is a slight time-lag in the passage of the nerve impulses, so that we can never hear what is being said to us now, but only what has just been said to us. Waves that are of a length that human ears react to we call sound waves. Pigeons however are able to react to extremely long wavelength 'infrasounds' that we cannot hear while dogs are able to react to air waves of shorter wavelengths than we can perceive. Sheepdog trainers become applied scientists when they make whistles of a wavelength so short that only a dog can hear them. Putting it again only apparently paradoxically, our ears are deaf to very nearly every-thing around us. Were our ears not as they are, we should not experience what we do.

To sum up, there is much of the world that we do not, indeed cannot, perceive because of the limitations of our sense organs. More significant when considering the conditions which must hold for language to operate, however, is whether the sense organs of different individuals are sufficiently similar for us to assume that language users see the world and hear its sounds in a way that is broadly comparable. We can never be certain of the answer to this question. We know that there are quite noticeable differences between the neurophysiological systems of some individuals. There are, for example, well known differences in perception of colour, most dramatically apparent in cases of colour blindness. The experience we call colour blindness results from the failure of the eye of the colour blind to respond to a small difference in wave length between the waves that the non-colour blind call 'red' and those they call 'green'. We know, too, that individuals' response to music, for example, or temperature, may differ considerably. The evidence of our everyday experience does suggest, on the other hand, that there are still considerable similarities in individuals' perception of the physical world.

Suppose we assume that the sense organs of individual lan-guage users give them the capacity to perceive the world in a way that is broadly similar to one another. There remains the fact that these individuals are not simply passive recipients of sense data. On the contrary, interacting with our direct perception of the world are further processes which determine what we notice, find relevant, take as salient, pay attention to, or see as foregrounded. We do not know much about these processes except to say that they are active and exploratory and interact with our neurophy-siological system to determine what we call knowing something.

It is thus only as a result of an interaction between both sensory and other attention-directing processes that individuals may be said to perceive the world. It is on this basis that they develop what we have called their 'store' of accumulated and generalised experience. Cognitive psychologists and others interested in the acquisition and organisation of knowledge have used other terms: they have referred to cognitive maps, models of the world, models of self, images, cerebral representations, frames. All these expressions are attempts to characterise the complex structures which result from the interaction of neurophysiological, cognitive and affective processes, structures not themselves fixed but being constantly modified through fresh experience.

Language depends for its operation on these highly complex structures which may be said to make up an individual's 'store' of accumulated and generalised experience and thus condition his perception of the world. It is extremely unlikely that these cognitive structures do not differ, sometimes considerably, across individuals. Although the sense organs of individual language users may give them the *capacity* to perceive the world in a similar way to one another, the interaction of sense perception with other attention-directing and affective mechanisms is bound to lead to considerable differences as well as the obvious similarities between individuals. Attention-directing processes in particular are closely tied to an individual's specific experience and highly influenced by his affective states.

For understanding language functioning this leads to a problem. If language is a means whereby one language user causes another to access his 'store' of accumulated and generalised experience, and if the 'stores' of particular individuals do differ significantly, how then can language work?

Part of the answer is to recognise first that language on many occasions does not work particularly successfully. And second, when it does work, we must assume that the interlocutors share broadly similar cognitive structures at least for the specific area of experience to which their utterances relate. This would mean, to return to an earlier example, that two professional golfers could use language to communicate highly successfully about golf even if their perception of other aspects of the world were very different.

Thus the principal condition for the successful operation of language *on any one occasion* is that interlocutors have a similar perception of the particular area of experience or aspect of the world to which the linguistic exchange relates. The fact, therefore, that individuals differ as regards the overall content and structure of their 'stores' of accumulated and generalised experience does not mean that they cannot use language to communicate reasonably successfully, in many areas. Language may thus be said to work with different degrees of effectiveness.

There are in addition aspects of everyday experience for which most individuals within a linguistic community would be likely to share broadly similar cognitive structures. If the study of language functioning is restricted to the analysis of linguistic exchanges relating to everyday occurrences such as eating, buying and selling or watching television, then language may appear to relate fairly directly to a shared world and thus be seen as an extremely effective medium of communication. If, on the other hand, language were studied as a teaching medium, whereby one individual attempts to use words to cause other individuals, with varied backgrounds and experience, to add to their 'data stores', then a very different picture of its effectiveness would emerge.

The dependence of language for its functioning on the perception of the world of individual language users as well as its uneven effectiveness as a medium of communication have been generally set aside by linguists and philosophers. This is largely because they have assumed that underlying the complex processes involved in language in use there is an entity which may be abstracted and characterised. Saussure called it 'langue', Chomsky 'linguistic competence'. The result has been, as we suggested earlier, that the problems and mysteries of how language in use actually works have not been tackled. Another way of looking at it is to say that they have been reformulated to fit within a theoretical framework which assumes that language may be usefully studied independently of its users.

Rejecting such an assumption does not mean denying that it is possible to categorise and classify, for example, the inflectional patterns of various languages or certain characteristics of their sound patterns. It means that categorising language forms is unlikely to throw much light on what happens when, by way of sound or written symbols, individuals appear to communicate or on the conditions under which language is able to function effectively.

The aim of this part of the book has been to argue that language users should be recognised as crucial to linguistic study. If this were generally accepted among linguists it would mean that linguistics would have to abandon any pretensions it may have to being a science akin to the most sophisticated of the physical sciences. It would mean that linguists would have to abandon, at least for the time being, attempts to construct deductively formulated explanatory theories. The knowledge, beliefs and expectations of language users cannot at this stage of our ignorance usefully be reduced to a suitable formal notation.

Linguistics as a science is at a stage that calls for careful, detailed analysis of specific problems in language use. The systematic investigation of these problems needs working theoretical constructs whose usefulness lies in clarifying the character of the problem and making it clear what further data is required. It is a time furthermore when Northrop's injunction against skimping the natural history stage of enquiry and moving too rapidly to the stage of deductively formulated theory needs to be heeded lest theoretical linguists indulge in 'immature, half-baked, dogmatic and for the most part worthless theory' (Northrop, 1959:37–8). The level of explanation achieved in linguistics will almost certainly not have the scope and generality of formal theories in some of the physical sciences. The style of explanation for linguistics, moreover, is likely to be teleological rather than reductive in character. But it should gain immeasurably in being more appropriate to its subject matter and thus much more likely to begin to offer plausible answers to the major unresolved questions of language in operation. In the final chapter we discuss some of the more significant of these questions.

Notes

1. R. G. Collingwood in his *An Essay of Metaphysics* which, in ordinary use is neither an essay nor on metaphysics, discusses clearly and eloquently the central significance of what he calls 'absolute presuppositions' in any type of enquiry.

2. Indexical or deictic terms came to be assigned to pragmatics.

3. It is customary in more detailed accounts to distinguish between sentences and propositions. It is then said that sentences express propositions; the proposition designates what the sentence states about the world. In this terminology, the problem of sentence meaning as we have expressed it is redescribed as the problem of the meaning of propositions. The problem remains, however, that of characterising the meaning of propositions in terms of a relation between two other terms; propositions and the objects, events etc. about which propositions are asserted or denied.

4. Apart from aspects of meaning in natural language that are not included within formal logics – we have in mind particularly the differences between valid inferences and the kind of 'practical' inferences made in natural language utterances – it is also widely recognised that the semantics of logical negation, logical conjunction and disjunction, and logical conditionals do not do justice to the complex use of negation, conjunction, disjunction and conditionals in natural languages. By the late sixties, logicians such as Kripke, Prior, Hintikka and Montague had extended the range of syntactic constructions of which they appeared able to give a semantic account. As far as we can tell the same problems of treating natural language phenomena in ways that are unrevealing about its character remain.

5. The founders of formal semantics, Frege, Russell, Carnap and Tarski, repeatedly drew attention to the 'vagaries' and 'illogicalities' of natural languages as they saw them that make the conversion task seem impossible.

6. As Church has noted:

> To adopt a particular formalised language thus involves adapting a particular theory or system of logical analysis – (this must be regarded as the essential feature of a formalised language, not the more conspicuous but theoretically less important feature that is found convenient to replace the spelled words of most written natural languages by single letters and various special symbols). (Church, 1965:3)

7. Amongst other problems, it should be noted that the logical *and* is a-temporal. Consequently the same truth value is assigned to *Alice married and had a baby* and *Alice had a baby and married*.

8. Frege set the direction when he wrote that it would be the reader's task to make clear to himself each proposition.

9. Students of linguistics are often uncomprehending of the significance of the formula: 'snow is white' is a true sentence if and only if snow is white.

10. Carnap in a similar vein observed: 'In consequence of the unsystematic and logically imperfect structure of the natural word-languages (such as German or Latin) the statement of their formal rules of formation and transformation would be

so complicated that it would hardly be feasible in practice.'
(Carnap, 1937:2)

11. See, for example, Marion Owen's work on topic organisation in conversation.

12. One striking difference is the frequent use in written language of the non-restrictive relative clause to introduce
parenthetically new information. In the spoken language,
nonrestrictive relative clauses rarely occur. Instead a number of phrases such as *by the way, you know, anyway* and regular
hesitations, the so-called 'ums' and 'ahs' are used to structure the parenthetic addition of new material. In the case of a
great deal of Chomsky's data, it has often been difficult to
know whether the sentoids output by the model were to be
put in correspondence with sentences of written or spoken
language. The uncertain position of intonation within transformational generative grammar is a further indication of the
uneasiness many generative linguistics have felt about
whether their analyses bear on spoken or written language.
Despite references from time to time by Chomsky and others
to 'normal intonation', it has often been difficult to decide
what intonation pattern should be assigned to crucial pieces
of data.

13. In their book *Gestures*, Desmond Morris *et al.* discuss the
culture-dependent nature of the interpretation of some 20
key gestures in 40 locations throughout Europe.

5 The Consequences of Variability

Speech is the only window through which the physiologist can view the cerebral life . . . and the problems raised by the organisation of language seem to be characteristic of almost all other cerebral activity.

Karl Lashley

In the last chapter we discussed our reasons for believing that language is inextricable from the accumulated and categorised experience of language users. A consequence of this view is that any theoretical work in linguistics based on idealising away from language users must lack both congruence with the object of enquiry and relevance to the puzzles and mysteries of language in use. The real difficulty here is not with accepting the importance of language users and their knowledge, beliefs and expectations to an understanding of language functioning: it lies rather in defining an investigatable domain once these are accepted as central.

Chomsky's view is that if it were to prove necessary to reject the 'initial idealisation to language, as an object of study' then he would conclude that 'language is a chaos that is not worth studying' (Chomsky, 1979:152–3). This view in various guises is widespread among theoretical linguists. Many continue to believe that the real strength of formal models such as Chomsky's, despite their limitations, lies in the rigorous framework they provide for the investigation of aspects of language. This belief is further reinforced by the assumption that the only alternative to deductively formulated theory would be a return to vague and anecdotal methods of study.

Such views have the weakness of being based on an extremely narrow view of scientific enquiry. They fail for example to recognise that the methods used in the physical sciences are diverse, much more so than is sometimes evident to those educated primarily within the humanities. Furthermore, they take insufficient account of the fact that an appropriate scientific approach is determined largely by the nature of the particular problem under investigation. There is no single 'correct' scientific method. Finally they overlook the stages that are necessary in any scientific enquiry. The same methods are not necessarily appropriate at every stage.

These points, in particular the notion of stages of enquiry, provide the theme of the work of F. S. C. Northrop, discussed briefly in the Prologue. In *The Logic of the Sciences and the Humanities*, Northrop writes:

> Again we see the importance ... of emphasising the different stages of scientific enquiry. We note also the importance of not supposing there is but one scientific method for all subject matters or for all the stages of enquiry of a single subject matter. Scientific methods, like space and time, are relative. A scientific method is relative to the stage of enquiry with which one is concerned as well as to the type of problem. The scientific method appropriate for the second stage of enquiry is different from the scientific method appropriate for its third stage. Moreover, the method of a later stage, to be effective, presupposes the method of the earlier stage. (Northrop, 1959:38)

With the perspective afforded by Northrop's analysis of scientific enquiry, it is possible to see that theoretical linguists working in the Chomskyan tradition have skimped the crucial first stage of enquiry – the analysis of the problem stage – and further that they have assumed that the existence of 'traditional' grammars was evidence enough that linguistics had all but passed through the second stage, the natural history stage. They thus moved far too readily to the final stage of enquiry, the stage of deductively formulated theory.

One of the main reasons that the resulting theories have been so unrevealing is that, in skimping the initial, crucial analysis of the problem stage, contemporary theoretical linguists have underestimated the importance of starting from reasonably well-defined problems. As we emphasised in Chapters 2 and 3, the problems that have come to interest Chomsky emerged from, rather than provided the basis for, his attempts to apply deductively formulated theory to the description of restricted aspects of language form. His interest in explaining the notion 'grammatical in language' for example appears to have arisen, we have argued, from his efforts to justify a model he had already devised.

As a result of developments within theoretical linguistics over the last twenty-five years – the fragmentation of the field, the absence of satisfying solutions to agreed problems, the general divergence of linguistics from its subject matter – we are particularly conscious of the need, in shifting the emphasis away from deductively formulated theory, to dwell at length on the analysis of the problem stage. It is, after all, this stage that gives point and relevance to more detailed work by providing tentative hypotheses and provisional working concepts. These may then be tested painstakingly and systematically against wider ranges of relevant data during the second or natural history stage.

In this chapter we embark on the analysis of the problem stage by firmly abandoning the idealisation to language as an independent object of study and by accepting that language users and their accumulated and generalised knowledge and experience must be taken into account if language functioning is to be understood. Taking the view that language is epiphenomenal on the 'states' and 'data stores' of language users raises the question: what types of relation hold between words and expressions and these 'states' and 'data stores'? In attempting to unravel the intricate factors involved in this problem, it became increasingly transparent that there was no simple, direct relation between a word and a particular location in a language user's 'data store'. This was driven home to us by the constant recurrence in all manner of language use of a certain type of unit that we have come to term 'variable'. A variable unit is one whose meaning cannot readily be characterised independently of its occurrence in combination with other units. A typical instance of such a variable unit would be 'put on'. 'Put on' can combine with an extremely wide range of *other units* such as:

> Put on the television/your socks/a big smile/the
> tablecloth/the milk/the brake/the dinner

It would be understood differently in each case, apparently taking on its meaning in relation to the other units in the combinations in which it occurs. 'Put on' is a typical example of a variable unit, as would be 'have', 'take', 'do', 'cut', 'in', 'round', and innumerable others. We believe that most units are variable to some degree and we suspect that all units are potentially variable.

The significance of variable units is that they provide language with its necessary indeterminacy. In a general way it is to be expected that the units of language will be indeterminate in that they must satisfy the needs of countless individuals within a speech community in relation to experience which for each of them is constantly shifting. The world perceived by language users is neither static and fixed for any one individual, nor uniform across individuals. This means that linguistic units have to be sufficiently flexible to enable users to adapt them to fresh visions of the world and new, unforeseen sets of circumstances. It is therefore to be expected that words and expressions will constantly occur in new or unusual combinations, or else in apparently familiar combinations which are understood in new or unusual ways.

Were there to be no indeterminacy, it is difficult to see how language could serve as a medium of communication across different individuals with their distinct, if related, experience of the world. Once indeterminacy is recognised as a fundamental property of language, the long-standing idealisation in theoretical linguistics to an abstract, user-independent, homogeneous body of knowledge must be called into question. The conception of language it provides is so far removed from the realities of its use that it is virtually impossible to see how it could account for the actual workings of language.

We assume that while specific linguistic units will generally be variable, they will be variable to different degrees. Units variable to a low degree would be those which may be fairly readily associated with some clearly defined aspect of most language users' world. Linguists have tended to concentrate their semantic analyses on such units – often the names of commonly found physical objects. We want to concentrate on units variable to higher degrees since it is these which highlight the difficulty of arriving at a satisfactory account of the relation between words and expressions and the 'states' or 'data stores' of language users. Highly variable units cannot be related directly to areas of 'data stores'. They thus give rise to a puzzle, a mystery: how is it that speakers, restricted to using a limited number of variable linguistic units, are able nevertheless on many occasions to cause hearers, in understanding, to access areas of their own 'data stores' that are generally appropriate?

This puzzle, this mystery appeared to be so fundamental that we recast the broad question of how does language operate in terms of an underlying sub-question: how does the variability of linguistic units affect the operation of language

In the course of analysing this sub-problem, we made two hypotheses:

(i) Most linguistic units are variable, but to different degrees. Processing of combinations of units involves the interaction of units of different degrees of variability. The meaning of a combination emerges partly from the interaction of differently variable units.

(ii) Some utterances occur repeatedly in the 'same' situational context; such utterances constitute an imprecisely defined special case which we call 'familiar'. Each individual will have a stock of familiar utterances which will differ from that of another individual. Such utterances may be processed somewhat differently to non-familiar utterances.

Variability of linguistic units: the analysis of the problem

The problem of variability may be best sharpened by considering a very simple example, an utterance:

Put on the television

in an everyday domestic situation. Suppose one argues as a first approximation that the unit 'television' is processed such as to enable an understander to identify an object in his immediate environment: one might then be tempted to make the very simple observation that he has learnt to associate the combination of sounds in the word 'television' with a type of object with which he has become familiar. Setting aside the definite article for a moment, it is clear that a parallel account of the understanding of 'put on' is much less plausible. It would be difficult to argue that an understander has learnt to associate the combination of sounds in the expression 'put on' with a type of action (the manipulating of a switch, combined, depending on whether this has or has not already been done, with the inserting of a plug in a socket) with which he is familiar. It would be difficult because if the utterance were to be: 'Put on your shoes', the type of action with which the understander might be said to associate the combination of sounds would have no identifiable characteristics in common. It would be different again if the combination were to be: 'Put on the tablecloth', and different yet again for: 'Put on a big smile' and so on down the list of examples suggested above. It seems more likely that the understander is able to interpret the utterance and consequently perform the task he is asked, because he is able to understand 'put on' in relation to an object in his immediate environment which he has been able to identify via the unit 'television'. In this particular example, it would appear that there has been an interaction between two somewhat different processes, the process of identifying an object in the immediate environment and the process of identifying what to do with it, i.e. interpreting the expression 'put on'. In this case, the nature of the physical object picked out from the immediate environment would appear to have been instrumental in fixing the interpretation of the variable unit: 'put on'.

If we accept this analysis, then it follows that the relation of the linguistic unit 'television' to the language user's data base and that of 'put on' are different. A way of looking at the processing involved in understanding is to see it as exploiting this difference.

We want to further complicate our initial, very simple analysis by observing that the unit 'television' itself is to some degree variable in that it would not serve to pick out an object in the immediate environment of speakers in every combination in which it occurs. This would not be the case in an utterance such as:

Television encourages violence

for example which might be uttered from any television set, and is likely to be understood as referring to something rather more complex and less easy to specify than the simple physical object: television. Thus an understander would have to bring to bear processing strategies of a somewhat different type to the understanding of 'television' in the second example. These strategies would enable him not to identify an object but rather to access an area of experience which is related to the physical object, television, but is much less precise. In addition, there is likely to be a greater degree of similarity across individuals in understanding 'television' in the first than in the second example. The 'television' may also be thought of as a variable unit, but with a lower degree of variability than 'put on'. Broadly we suggest that language production and understanding require units with different degrees of variability to adjust to one another. In exploring this idea we refer to such adjustment as the modulation effect.

It might be argued, of course, that understanders recognise

this difference in the contribution of the unit 'television' to these combinations, according to whether or not it is accompanied by a definite article. Undeniably, in this case, the distinction does correlate with the presence or not of 'the'. However, it would be hasty to conclude from this that the presence of a determiner marks a semantic distinction between the use of a word to pick out a physical object, and the use of the same word in a related but more abstract sense. After all, for some people:

The television encourages violence

would be as acceptable as:

Television encourages violence

Futhermore, some of us spend our evenings 'watching television', others 'watching the television', apparently the same activity. The question of the weighting of the contribution of syntactic information such as the presence or absence of a determiner to the understanding of utterances is not a straightforward one. Our view is that the significance of syntactic information has often been overestimated, simply because its manifestations, be they in the form of morphological markings, word ordering conventions or other devices, are relatively easy to observe and classify. Utterances apparently contain what may be seen as a mass of syntactic information which it is easy but misleading to claim is crucial to their understanding. In a later section we explore some of the consequences for understanding of stripping away much of this information.

Over the years, strenuous efforts have been made by linguists and philosophers to wish away the problems posed by what we have called the variability of linguistic units. The most obvious way of doing this has been to assume that the modulation effect can be reduced to manageable proportions by acknowledging that some words have a number of senses and by taking for granted that these may be distinguished from one another and listed. Dictionary writers as we discussed in the Interlude certainly adopt this view in response to the practical problem of producing a rough and ready guide to the uses of words. Linguists attempting to provide a formal account of word meaning have of necessity idealised away from indeterminacy and adopted a position close to that of the lexicographer. The limitation of their 'dictionary approach' to variability is that it takes for granted the container view we discussed in Chapter 4, i.e. that meaning is an inherent property of words rather than an emergent property of utterances. As such it conceals fundamental characteristics of meaning. As an illustration, we compare a container account and an emergence account of the same set of examples. Consider the following three sentences, assumed to be uttered once again in an everyday domestic context:

(i)   Put on the television
(ii) Put on the gas fire
(iii) Put on some music

A container view of variability

In the container view, many words and expressions are seen as having a number of distinguishable and specifiable senses. It follows therefore that it should always be possible, given an occurrence of a word or expression, to relate it to one of its specified senses. If 'put on' is one such expression, then it is arguable that in each of the above occurrences it may be related to the same sense characterisation in the list: this sense we might roughly characterise as CAUSE TO WORK. Thus, on this view, an account of the meaning of (i) would include its being a command to CAUSE TO WORK a physical object with the properties appropriate to a television, an account of (ii) would include its being a command to CAUSE TO WORK a physical object with the properties of a gas fire, an account of (iii) would have to gloss over the fact that what is in fact CAUSED TO WORK is not the music so much as the source of the music. An alternative would be to say that 'put on' in (iii) is different to the other two examples; that it would have to be related to another sense from a list of pre-specified senses. It is not clear what such a sense would be.

An emergence view of variability

The emergence view would focus attention on the observation that, in spite of the occurrence in each of the examples of the same unit, 'put on', a language user who understood (i)–(iii) would perform a different action in each case. In addition, the action he performed would itself depend both on his own knowledge and expectations and on the state of the environment – whether in (i) the plug is in or out, in (ii) what kind of gas fire it is, whether for example it requires a match, in (iii) what the available sources of music are and whether there is more than one. If a different set of examples were chosen:

Put on the tablecloth
Put on the potatoes (to cook)
Put on the car (add to the list)

the emergence view would draw attention to the fact that a different set of actions would result, themselves dependent on the expectations of the understander and the state of the environment, actions bearing little resemblance either to one another or to the first set of examples. The emergence view assumes that this diversity needs to be accounted for, and suggests that the interpretation of (i) – (ii) emerges from the modulations of units of different degrees of variability. It would appear that different types of processing mechanisms are involved. These would have to include picking out objects from the immediate environment and identifying appropriate actions in relation to them. A vital element in this modulatory process would be the state of the environment and, in particular, the state of the object picked out. Looked at in this way, the meaning of 'put on' *an any case* may be said for the understander to emerge as a result of its interaction with other units with a lower degree of variability.

When these two accounts are compared, then the following points emerge:

The container view of variability assumes what we have argued that most linguistics of this century have assumed, i.e. that language may be isolated from language users as an object whose characteristics may be independently described. Among these characteristics is word meaning. The container view is essentially a dictionary view in which giving an account of word meaning involves deciding that various uses of word have something in common, i.e. that in each of a number of cases the word has basically the 'same meaning', and then giving that 'something' a label. In the example we considered, the label was (CAUSE TO WORK. There are however a number of serious limitations connected with this approach. Perhaps the most important is that it considers words and expressions in isolation, largely setting aside their affects on each other in combinations. The container view thus leaves untouched the central problem of language in operation, that of how units of different degrees of variability adjust to one another in combinations and are interpreted through their interactions with language users' perceptions and expectations.

In assuming that words and expressions have a set of meanings, fully specifiable independently of their occurrence in combination with other units in particular contexts, the container view overlooks one of language's most fundamental characteristics: the capacity of language users, with a relatively limited vocabulary, to reflect a potentially limitless variety of human experience. The ways in which they do this constitute the true innovative and creative use of language. An excess of this type of creativity on the part of one speaker may make it impossible for another to identify anything in his own experience that relates to the language he hears. As we discussed in Chapter 4, what constrains the creativity of individual language users is the degree of agreement, tacit and largely unconscious as it is, that holds between interlocutors sharing similar beliefs, experiences and expectations of the world. In general, the closer interlocutors are in occupation, social class, regional origins, education and age, the more likely they are to be able to follow the adjustments they are each making.

A further more specific limitation of the container view is that of drawing boundaries between different meanings of a word or expression. In example (iii) 'Put on' is neither clearly parallel, nor clearly different to the 'same' expression in (i) and (ii). If 'put on' were to be further investigated, then questions would have to arise as to whether, for example, 'put on' in 'put on your shoes' should have the same label as 'put on' in 'put on a bandage', or whether there was anything in common between 'put on' in 'put on some coal' and 'put on the lid'. Those who have taken the validity of this approach for granted have never tried to establish rigorous procedures for drawing distinctions between what on this view are seen as different meanings of a word or expression. The container view is thus insecurely based, and at its worst gives rise to empty speculation as to whether a word in one combination is or is not 'really the same as' that word in another.

The emergence view of variability has the drawback of being difficult to formulate precisely. It is an emergence view rather than an emergence theory of meaning. It does however have the important advantage of constituting a much less restrictive idealisation than the container view. It recognises the need to take into account the state of the environment in which an utterance occurs as well as the state of the 'data base' of the understander in attempting to elucidate the interactive processes which constitute language in operation. Furthermore, it largely eliminates a problem which arises with an essentially container view of variability. On that view, variable items are assumed to have associated with them a number – sometimes quite a large number – of distinct meanings. Understanding utterances of combinations of items has then necessarily to involve selection from among the possible meanings of the variable items in the utterance. In an utterance with several variable items the result could rapidly be a combinatorial explosion. There is however no evidence to suggest that such an explosion actually occurs. The emergence view circumvents this problem by assuming that the expectations of language users as well as the state of the environment allows an appropriate interpretation of utterances to emerge. It does moreover bring into the open a characteristic of language that the container view conceals. In focusing attention on variable units, it highlights the indeterminancy we have argued is inherent in language, enabling it to operate across individuals who have only partially overlapping perceptions of the world. This at the same time poses a problem, an unresolved problem that the container view simply avoids: if the meaning of a variable item such as 'put on' emerges for the understander as a result of its interraction with units of different degrees of variability, the state of the environment and the expectations of the understander, does this amount to accepting that variable items may assume potentially any meaning at all? Intuitively, the answer would seem to be that they may not. Generally we would not want to claim that variable items have potential for infinite meaning. It is likely that the higher degree of variability of an item, the broader the range of potential meaning that may emerge. Although the problem of how to establish more precisely the bounds on variable items is still unresolved, the emergence view at least serves to bring the problem into the open.

Finally, the emergence view concentrates attention on the question of how units with different degrees of variability come to 'fix' the interpretation of the combination in which they occur. Much of the rest of the book is devoted to exploring this question of 'fixing' interpretations in the framework of an emergence view of meaning.

Before going on to look more closely at the implications for processing of the variability of linguistic units, we should like to add one further dimension to the problem in the form of a distinction between two types of utterance: those which are produced, heard and understood frequently in the context of everyday activities, and those which are not.

We call utterances which fall into the first category, *familiar* utterances, those in the second, *non-familiar*. Some familiar utterances are likely to be used daily by millions of people, 'Can I have . . .', 'Give me . . .' at mealtimes, or 'Do you want . . .', Would you like some . . .' or 'Turn it up/down' in relation to television or music, 'What time is it?' by those late or at a loose end. Some will be used frequently within much smaller groups. There are many such utterances, apparently processed very readily by language users. Indeed one of the reasons we are considering them is that their existence may blur the complexity of the processes involved in language use by making it appear more straightforward and precise than in many cases it is.

Familiar utterances may be thought of as constituting an imprecisely defined special class, imprecisely defined because their characterisation is simply in terms of 'familiar' and 'every-day'. It is important to note that utterances fall into this class, not because of particular linguistic characteristics, but because they occur repeatedly in the 'same' situation. A further reason for giving attention to familiar utterances is to counterbalance the emphasis we have given to the creative use of language by taking into account the existence of a large class of utterances that language users produce and understand time and again.

Familiar utterances are difficult to characterise very closely. There are a number of reasons for this, but probably the most important is that they are individual-dependent. One language user's familiar utterance may well be non-familiar to another. This means that language itself cannot be separated into familiar and non-familiar utterances in any pre-determined way.

What linguists have traditionally done is to acknowledge the existence of fixed or ritual expressions in languages. These gener-ally include greetings, oaths, politeness formulae – 'I'd be grateful if . . .', 'Sorry to keep you waiting . . .', – conventional opening remarks, 'Nice day, isn't it' and so on. What they have not taken into account is that for each individual, such 'fixed formulae' are only a sub-class of a much broader set of utterances which are produced and understood time and again. As a sub-class, fixed or ritual expressions have the special characteristic of being shared by almost an entire linguistic community. In addition to this sub-class, however, there are utterances produced and understood time and again within quite small groups, people who work together, for example. Such utterances would not constitute the 'fixed expressions' of a language, but of a group of speakers within a particular situation context. I an office, such 'familiar utterances' may be:

> Will you check this?
> Have you time to get this done today?
> The paper's run out
> I've got some work for you
> Can you come in for a moment?

and a host of others. Some individuals may invariably use the same combination whenever the 'same' situation arises, others may select from a number of variants. What must be borne in mind too is that the utterances produced and understood time and again within a group, the familiar utterances of that group, are employed by individuals who are likely, at the same time, to be performing some action, holding out a piece of paper or putting it down in front of the understander or beckoning for example. Familiar utterances are likely to be heavily supported. They are familiar by dint of their repeated occurrence within a particular supportive framework, and not because they exhibit characteristic linguistic attributes. People who live together, families, couples, friends, are equally likely to share sets of familiar utterances as indeed are any groups of individuals, however small, who share some activity.

The distinction between familiar and non-familiar utterances is a very informal one. We have included it, however, because it would seem, even at this level of generality, to have implications for the understanding of linguistic processing. The most important of these is that the amount of analytic processing required in the understanding of familiar utterances is likely to be less than that required for non-familiar utterances. One way of looking at it is to suggest that in understanding familiar utterances the processing mechanisms are in some way telescoped. This simple hypothesis might seem relatively easy to test by measuring the response times of language users to familiar utterances and comparing them with the response times to other utterances. It would, however, in practice, be extremely difficult precisely because familiar utterances, if they are readily processed, are so processed because they occur often in frequently repeated situational contexts, and not because of their inherent semantic or syntactic simplicity. Such contexts would be extremely difficult to recreate experimentally. Uttered outside its familiar, often repeated situational context, a familiar utterance may no longer be processed as one, and may be processed differently. Therein lies the mystery. Not only different individuals likely to process the same utterance differently according to whether or not it constitutes part of their set of familiar utterances – a stranger walking into an office for example and observing what is happening may process at least part of what he hears more slowly than the participants – but in addition, the same individual may process the same combination of words differently according to whether it occurs within a familiar, often repeated context and thus constitutes a familiar utterance or whether it occurs in some other situation. The expression 'processed differently' cannot really be made much more precise, except to repeat that for understanders familiar utterances are likely to require less analysis than non-familiar ones. It may be the case that, for each individual, the meaning of familiar utterances has, by dint of constant repetition in the same situation and environment, been absorbed. Or rather, it may be that the degree to which the processing mechanisms are telescoped, making understanding appear automatic, depends on the degree of familiarity of the utterance-in-context concerned.

The possibility that for each individual processing may differ according to whether or not an utterance-in-context is a member of his set of familiar utterances bears crucially on the question of determining basic units of analysis. The question it raises is the following: how does the brain store and allow access to linguistic information such that the same linguistic unit is able to occur as:

(i)   an inextricable part of a familiar utterance?
(ii) part of the same combination used in an unfamiliar context

and thus processed as a non-familiar utterance?

(iii) part of other combinations, familiar and non-familiar, in which its contribution to the interpretation of the whole differs?

How is it, in other words, that an English-speaker stores and accesses a linguistic unit, such as 'Check', which may occur:

(i)   In a familiar utterance: 'Will you check this?' in for example a work supported by the material to be checked?

(ii) In a non-familiar utterance: 'Will you check this?' as part, for example, of a telephone conversation relating to what someone was purported to have said?

(iii) In another utterance: 'We'll have to check this' referring to some part of abuse which needs to be stopped and thus representing a different type of activity to (i) and (ii)?

The concepts which have been thrown up in the course of analysing the problem of variability – emergence, familiarity, modulation – serve to reinforce our decision to set aside the idealisation to language or linguistic knowledge as a self-contained system. In the following section we consider some of the implications of our initial analysis for the understanding of the brain's storage and accessing facilities. It is not our intention, in spite of this terminology, to draw extensive parallels between the brain and a computer, further than to assume grossly that the brain stores information in some form which the individual, selectively, makes use of. In order to do this, he needs to be able to locate the information he requires in a particular situation within his complexly structured 'store'. Language production and understanding represents a situation in which this accessing facility is crucial. We should like to emphasise once again, that 'store', if it suggests something fixed and static, is misleading; we use 'store' to refer to an individual's 'accumulated and partially generalised knowledge of the world as he perceives it'. This 'store' may, as we suggested earlier, be in a constant state of excitation; it may be continuously being modified in minute ways. The nature of the 'store' remains in the present state of our knowledge, almost a total mystery. This does not mean that some psychologists, some philosophers, some workers in artificial intelligence have not been addressing themselves to the question of what is sometimes called 'the structure of knowledge': it is, however, probably fair to say that investigation of this area is still very much in its early stages.

Variability of linguistic units: implications for language processing

We start from the position that very little is known about the brain's storage and accessing mechanisms. This means that there is much to be discovered about the processing of even the simplest utterances. With this in mind, we concentrate on a small sample of apparently simple utterances in everyday contexts in order to bring out the complex factors which must be involved in processing what appears straightforward. Concentrating on understanding processes, we explore the general question of how an utterance is processed by considering:

(i)   what type of information the linguistic units constituting the utterance enable the understander to access.
(ii) the interaction of the various types of information.
(iii) the role in understanding of the environment of the utterance.
(iv) the factors involved in assigning a weighting to the importance to understanding of the various types of information an understander has at his disposal.

The first case we shall consider is that of a married woman, opening the door of her home to a caller, who asks:

Is your husband in?

This apparently banal exchange becomes less banal once we learn to see it as a physical transaction between two complexly structured organisms in a complexly structured environment. One complexly structured organism puts out a string of sounds; the other complexly structured organism takes in some subset of this string of sounds as input. In nearly all cases imaginable, the receiving complexly structured organism would be taking in other sensory input at the same time. The input data is then processed according to the state and structure both of the environment and of the 'data store' of the complexly structured organism at the time the input is received.

When the phenomenon to be investigated is presented in these terms, it can seem intractable. It is certainly possible to argue that far from being simple, such an exchange between complexly structured organisms contains so many factors which are idiosyncratic that no useful generalisations can be made. The other way to proceed is to accept the complexity of the phenomenon, but to attempt nevertheless, hesitantly and tentatively, to isolate what appear to be some at least of the non-idiosyncratic features.

The first broad simplifying assumption we must make is that the exchange is a 'normal' one, that neither of the participants is unusual, that neither the voice quality of the caller nor the tone of his question are such as to divert the woman's attention from her primary task: understanding. Without such an idealisation, we could not proceed at all.

If one accepts this idealisation to a 'normal exchange', then the next step is to consider the woman as 'understander'. As understander, she must use the string of sounds she receives as input to access what we shall loosely call information enabling her to interpret the combination of units making up the utterance. Assuming these units to be 'is', 'your husband' and 'in', we must further take into account the fact that she recognises she is being asked a question.

The first observation to be made is that for this particular understander, the units making up the combination would enable her to access 'information' corresponding to specific and well-defined aspects of her own experience: they would enable her to identify a specific individual, present or not, with a clearly defined relation to herself, as well as a specific area of her environment: her own home. Another way of putting it, very tentatively, might be to say that the utterance constitutes input patterns which are so converted within the brain as to hook up with, or in some way link up to, traces corresponding to 'specific' (as opposed to 'generalised') knowledge.

It is important to note that there is no necessary connection between processing which results in access to 'specific knowledge' and the particular linguistic characteristics of utterances. A linguist might want to argue, for example, that 'your' and 'husband' are separate units and that the possessive pronoun supplies the information that the husband being referred to is a specific one, that of the addressee, in other words, that the sentence contains a deictic expression the interpretation of which is resolved by context. The problem here is not that it is wrong, but that it is unilluminating. Suppose the woman who answers the door is unmarried and lives alone. In order to respond to the question, she still has to process the utterance: 'Is your husband in?' This raises the question of what type of information, the unit 'your husband' enables *her* to access. Clearly it cannot enable her to locate 'information' corresponding to a specific individual since no such individual exists. She is nevertheless likely to understand the question addressed to her. We must therefore assume that in this case, the string of sounds constituting the utterance enables her to access more 'generalised' information as to the characteristics of husbands. Thus, the first tentative conclusion we might draw from this example is that we have knowledge of at least these two different types: specific and generalised. Furthermore, the particular type of knowledge located in any one case varies not according to the characteristics of the utterance but to the state of the understander and the environment.

The second observation concerns the interpretation of the unit 'in', which in this case would be likely to be understood as 'at home' or 'there'. We use the expression 'in this case' advisedly since 'in' would not, of course, be understood as 'at home' in all combinations in which it occurs. 'In' is a highly variable linguistic unit. An understander is nevertheless able to interpret 'in', more or less appropriately, in most of the utterances in which it is likely to be found.

The variability of units such as 'in' presents a strong challenge to any linguistic theory which includes a lexicon. In recent versions of Chomsky's theory, the lexicon has come to play a more and more prominent role. In a recent textbook on the consequences for linguistics of Chomsky's work, it was claimed that:

> . . . a grammar designed to give a full account of linguistic knowledge will simply have to list in the lexicon for each word of the language the sum total of its syntactic, semantic and phonological properties. (Smith and Wilson, 1979:53)

The view that the linguist's task is to give a full account for each word of a language of its syntactic, semantic and phonological properties fails entirely to come to grips in an illuminating way with the problems posed by the widespread variability of linguistic units. This emerges very clearly if we were to attempt seriously to list the 'sum total' of the various properties of a highly variable unit such as 'in'. The phonological properties appear to present the least difficulty. It would be possible to give some characterisation of the two sounds making up the item 'in'. More problematic, however, would be listing the environments which could cause these to be modified since this would involve taking non-phonological factors into account.

More difficult would be listing the syntactic properties: these should include the possible syntactic categories to which 'in' may be assigned, among which would be at least the category adverb and the category preposition. That is, on the basis of a mixture of intuition and 'traditional grammar' we associate 'in' with being a preposition or an adverb. If in addition we consult a dictionary we are likely to find that 'in' may also be an adjective and, generally in the plural, a noun. To say that a linguistic unit may be an adverb or an adjective, a noun or a preposition is only revealing if we have some way of establishing what it is that 'makes' it adverb, adjective, noun or preposition. We discussed this problem at some length in Chapter 2. It might be argued, for example, that 'in' is a preposition when it occurs in prepositional phrase, i.e. when it is followed by a noun. Thus, in an example such as 'Is the chicken in the oven?' 'in' is being used prepositionally. But suppose the example were to be 'Is the chicken in?' Is this an occurrence of 'in' as an adverb? Or is 'in' to be understood here as 'in the oven', a prepositional phrase with the noun phrase deleted? Then again, 'in' in 'Is the chicken in?' would not always be interpreted as 'in the oven'. Once one starts inventing scenarios, then 'Is the chicken in?' may be interpreted as for example: Has the cost of the chicken been taken into account in the budgeting? – in this case, is 'in' an adverb or preposition? It would be easy to go on at considerable length raising questions of this kind. We want to emphasise here the vacuity of simply stating that a word may be assigned to a number of syntactic categories in the absence of criteria for establishing, for, any given case, what its category is. It is particularly vacuous for a highly variable linguistic unit such as 'in' where whether it be 'called' prepositional or adverb may, in any particular case, be largely a matter of expediency. A linguist may, for the purpose of his analysis, have simply to deem 'in' to be a preposition in one case, perhaps an adverb in another. And he is most likely to do this as we illustrated in Chapter 2 on the basis of his intuitive appreciation of the meaning of the sentence or utterance in question.

Given its high degree of variability, it would be difficult to decide what could constitute the 'sum total' of the semantic properties of 'in'. The textbook from which we took the statement on the contents of the lexicon accepts the conventional distinction between literal and non-literal meaning and argues that meaning should be described in terms of entailments. This approach, however, is firmly within the assumptions and idealisations of the container view that we discussed in Chapter 4. It assumes that the meaning of a sentence may be regarded as a set of propositions expressed by the sentence and that the task of 'semantics proper' (Smith and Wilson, 1979:150) is the statement of the entailments of one specific sentence type, the simple declarative sentence. Entailments are said to be those propositions that can be inferred from a declarative sentence in isolation from any context. In the examples given 'that is a horse' entails 'that is an animal' and 'I bought a horse' entails 'I bought an animal', and so on.[1] On this view of the meaning of sentences, the meaning of a particular word is seen as the contribution it may or must make to the entailments of the sentences in which it occurs.[2] The importance of variable units such as 'in' is that they pose not merely a practical but an in principle problem for such approaches. Since in any one case, their contribution to the meaning of a sentence emerges as a result of their interaction with other units in the combination, their semantic properties cannot be reduced to a list of statements prespecified in a lexical entry.

Variable units such as 'in' thus call into question attempts to explain linguistic knowledge by giving 'the sum total' of each word's syntactic, semantic and phonological properties. An alternative approach, in keeping with the emergence view of meaning, would see linguistic units as of different types, such that some types 'fix' the interpretation of utterances in which they occur much more than others. Very generally, we might say that the extent to which a unit fixes the interpretation of an utterance is related to the degree of its variability. On this view, in the 'Is your husband in?' case, the unit 'your husband' may be seen as acting as a 'fixing' or 'anchoring' unit in relation to which the rest of the utterance is understood. This unit acts in this capacity by enabling an understander to gain access to 'information' specific or generalised, which may be characterised reasonably precisely. The unit 'in' would count as a non-anchoring unit in that it would not enable an understander to gain direct access to 'information'.

Instead, its interpretation would emerge as a result of a number of factors which would include:

(i)   the processing of the anchoring unit, processing would also involve establishing the relations between units.
(ii)   the expectations of the understander and the extent to which these are satisfied. In the case in question, the understander in going to the door, will have expectations of what an appropriate or likely style of exchange in these circumstances will be. In more complex cases, expectations, will be aroused by the nature of the exchange which has already taken place.

The distinction between anchoring and non-anchoring units is not a clear cut one. We have taken what seems like clear cases: 'husband' and 'in'; there are likely to be other cases in which it would be more difficult to assign units definitely to one or other category. We nevertheless consider it worthwhile to explore such a distinction as part of an attempt to break free from the mental straitjacket which traditional grammatical categories and relations, and dictionary approaches to meaning have imposed. By stating our problem in processing terms, we are then obliged to define units which are significant for the understanding of language operation.

The particular significance of the anchoring – non-anchoring distinction lies in the light it could help to throw on the nature of the 'knowledge store' or 'data base' which a language user calls upon in understanding language. In order to see this more clearly, consider a metaphor we used earlier whereby we suggested that the sound patterns constituting input to an understander might be so converted as to hook up with 'traces' laid down in the brain as a consequence of experience. If we carry this metaphor further, we might say that in the case of anchoring units, the 'hooking up' may be thought of as direct in that the brain 'stores' reasonably precise information corresponding to their sound patterns. In the case of non-anchoring units the 'trace' may be thought of as ill-defined, only becoming well-defined as a result of a complex series of interactions. Some of these interactions would be those between anchoring and non-anchoring units; others would somehow relate to the state of the understander, his expectations and the state of his environment. These factors are difficult to discuss more specifically in processing terms, yet they are crucially important to the interpretation of non-anchoring units – and, if we think of non-anchoring units as that part of language which is most flexible, then these factors are indispensable to the entire operation of language.

Suppose we return to the example: 'Is your husband in? and vary the environment of the utterance, and consequently the expectations of the understander. We would expect this to affect the interpretation of the anchoring unit, 'your husband', less than the interpretation of the non-anchoring unit 'in'. If the lady were watching a cricket match in which her husband were playing, for example, and were asked: 'Is your husband in?' then the anchoring unit 'your husband' would once again enable her to identify a specific individual, at that moment engaged in a particular activity. The interpretation of 'in' as 'batting' might then be said to emerge as a result of the interaction of this information and the expectations set up by the environment and the interlocutor.

If we were to vary the anchoring unit and consider the example: 'Is your application in?' then the interpretation of the non-anchoring unit 'in' might again be quite different. It might be said to emerge in relation to:

(i)   the 'information' accessed by the unit 'your application' which would be likely to enable the understander to identify a particular application, at a particular stage of submission.
(ii) the related generalised information about applications and what one does with them.
(iii) the person of the questioner, his status, whether he has anything to do with the application, and so on. The interpretation which emerges would not necessarily bear any readily discernible resemblance to the interpretation of 'in' in another utterance with different anchoring units.

One final observation we should like to make on the anchoring–non-anchoring distinction is that non-anchoring units are in some sets of circumstances, readily interchangeable with other non-anchoring units. In the example of the lady going to the door and being asked: 'Is your husband in?' the non-anchoring unit 'in' may be replaced by other units such as 'around', 'about', 'there', 'here', 'out'. Yet 'in' would not be considered as generally synonymous with 'out' or 'about'. A way of looking at it is to say that 'in' shares certain types of potential with other units, that the emergent meaning of 'in' and the emergent meaning of a number of other items may be similar in combination with certain anchoring units in certain situations. In the cricket match case, on the other hand, 'in' could be replaced by an anchoring unit 'batting'. A language user who chooses this option may be said to be being more explicit than one who chooses a non-anchoring unit. A way of exploring the notion 'explicitness' might be to see it as the use of more anchoring units than may be necessary for some interlocutors.

In considering the anchoring–non-anchoring distinction we have concentrated on the interaction between different types of units within an utterance. Before leaving this example, we want to raise one further issue: how is it that the understander recognises that she is being asked a question?

It would normally be agreed straightforwardly that language users make use of different ways of asking questions: they may introduce question words, or inflexions; they may adopt a particular word order, they may use a characteristic intonation pattern. The example we are considering is apparently a straightforward case of what is sometimes known as a yes-no question. In English, these questions are generally characterised by the presence of an auxiliary verb in the initial position:

Do you want to go?
Has he gone?
Will he arrive on time?

and so on. In this particular case in which the verb is 'be', the verb itself comes first. Another technique an English speaker may adopt in asking a question is to order the elements of the sentence as for a declarative sentence but to use a rising intonation pattern. Thus, in this case, the caller could say: 'Your husband is in?' (rising intonation). In practice, however, this would be somewhat unusual. These two ways of asking the question are not simply variants of one another. Intuitively, we feel that the second way is less usual than the first, although it is probably the case that it would be more unusual as an opening question without preamble than at some later point in a conversation. Whether this is actually so would be a matter for empirical investigation. What would not be unusual as an opening question would be for the copula to be entirely (or almost entirely) absent: 'Your husband in?' (rising intonation). The constraints on the use of this form would once again be a matter of empirical investigation.

In the light of these observations the first point we want to bring out is that questioning is a matter of some complexity such that simply listing the possible forms, which is what traditional grammars have always done, and which Chomsky has, in a more sophisticated way, continued to do,[3] is no more than classificatory task which does not enable us even to scratch the surface of the problem. The question we should like to raise very tentatively is the following: languages may certainly be characterised in terms of the ordering and/or intonational conventions which their users adopt to ask questions, give information, commands and so on. However, does it necessarily follow from this that language users recognise they are being asked a question or given information as a result of their perception of characteristic word orders or intonation patterns? In other words, if we are looking for an explanation of the processes involved in language understanding, what weighting do we give to the observation that languages exhibit characteristic forms which correspond in a number of cases to particular functions? In the case of the example in question, that of a married woman opening the door to an unknown caller who asks: 'Is your husband in?' we should be tempted to weight the role of the syntactic structure of the sentence as very low in importance. The reason for this is not that the utterance is a very simple one. It is that, given the units to be processed, and given the fact that in 'normal' circumstances an unknown caller would not be in a position to inform her that her husband is in, a question is the most likely possibility. She might then be said to expect the utterance 'Is your husband in?', which she anticipates to be a question, to correspond to a particular conventionalised pattern. It is a subtle distinction: do you recognise a question because the utterance has the order and/or intonation pattern characteristic of questions, or do you expect a question and find in many cases that the order and/or intonation pattern confirm your expectations? It is possible that, to pursue this question profitably, word order and intonation need to be carefully distinguished. It may well be that prosodic features play a role in processing which ordering conventions do not. We emphasise this point in order to raise not to answer questions about the relative weighting of syntax and phonology. Clearly, aspects of languages can be described in terms of structural patterns, which may be related to morphological markings of various sorts, or to word order or to both. The question we want to raise is the extent to which these markings and other conventions have to be interpreted by language users in order to process successfully, and the extent to which they simply correspond to expectations aroused as a result of other factors.

We shall return to the question of weighting of different types of information in the course of discussing the following example. Consider the case of a mother who has moved into a new area. She meets, perhaps for the first time, one of her neighbours who asks:

Does your son go to school yet?

This utterance is once more a question, once more apparently banal, once more highly complex.

Under the idealisation that the participants are engaged in a 'normal' conversational exchange, the first point we want to make is that there could well be a difference in processing according to whether the answer to the question is positive or negative. Whereas in both cases, as in the previous example, the unit 'your son' would enable the understander to pick out a specific individual, the interpretation of the unit 'go to school', on the other hand, is likely to differ. The difference would be in whether the 'information' accessed were specific or generalised. If we suppose the answer is no, then the string of sounds 'go to school' could only enable the understander to gain access to generalised 'information', since there is no specific 'son + school-going' to be located in the experience of the understander. Processing in this case would thus involve the combined accessing of different types of information: generalised and specific. If, on the other hand, the answer is yes, then the processing of 'your son' and 'go to school' will involve the understander gaining access to 'information' corresponding to the particular school-going activities of a particular individual, i.e. specific information only.

School-going, however, is not a uniform, readily definable activity, and this must complicate any account of the 'information' accessed by the unit 'go to school', whether it is generalised or specific. School-going has many facets such that there would be likely to be considerable variation across individuals with respect to the 'information' accessed through such a unit. Such individual variation would be difficult to investigate empirically. Asking subjects to write down what they think they understand by school-going, or what they associate with the unit 'go to school', would be clumsy. It would be necessary to devise experiments whereby subjects would give evidence of what they understood without themselves consciously introspecting. We would expect individual variation to be more marked in cases where understanding involved access to generalised than to specific information. However, even when a particular child attending a particular school is in question, the specific 'information' located in the course of understanding would still have to be some kind of summation of a particular, though still multifaceted, experience of school-going.

The main point to emerge from these observations is that the specific information which we, as understanders, locate and use in much of our everyday exchanges is itself likely to be of different types. We have up to now discussed two distinct types: information enabling an understander to pick out a specific individual, and information corresponding to a specific, though non-uniform activity. We should like to emphasise once again that the distinctions we are making are not part of a new linguistic theory, but are rather part of an attempt to discuss linguistic units and their interactions in terms relevant to the understanding of language processing. Note that we have assumed that, for processing purposes, 'go + to + school' would constitute a single unit. This is an assumption which would require further substantiating. However, it reflects an attempt to get away from a static container view of language whereby language users have at their disposal a kind of mental dictionary where individual words with pre-specified lists of properties are stored.

A further point we want to raise in relation to this example is that once again we are dealing with a question. The utterance has the syntactic form appropriate to a yes-no question; in 'normal' circumstances, and given these units, 'your son' and 'go to school', a question is the only real possibility, since a stranger would not normally be in a position to inform one about the school-going activities of one's own son. In addition the unit 'yet', in this particular type of combination, may be seen as marking a question. Thus, at least four different factors – syntax, intonation, question marker, expectations – may be correlated with the fact that a question is being asked. Such massive redundancy makes the relative weighting of the various factors quite difficult. These

factors are all subordinate to the accessing of information resulting from the processing of the units 'your son' and 'go to school'.
Suppose however that we remove the unit 'yet', thus leaving
ourselves with:

Does your son go to school?

same structure, same intonation pattern, same circumstances and
expectations. This would seem to make very little difference to the
interpretation of the utterance as constituting a question,
suggesting that we should weigh the presence of 'yet' as a question
marker as of low importance. Suppose we then alter the syntactic
structure such that the auxiliary is no longer in its characteristically initial position:

Your son go to school (yet)?

Same rising intonation, same circumstances and expectations.
This would not be an unusual form of question, which might just
as easily be:

Your son goes to school? (same intonation)

Indeed, if the boy is present, then a nod in his direction and:

Go/goes to school? (rising intonation)

would be easily understood. This would suggest that the syntactic
structure of the utterance should be assigned a low weighting.
Suppose now that the neighbour asking the question is a
non-native speaker of English and ask the question:

Your son go to school?

with the falling intonation characteristic of a statement. Whether
this would mean that the utterance would be misunderstood as a
statement would be a matter for empirical investigation. What we
think would happen is that the expectations arising from the
particular combination of units, the circumstances and relation
between interlocutors would override the intonation pattern such
that the remark would still be interpreted as a question. This does

not mean that we would generally assign a low weighting to intonation but rather that the information accessed by the units of the utterance, plus the other circumstances, would in some cases even be sufficient to override the interpretation which would be congruent with the intonation pattern actually used.

The question of relative weighting we consider an important one for linguists to address themselves to. It is an area in which empirical work should be possible, and should enable us to gain insight into the interactive character of language use.

A further pair of examples we want to consider briefly relates to the fact that the language user's information base is constantly being modified in a way which makes it difficult to establish firm links between the form of utterances and the way they would be processed. The 'same' utterance (i.e. the same combination of units) may be processed differently by the same individual on one day to the next or even from one moment to the next. Consider the case of someone looking around at cars with the intention of eventually buying one, and his processing of the utterance:

   I hear you've got a new car

One of the interesting points raised by this example is whether the unit 'a new car' would cause an understander to access 'generalised' information about cars, or rather more specific information enabling him to pick out a particular car, which is not his new car, but for example, one he has just looked at and has not yet decided whether to buy. What is not clear either is whether, if the same observation were addressed to him on some other occasion, he would access 'information' relating to the car he has seen most recently, or whether if he had in fact stopped looking at cars, he would then access generalised rather than specific 'information'. If a car had actually been bought another factor would be the variation in the emergent meaning of the unit 'got' in relation to how recently the car had been acquired. 'Got' would generally act as a non-anchoring unit, and which, in this combination, would be likely to vary in relation to the state of the understander's world. If he has just bought a car, then this set of circumstances would probably mean him interpreting 'got' as 'acquire'. If he has had the car for some time, then he may be more likely to interpret 'got' as 'possess'.

Finally, suppose the utterance were:

I hear Fred's got a new car

then the initial processing might, if the understander is unaware of what Fred has been doing, involve a combination of access to specific information (specific individual: Fred) and access to 'generalised information' relating to possession and new cars. Suppose, however, that Fred does in fact have a new car. If prodded, the understander might recall Fred's situation sufficiently to re-process the utterance – whether or not it is repeated – this time locating specific information relating to Fred and his car. This two-stage processing is not uncommon and constitutes another factor to be taken into account in the investigation of the relation between language and the data bases of language users. Such an investigation would relate in part to work done in psychology on the characterisation of different types of memory. However, as yet, this work has not been sufficiently clearly linked to the detailed understanding of language processing.

To widen the analysis of the problem of variability and to extend its implications for language processing, we want to look afresh at a traditional problem in linguistics, the interpretation of different verb forms, from the perspective provided by the emergence view of meaning.

Traditionally grammarians have observed that verbs occur in different forms and have attempted to classify these forms and find some correlation with meaning. For a language such as English, it is customary to make an initial distinction between tense and aspect. Tense is commonly sub-classified into past, present and future; aspect into perfect/imperfect, progressive/non-progressive etc. The difficulty arises, not with making distinctions which can readily be done on the basis of form, but in correlating meanings with the various forms. In his book on aspect Bernard Comrie, for example, attempted to do this by drawing a sharp semantic distinction between tense and aspect, arguing that tense is a deictic category that locates situations in time – past, present or future – whereas aspect is concerned with the 'internal temporal constituency' of a situation (Comrie, 1976:5). The difficulty with attempting to characterise tense and aspect in this way is finding regular correlations between forms and meanings. If the range of verbs is kept quite small it is not impossible to find some correlations. Typically, for example, the present perfect:

   Max has painted the gate

is often said to indicate 'current relevance' as opposed to the simple past:

   Max painted the gate

   It is not however difficult to find sentences where the idea of current relevance does not seem to apply. The sentence:

   Max has got up at 6 a.m. in his time

for example places Max's activities firmly in the past.

   The root of the problem appears to be that an interpretation of a form of a verb does not depend in any simple and direct way upon the form itself, but upon the particular verb, upon the other units in combination with the verb, and upon the experiences and expectations of the language user in each individual case. The limited interest of the traditional grammatical distinctions for providing a basis for correlating forms and meanings becomes particularly apparent when variable units are taken into account. One highly variable unit is 'have'. Consider the pair:

(i) Alice has a bicycle
(ii) Alice is having a bicycle

where the only difference is in what would traditionally be called aspect: (i) is in the non-progressive form, (ii) the progressive. The different forms of 'have' illustrated by this pair do not readily correlate simply with a difference of 'internal temporal consti-tuency'. Instead, the form 'has' would be likely to cause the emergence of one meaning, 'possess', in combination with Alice and bicycle. The form 'is having' in the same combination would be likely to cause the emergence of a distinct meaning, 'acquire'. In addition, the 'is having' form would generally be associated with future time in this combination.

   It would not however be possible to generalise from this case and assume that the different forms of 'have' regularly correlate with this distinction in meaning and time. If we consider the pair:

(iii) Alice has a problem
(iv) Alice is having a problem

no comparable distinction in meaning hold. Nor would the 'is having' form in this second combination be likely to be associated with future time. Furthermore, if we go back to the original pair and place them in an appropriate context rather than treat them as independent entities, then the interpretation of the form-meaning correlation we did observe is again affected.

Suppose for example we placed these utterances in a context – in which they could easily fit – of parents listing the Christmas presents they have bought for their children:

(Max has football boots) Alice has a bicycle
(Max is having football boots) Alice is having a bicycle

In this context there is no longer a clear distinction to be observed either in meaning or in time. Both could readily be interpreted in the same way as 'is to acquire'. The understander, in this case one of the parents, has two anchoring units, 'Alice', specific individual, and 'bicycle', specific object with particular characteristics, bought for a particular purpose. These two units and the expectations they give rise to when processed together would clearly override any aspectual information a traditional grammarian might wish to argue is present.

This does not mean of course that form cannot be character-ised. It means rather that in attempting to explain the operation of language not simply describe its external manifestations, classi-fications based on form are likely to be far too rigid. Traditional characterisations of form could not for example give any account of what it is that would be likely to locate:

Alice is having a bicycle

in future time, and:

Alice is having a problem

in present time. This question has rather to be placed in the broader context of how meaning, in any one instance, emerges for an understander from a combination of linguistic units.

In this case, we could say that 'Alice + bicycle' and 'Alice + problem' are anchoring units. In understanding 'Alice + have + bicycle' a language user would access quite a different area of his 'data store' to that accessed in understanding 'Alice + have + problem'. In other words, 'having bicycles' and 'having problems' are quite distinct areas of most individuals' experience, and this difference would be reflected in the interpretation of the variable unit 'have' in either case. Whereas in:

Alice is having a bicycle

the emergent meaning 'is to aquire' is quite compatible with what language users known about the relations between individuals and readily obtainable objects, in:

Alice is having a problem

such a future time meaning would be less likely to emerge. Problems are states or experiences not normally planned in advance. In the second case, therefore, the anchoring unit 'problem' would be likely to cause the emergent meaning of the present progressive form of 'have' to be 'experience + present time'.

In considering these examples we have attempted to show just some of the difficulties inherent in correlating verb form with meaning.[4] A tentative conclusion might be that if there are any regular correlations between verb forms and meanings, these cannot be established independently of language in use but would have to be responsive to the nature of the area of experience accessed by the entire combination in which a verb form occurs.

In an attempt to see what such a regularity might look like, we could use the 'Alice is having a bicycle/problem' case to suggest that language users might expect BE (PRES) + ING forms to be associated with future time only when the area of experience accessed in the course of understanding is one that can be controlled or possibly is one that involves intention. Thus, in the 'Alice is having a bicycle' case, the acquiring of the bicycle is clearly under some individual's control. Someone must intend Alice to acquire a bicycle. In the 'Alice is having a problem' case, on the other hand, no such control or intention would normally be found.

This conjecture would be generally in line with the observation that, in response to the question, What is Max doing tomorrow? the answers:

Cutting the grass
Giving a lecture

would access areas of experience under Max's control, and thus correspond more closely to most understanders' view of a coherent world than responses such as:

Going to pieces
Taking offence

areas of experience not normally allowing of intention, and, if this proposed regularity were valid, not normally to be associated with future time.

Suppose we consider another 'is having' example with a different anchoring unit:

Alice is having big eyes

Taken in isolation this sentence would be said by many linguists to be deviant in that what is called inalienable possession is incompatible with a progressive aspect. If, on the other hand, the sentence is assumed to be uttered in the context of, say, a pantomime or play, then the combination of 'Alice + have + big eyes' would be straightforwardly interpretable. The unit 'big eyes' would allow an understander to access a very specific area of his 'data store'– the big eyes Alice is to be wearing in the pantomime – and this, combined with the specific information accessed by the unit 'Alice', would easily allow the future time 'is to acquire' meaning of 'have' to emerge. Set in this context the units 'Alice + have + big eyes' would allow an interpretation in which someone, perhaps Alice herself, intends that Alice shall have big eyes, giving further support to our very tentative suggestion of what a language user's world responsive regularity might be.

Finally we return to 'Max' examples and assume that the responses to the question: What is Max doing tomorrow?

Going to pieces
Taking offence

We first note that a future time interpretation of the BE (PRES) + ING verb form has been imposed on the combination by the occurrence in the question of 'tomorrow'. If our suggested regularity holds and language users do expect a future interpretation to relate to activities involving intention, then they would, in making sense of these responses, have to impute intention to Max. In other words, they would infer that Max intends to assume states not normally under an individual's control. The particular context of utterance would determine how easy this was and how far humour was intended.

The purpose of this final section has been to add a further dimension to the notion 'emergent meaning' by discussing some of the problems involved in attempting in any regular fashion to correlate verb forms with meanings directly. We have touched briefly on some examples involving the present progressive aspect. In each case we have argued that the area of experience accessed by the combination of units in the utterance, interacting with other experience and expectations of the understander, would play a determining role in the interpretation of the verb form. In isolating language from its users and in concentrating attention on those semantic distinctions that are grammaticalised in syntactic or morphological forms, linguists have been forced into classifications that are unilluminating for language in operation.

Conclusion

In this part of the book we have, in Northrop's terms, returned to the first stage of enquiry, the analysis of the problem stage. We have done so partly in order to begin the process of marking out for theoretical linguistics a fresh domain of enquiry. We have become convinced that traditional grammatical analyses – much of which Chomsky incorporated into his own 'revolutionary' theory of grammar – have been misleading in focusing undue attention on formal features that are easy to identify and appear to grammaticalise semantic distinctions. In attempting to understand how language works, we do not idealise away from language users. On the contrary, we approach our analysis of the domain of enquiry by considering how language users' data bases might be organised and what factors need to be taken into account if their interpretative strategies are to be understood.

In the course of our analysis we have made some basic assumptions and developed a number of working concepts. The most fundamental of the assumptions is that meaning should not be viewed as an inherent property of words, but as an emergent property of utterances. We called this the emergence view of meaning. Closely associated with the emergence view was the notion of the variability of the units of language. In illustrating this notion, we argued that although many linguistic units were variable, they did not vary uniformly but to different degrees. We suggested that these differences in variability might be exploited in the course of language processing. In exploring the implications of variability, we made use of further concepts such as anchoring and non-anchoring units, modulation effects, familiar and non-familiar utterances and, very briefly in discussing control and intention, began to consider whether regularities might be characterised that were sensitive to a language user's perception of the world.

These working concepts are still tentative. They do however represent a departure from traditional linguistic analyses in attempting to grasp the nettle of language users' involvement in the operation of language. They do moreover suggest ways in which the new questions that have emerged might be tackled. Foremost among these questions are:

(i)   How is it that separate individuals, unable to know directly what analysing and synthesising processes are going on in each other's heads, and trapped within the confines of their own 'data stores' are able on many occasions and to various degrees to understand one another?
(ii) What is the relation between an individual's accumulated and categorised experience, his 'knowledge store' or 'data base', and the language that enables that data base to be accessed?
(iii) How is it that for an individual the same words in different combinations enable him to access information corresponding to such widely different areas of experience?
(iv) How is it that for an individual the same combination of words can enable him to access different types of information on different occasions?

These questions are not a re-statement of the age-old question of the relation between language and the world, a question that almost invariably seems to assume an 'objective reality' to which words and sentences somehow correspond. They are different and extremely puzzling questions concerning the relations for each individual, between what he knows and remembers, and the combinations of words which enable him to pick out, from the complex mass of accumulated knowledge and experience, the particular area to which the words relate. This would not be such a difficult relation to comprehend if there were a regular and systematic relation between particular words and parts of an individual's 'knowledge store'. But, as we have tried to bring out in the course of discussing even apparently simple examples, this is not the case.

The answers to the questions we have raised are largely shrouded in mystery. It may moreover be argued against us that we have made their investigation even more difficult if not impossible by insisting upon the extent to which language processing depends on the state of the world as experienced and perceived by individual users. It may even appear that we have sunk into an extreme form of solipsism. Against that charge we would argue that in attempting to throw some light on the mysteries of language in operation, we have assumed that while the processing of a linguistic unit or combination of units may depend *in any one instance* on the state of a particular individual, such processing will nevertheless still operate according to general principles. It is these principles we would wish to see characterised.

Our belief is however that explanations of these principles will not take the form of deductively formulated theory, but be teleological in character. We expect appeals to the purposes, beliefs, knowledge and expectations of users to be vital elements in explaining the way language-in-use works. In developing adequate explanations of this sort, we anticipate a prolonged period of root and branch studies at the first stage of enquiry, the analysis of the problem stage, followed by the steady, painstaking and rigorous testing of concepts and hypotheses during an extended natural history stage. There would be some reason to hope that, out of such a framework of enquiry, linguists would develop insightful and revealing explanations of the operations of language.

Notes

1. In the book it is clear that the authors are well aware of the

serious limitation of an approach to meaning through a simple listing of the entailments of sentences.

2. Since the authors are, in their own words, inclined to be conservative about the degree of linguistic knowledge to be assigned to a semantic entry, they make the startling assumption that 'the semantic relation between horse and animal is the only one available in the lexical entry for horse' (Smith and Wilson, 1979:167).

3. Chomsky has not been reluctant to take over 'the kind of information presented in traditional grammars'. he further wrote that such:

> ... information ... is without question, substantially correct and is essential to any account of how the language is used or acquired. The main topic I should like to consider is how information of this sort can be formally presented in a structural description, and how such structural descriptions can be generated by a system of explicit rules. (Chomsky, 1965:64)

4. It would not be difficult as linguists know to multiply instances of counter-examples to alleged correlations between verb forms and meanings. The verb 'hear' for example, a less variable unit than 'have', is frequently described as a 'stative' verb, that is a verb, unlike 'listen', referring to a state not an activity. It is said to be a characteristic of stative verbs that they do not occur in the progressive form; 'Max was listening to the music' is acceptable, but not 'Max was hearing the music'.

Comrie argues that:

> ... verbs tend to divide into two disjoint (non-overlapping) classes, those that can appear in the progressive forms, and those that cannot. Moreover, this distinction corresponds to that between stative and nonstative verbs. Thus we can give the general definition of progressiveness as the combination of progressive meaning and nonstative meaning. Naturally, then, stative verbs do not have progressive forms, since this would involve an internal contradiction between the stativity of the verb and the nonstativity essential to the progressive (Comrie, 1976:35).

The claim that stative verbs do not have progressive forms is in keeping with the assumption that there should be direct correlation between form and meaning. But, as Comrie is well aware, it is not difficult to find occurrences of 'hear' in the progressive form. Consider the example:

The judge is hearing the witnesses.

In an appropriate context an understander is unlikely to note as unusual the occurrence of 'hear' in the progressive form, nor is he likely even to notice that the sentence may be interpreted in a number of ways. If he is a barrister, addressed by another barrister, he is likely to interpret the utterance as a remark about the judge's powers of hearing (which must have been failing to make the remark appropriate) since he would not expect to be instructed by a colleague on what is going on in the courtroom. If on the other hand the understander had never been to court before and was being given information about legal processes, his expectations would be likely to lead to him to interpret the sentence as a remark about legal procedure. In other words, the anchoring units 'judge' and 'witness' and the expectations of the understander in each case would enable a different interpretation of a form to be arrived at quite readily.

Epilogue

This book began as an attempt to understand why theoretical linguistics had become such a fragmented field, why, in spite of its sophisticated techniques, it had provided so little insight into the workings of language. It has ended by offering a re-analysis of the domain of theoretical linguistics, a re-analysis in which language is no longer seen as a self-contained system but as inextricably bound up with the world as perceived by individual language users.

We had become convinced quite early on that a key factor in the fragmentation of the field had been the extent to which theoretical linguistics had diverged from its subject matter, language. We traced the more immediate roots of this divergence to the origins and motivation for Chomsky's theory of grammar, sometimes misleadingly called a theory of language.

If we were to uncover beneath the weight of subsequent modifications, revisions and refinements, the reason why Chomsky had moved theoretical linguistics in the direction he had, it seemed essential to go back to the very early stages of his theory. We began therefore with Chomsky's links with his immediate predecessors, the North American descriptivists. We showed that it was these links, in particular with Harris, that led him to seek a firmer theoretical basis for their work on constituent structure grammars. As a result of that work, Chomsky introduced into linguistics a new style of explanatory theory: deductively formulated theory. We then explored some of the effects of the introduction of the hypothetico-deductive approach into linguistics.

We argued that while deductively formulated theory may be appropriate for subject matters reasonably well-understood and well-defined, and readily reducible to a formal notation, language is not such a phenomenon – unless it is reduced to a pale shadow of itself. In attempting to force language into the mould required by the deductively formulated approach Chomsky was obliged to pay exaggerated attention to the distribution of forms in structures, insufficient attention to meaning. This was imposed upon him since forms and their distribution in structures lent themselves to formalisation of the theoretically required type in a way

215

that the alleged vagueness and indeterminacy of meaning did not. Our conclusion was that within linguistics the demands of a particular theoretical approach have been allowed – much more than is warranted by the subject matter – to shape the domain of enquiry. There may we suspect be lessons to be learnt here for human and social sciences other than linguistics.

There were however deeper roots to the divergence of linguistics from language than are apparent from an analysis of the origins and motivation of Chomsky's theory of grammar. These roots lay in a belief that has been widespread for almost the whole of this century, the belief that language may usefully be studied as a self-contained system. It seems to have been an article of faith, at least since Saussure and Meillet, that language is best treated as an entity independent of individual users. This has been reflected in linguistic studies of meaning in the assumption that sentences could be treated as if, in themselves, they 'contain' meaning which they are able to 'convey' and that words 'have' or 'bear' meaning. Metaphors of containment and transport have – as we pointed out in Chapter 4 – been rife in nearly all studies of meaning.

Our conviction is that this 'container' view has had an insidious effect within both linguistics and philosophy. In distancing ourselves resolutely from this view we placed language in a different perspective. We started from the assumption that language is inextricably bound up with users and their experience, expectations and perception of the world. Language is thus an epiphenomenon on the accumulated and generalised experience of its users. From this perspective language itself cannot 'do' anything; instead speakers in producing utterances make use of their 'stores' of accumulated and generalised knowledge and experience; the utterances they produce cause understanders, in interpreting them, to gain access to their own, possibly quite different, 'data stores'.

In approaching language as epiphenomenal on its users, we were led to an even more challenging conjecture: that meaning does not inhere in utterances but rather emerges from them. From the epiphenomenalist viewpoint, meaning is not an inherent but an emergent property of language. While this approach does not solve the problem of how language operates, it does shift the focus of attention. What now needs to be characterised is the relation holding between language and the accumulated and generalised experience of its users, their 'data stores'.

Our initial, tentative approach to characterising this relation led us to give particular attention to what we call variable linguistic units, units whose meaning cannot readily be characterised independently of their occurrence in combination with other units. The significance of variable units for the emergence view of meaning is that it is they that provide language with the flexibility that enables it to be used by countless individuals to reflect and comment upon countless fresh experiences and conjectures. We discuss units with different degrees of variability and suggest that such differences may be exploited in language production and processing. A general line of research the emergence view thus opens up is how units with different degrees of variability interact in the course of language use. A more specific problem is the relative weighting of the various kinds of knowledge that play a part in the emergence of degrees of understanding. We are particularly interested in the implications of variable units for the understanding of the brain's storage and processing strategies.

The ideas put forward in the second part of the book are tentative. They constitute a part of the 'analysis of the problem' stage of an enquiry. We believe nonetheless that variability is a key concept in understanding how language operates. The hypothesis that language in use depends upon the interaction of units of different degrees of variability is one however that needs to be explored in much greater detail. We would not wish to make claims for a 'variability theory' of language or for an 'emergence theory' of meaning, only for a variability and an emergence view. While views precede theories, they are not identical with them. In linguistics too many over-bold claims have already been made for too many over-hasty and ill-thought out theories. In converting views into theories we believe that linguists will need to employ very different methods of enquiry from those that have marked so much of the work in theoretical linguistics for the last quarter of a century. Following Northrop, we incline to the view that it is certainly premature and probably worthless to attempt to apply deductively formulated theory in devising generative rule systems or grammars to describe limited aspects of questionable 'linguistic' knowledge. Limited but satisfying explanations for the workings of language are much more likely to emerge from a problem-based approach that examines specific questions of language acquisition and use in relation to the purposes, beliefs, expectations and experience of language users.

We anticipate then that explanation in linguistics will be teleological rather than deductive in character. One effect of such a change in the mode of explanation would undoubtedly be that linguistics could no longer compare itself with the more sophisticated of the physical sciences. It might however end the long divergence of linguistics from its subject matter, and allow the field, however slowly to begin to converge with other related fields upon the study of language in operation.

References

Abbreviations

RIL: *Readings in Linguistics*, ed. M. Joos, New York: American Council of Learned Societies, 1957.
SL: *The Structure of Language*, eds J. A. Fodor and J. Katz, Englewood Cliffs, N. J.: Prentice-Hall, 1964.
(Page references in the text refer to these collections.)

Black, M. 1970, Comment on 'Problems of Explanation in Linguistics' by N. Chomsky in *Explanation in the Behavioural Sciences*, eds R. Borger and F. Cioffi.
Bloch, B. 1949, 'Leonard Bloomfield', *Language*, 25, 92–4.
Bloch, B. and Trager, G. L. 1942, *Outline of Linguistic Analysis*, Baltimore: Linguistic Society of America.
Bloomfield, L. 1914, *An Introduction to the Study of Language*, London: G. Bell.
Bloomfield, L. 1924, *Modern Language Journal*, 8.
Bloomfield, L. 1926, 'A Set of Postulates for the Study of Language', *Language*, 2, 153–64.
Bloomfield, L. 1935, *Language*, London: George Allen & Unwin.
Bloomfield, L. 1939, 'Linguistic Aspects of Science' in *International Encyclopedia of Unified Science*, ed. O. Neurath, University of Chicago Press.
Bolinger, D. 1965, 'The Atomization of Meaning', *Language*, 41, 555–73.
Borger, R. and Cioffi, F. 1970, eds *Explanation in the Behavioural Sciences*, Cambridge University Press.
Bransford, J. D. and Johnson, M. K. 1972, 'Contextual Prerequisites for Understanding', *Journal of Verbal Learning and Verbal Behaviour*, 11, 717–26
Carnap, R. 1937, *The Logical Syntax of Language*, London: Routledge & Kegan Paul.
Chomsky, N. 1955, 'Semantic Considerations in Grammar', Monograph No. 8, Georgetown Monograph Series.
Chomsky, N. 1957, *Syntactic Structures*, The Hague: Mouton.

Chomsky, N. 1962, 'Explanatory Models in Linguistics', in *Logic, Methodology, and Philosophy of Science*, eds E. Nagel, P. Suppes and A. Tarski, Stanford University Press.

Chomsky, N. 1964a, 'Current Issues in Linguistic Theory', SL, 50–118.

Chomsky, N. 1964b, 'A Review of B. F. Skinner's *Verbal Behavior*', SL, 547–78, first appeared: *Language*, 1959, 35, 26–58.

Chomsky, N. 1964c, 'The Logical Basis of Linguistic Theory', in *Proceedings of the Ninth International Congress of Linguists*, ed. H. G. Lunt, The Hague: Mouton.

Chomsky, N. 1965, *Aspects of the Theory of Syntax*, Cambridge Mass.: MIT Press.

Chomsky, N. 1966, *Cartesian Linguistics*, New York: Harper & Row.

Chomsky, N. 1967, 'Recent Contributions to the Theory of Innate Ideas', *Synthese*, 17, 2–11.

Chomsky, N. 1969, 'Comments on Harman's Reply', in *Language and Philosophy*, ed. S. Hook, New York University Press.

Chomsky, N. 1970, 'Problems of Explanation in Linguistics', in *Explanation in the Behavioral Sciences*, eds R. Borger and F. Cioffi.

Chomsky, N. 1971, 'Deep Structure, Surface Structure and Semantic Interpetation', in *Semantics*, eds D. D. Steinberg and L. A. Jakobovits, Cambridge University Press.

Chomsky, N. 1972, *Language and Mind* (enlarged edition), New York: Harcourt Brace.

Chomsky, N. 1975, *The Logical Structure of Linguistic Theory*, New York: Plenum.

Chomsky, N. 1976, *Reflections on Language*, London: Temple Smith.

Chomsky, N. 1979, *Language and Responsibility*, Hassocks, Sussex: Harvester.

Chomsky, N. and Hampshire, S. 1968, 'Discussion: The Study of Language', *Listener*, 30 May, London: BBC.

Church, A. 1956, *Introduction to Mathematical Logic*, Princeton N.J.: Princeton University Press.

Collingwood, R. G. 1940, *An Essay on Metaphysics*, London: Oxford University Press.

Comrie, B. 1976, *Aspect*, Cambridge University Press.

Fries, C. C. 1952, *The Structure of English*, New York: Harcourt Brace and World.

Goody, J. and Watt, I. 1972, 'The Consequences of Literacy', in

Language and Social Context, ed. P. P. Giglioli, Harmondsworth: Penguin.

Harris, Z. S. 1951, *Structural Linguistics*, University of Chicago Press.

Harris, Z. S. 1952, 'Discourse Analysis', *Language*, 28, 1–30.

Haugen, E. 1957, 'Directions in Modern Linguistics', RIL, 357–63, first appeared: *Language*, 1951, 27, 211–22.

Hill, A. A. 1958, *Introduction to Linguistic Structures: From Sound to Sentence in English*, New York: Harcourt Brace.

Hockett, C. F. 1957a, 'A System of Descriptive Phonology', RIL, 97–108, first appeared: *Language*, 1942, 18, 3–21.

Hockett, C. F. 1957b, A Note on "Structure" ', RIL, 279–80, first appeared: *International Journal of American Linguistics*, 1948, 14, 269–71.

Hockett, C. F. 1957c, 'Two Models of Grammatical Description', RIL, 386–99, first appeared: *Word*, 1954, 10, 210–31.

Hockett, C. F. 1958, *A Course in Modern Linguistics*, New York: Macmillan.

Hook, S. 1969, 'Empiricism, Rationalism, and Innate Ideas', in *Language and Philosophy*, ed. S. Hook, New York University Press.

Jardine, N. 1975, 'Model Theoretic Semantics and Natural Languages', in *Formal Semantics of Natural Language*, ed. E. L. Keenan, Cambridge University Press.

Jones, P. E. 'Materialism and the Structure of Language', Ph.D. dissertation, Cambridge University, forthcoming.

Joos, M. 1957a, 'Description of Language Design', RIL, 349–56, first appeared: *Journal of the Acoustical Society of America*, 1950, 22, 701–8.

Joos, M. 1957b, Editorial Comment to Bloch's 'Phonemic Overlapping', RIL, 96.

Katz, J. J. and Fodor, J. A. 1964, 'The Structure of a Semantic Theory', SL, 479–518, first appeared: *Language*, 1963, 39, 170–210.

Magee, B. 1978, *Men of Ideas*, London: BBC.

Miller, G. A. and Johnson-Laird, P. N. 1976, *Language and Perception*, Cambridge University Press.

Morris, D. *et al.* 1979, *Gestures and their origins and distribution*, London: Jonathan Cape.

Nagel, E. 1961, *The Structure of Science*, London: Routledge & Kegan Paul.

Northrop, F. S. C. 1959, *The Logic of the Sciences and the Humanities*, New York: Collins.

Owen, M. 1980, *Aspects of Conversational Topic*, Interim Report of the SSRC project on 'Topic Organisation in Conversation', Department of Linguistics, University of Cambridge.

Passmore, J. 1968, *A Hundred Years of Philosophy*, Harmondsworth: Penguin.

Polanyi, M. 1958, *Personal Knowledge*, New York: Harper & Row.

Quine, W. V. 1969, 'Linguistics and Philosophy', in *Language and Philosophy*, ed. S. Hook, New York University Press.

Sapir, E. 1963, *Selected Writings of Edward Sapir in Language, Culture and Personality*, ed. D. G. Mandelbaum, University of California Press.

Saussure, F. de 1959, *Course in General Linguistics*, eds C. Bally and A. Sechehaye, translated by W. Baskin, New York: Philosophical Library, First Edition 1916.

Sinclair, A. 1951, *The Conditions of Knowing*, London: Routledge & Kegan Paul.

Smith, N. and Wilson, D. 1979, *Modern Linguistics*, Harmondsworth: Penguin

Sparck Jones, K. 1965, 'Semantic Markers', Report M.L. 181, Cambridge Language (England) Research Unit.

Suppe, F. 1977, ed. *The Structure of Scientific Theories*, Second Edition, University of Illinois Press.

Tarski, A. 1956, 'The Concept of Truth in Formalized Languages', in *Logic, Semantics and Metamathematics*, translated by J. H. Woodger, London: Oxford University Press.

Watson, I. 1975, *The Embedding*, London: Quartet.

Watson, J. B. 1925, *Behaviorism*, London: Kegan Paul.

Weinreich, U., Labov, W., Herzog, M. I. 1968, 'Empirical Foundations for a Theory of Language Change', in *Directions for Historical Linguistics*, eds W. P. Lehmann and Y. Malkiel, University of Texas Press.

Index